CONNECTICUT ARCHITECTURE

Connecticut

Architecture

STORIES OF 100 PLACES

CHRISTOPHER WIGREN,

CONNECTICUT TRUST FOR

HISTORIC PRESERVATION

WESLEYAN UNIVERSITY PRESS   Middletown, Connecticut

Wesleyan University Press
Middletown CT 06459
www.wesleyan.edu/wespress
© 2019 Connecticut Trust for Historic Preservation
All rights reserved
Manufactured in China
Designed by Richard Hendel
Typeset in Miller and Klavika by
Tseng Information Systems, Inc.
Frontispiece: George Izenour House, Stony Creek. Tom Bernard,
Courtesy of Venturi, Scott Brown and Associates Inc.
Page vi: Warner Theatre, Torrington. William Hosley
Page 286: Willis Bristol House, New Haven. Patrick L. Pinnell

Library of Congress Cataloging-in-Publication Data
Names: Wigren, Christopher, author.
Title: Connecticut architecture : stories of 100 places /
Christopher Wigren, Connecticut Trust for Historic Preservation.
Description: Middletown, Connecticut : Wesleyan University
Press, 2018. | Series: Garnet books | Includes bibliographical
references and index. | Identifiers: LCCN 2018002991 (print) |
LCCN 2018004783 (ebook) | ISBN 9780819578143 (ebook) |
ISBN 9780819578136 (cloth)
Subjects: LCSH: Architecture—Connecticut.
Classification: LCC NA730.C8 (ebook) | LCC NA730.C8 W54
2018 (print) | DDC 720.9746—dc23
LC record available at https://lccn.loc.gov/2018004783.

Hardcover ISBN: 978-0-8195-7813-6
Ebook ISBN: 978-0-8195-7814-3

5 4 3 2 1

In memory of Elizabeth Mills Brown

CONTENTS

PREFACE

Connecticut's architecture tells many kinds of stories. Whether we are longtime residents, recent transplants, or visitors, we know the state first through its built environment—its buildings, landscapes, neighborhoods, and communities that embody the state's history and are essential components of its present-day character.

This book aims to introduce readers to Connecticut's built environment through stories about one hundred places, chosen to present a cross section of the varied architecture found in the state. It is not intended to be a "best of" state architecture. While I have tried to achieve a balance of well-known places and lesser-known ones, any reader with a passing knowledge of the state will find many favorite works missing. Rather, they were chosen to illustrate the wide variety of Connecticut's architecture, in terms of periods, building types, disciplines, geographical distribution, and expressive qualities. Above all, they were chosen because they had good stories to tell—about how they came to be, about the people who created or used them, about what they meant and how they fit into the state's overall development.

I hope that this book will provide new ways to understand the state's history and character, and will encourage the preservation of its historic places. I use the term "historic" very broadly, to encompass Colonial saltboxes, but also postwar Capes and industrial and agricultural sites. These sites are crucial to Connecticut's history, and many of them face increasingly uncertain futures because of changing tastes or declines in manufacturing and farming. Landscapes, townscapes, and cityscapes are often even more important to our sense of place than individual buildings. Preserving, enhancing, and, in some cases, reshaping these historic places enriches our present and can help us build a better future.

Each entry that follows includes basic information about date, designers or builders, and location. Many of these places are open to the public, and all are at least visible to the public. But please respect the privacy of property owners. In addition, each entry includes some sources of further information, including references to the National Register of Historic Places. The National Register is the fundamental nationwide listing of significant places, and it is easily accessible online. The quality of information in the Register varies; in general, the more recent nominations are more accurate and complete. Nonetheless, it is almost always a good starting point. When a place has a website, it usually is listed. But there are not a lot of other Internet references, since websites change so frequently that many would be out of date before this book is published.

Many sources and people have contributed to the telling of these stories. First and foremost is the late Elizabeth Mills Brown—Betty to almost everyone who knew her—with whom I worked for many years on a never-completed architectural guidebook. Although this work contains only a few short quotations from her insightful and lively writings, Betty is present on every page, thanks to the many lessons I learned from her. Moreover, she and her band of helpers generated much of the raw material that I drew on. I am eternally grateful to Betty's daughters, Lauren Brown, Valerie Brown, and Lila Brown, for generously allowing me to use her papers. Some of that guidebook material, we hope, will be made available electronically in a second phase.

This book would not have been written without the Connecticut Trust for Historic Preservation, in particular its former executive directors, Helen Higgins, who gave the project an institutional home, and, Daniel Mackay, who enthusiastically saw it nearly to fruition. The board of trustees, especially chairmen Edmund Schmidt, Charles Janson, and Garry Leonard; the Historic Buildings and Easements Committee, chaired by Richard Wies; and my board liaison, Caroline Sloat, gave official support and guidance to the project. My fellow staff members, Gregory Farmer, Michael Forino, Terry Grady, Wes Haynes, Charlotte Hitchcock, Todd Levine, Erin Marchitto, Jane Montanaro, Kristen Nietering, Brad Schide, Jordan Sorensen, Renée Tribert, and Kathleen von Jena, have unfailingly offered assistance, advice, or encouragement. Several of them reviewed drafts at various stages; Charlotte Hitchcock read it all. As deadlines approached, they selflessly covered some of my other responsibilities so I could write.

The staff of the Connecticut State Historic Preservation Office and its predecessor, the Connecticut Historical Commission, also helped, despite agency reorganizations, budget cuts, and chronic staffing shortages. Other valued input came from an advisory group that included Rachel Carley, Bruce Clouette, Jan Cunningham, Kathleen Curran, Rudy Favretti, Patrick Pinnell, Alan Plattus, James Sexton, Caroline Sloat, and Barbara Tucker. I am also grateful to the countless designers, builders, students, property owners, and stewards of Connecticut's architecture who took time to show sites and share their knowledge and enthusiasm.

Earlier versions of some entries appeared in the *Hartford Courant*'s "Place" section; I thank the *Courant* for permission to reuse them here and former "Place" editor Tom Condon for inviting me to write. Other material was test-driven in *Connecticut Preservation News*, the Connecticut Trust's newsletter.

Funding has come from the Connecticut Trust's operating budget, thanks to the Trust's generous members and donors. In addition, the project received grants from the Sons of the American Revolution in Connecticut and the Howard Gilman Foundation (special thanks to Garry Leonard for obtaining the latter).

Good illustrations are crucial to a book about architecture. Deb Cohen, Robert Egleston, Robert Gregson, Robert Grzywacz, and Patrick Pinnell all took multiple photographs, crisscrossing the state to capture the right place with the right light. Elizabeth Pratt Fox coordinated them all. In addition, she tracked down illustrations based on her extensive knowledge of archival collections throughout the state and beyond, made sure we had proper permissions, and kept everything in order. Diana Ross McCain edited copy before it was submitted to the publisher; an experienced historian as well as an editor, she caught and corrected numerous errors and offered valuable suggestions. Joan Shapiro's attention to detail made the index a valuable aid to using the book. Staff and editors from Wesleyan University Press and the University Press of New England have been unfailingly helpful and understanding of a first-time author's inexperience. I also thank the anonymous readers whose observations made the book much stronger. Of course, any errors are my own.

On a personal level, I must recognize the Institute

Library in New Haven, a little-known gem, which became
my asylum for writing and thinking. Finally, I thank
my partner, Mark, who generously put up with years
of reading, writing, and obsessing. How will I try your
patience now?

Hamden
February 2017

THE 100 PLACES

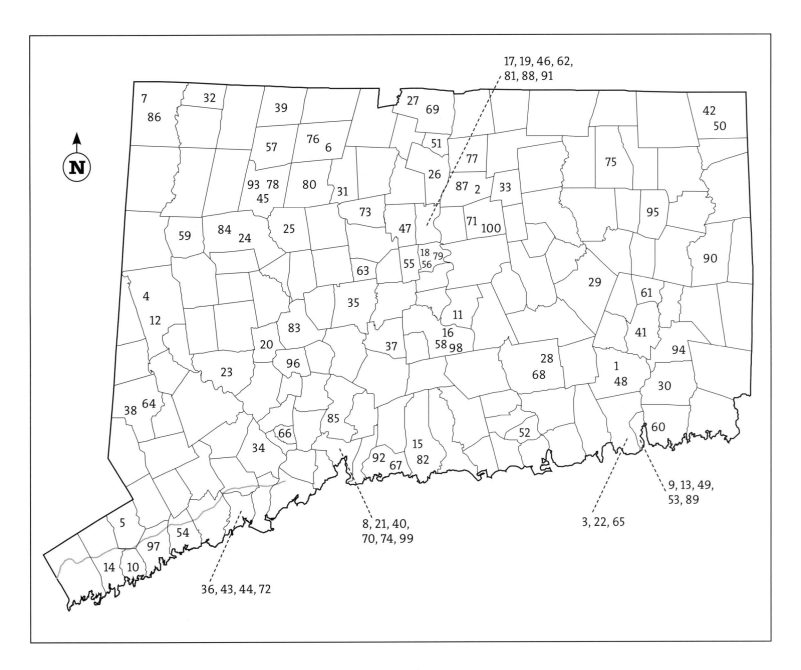

17, 19, 46, 62, 81, 88, 91

9, 13, 49, 53, 89

3, 22, 65

8, 21, 40, 70, 74, 99

36, 43, 44, 72

Colonial and Colonial Revival

79. Buttolph-Williams House, Wethersfield
80. Deacon Adams House, New Hartford
81. Horace Bushnell Congregational Church, Hartford
82. Hyland House, Guilford
83. Waterbury City Hall, Waterbury
84. Litchfield
85. Houses by Alice Washburn, Hamden
86. Salisbury Town Hall, Salisbury

Meaning and Message

87. Ebenezer Grant House, South Windsor
88. Old State House, Hartford
89. United States Custom House, New London
90. Two Houses, Plainfield
91. Connecticut State Capitol, Hartford
92. James Blackstone Memorial Library, Branford
93. Villa Friuli, Torrington
94. Mashantucket Pequot Museum and Research Center, Mashantucket

Transformations

95. Taintor House, Hampton
96. Downtown Naugatuck
97. Canaan Institutional Baptist Church, Norwalk
98. Wilcox, Crittenden & Company Factory, Middletown
99. Dixwell Plaza, New Haven
100. Cheney Yarn Dye House, Manchester

OVERVIEW

CONNECTICUT AND
ITS PLACES

Through Connecticut's long history its people have shaped the place in which they lived in rich and varied ways. They have worked and transformed the land, erected high-style and utilitarian buildings, grouped them into towns and cities, and engineered bridges and dams and roads. These works reflect and reveal the evolving history of the people of Connecticut, and they make the state a place that is distinct from any other.

All this activity can be grouped under the term "architecture," which might be defined as "the art and science of making places." In this definition, "science" refers to the practical or technical aspects of architecture. First and foremost, architecture has to accommodate the activities of human life, such as dwelling or working, worshipping or playing. It may do this in artistic ways, but its primary task is functional. "Science" also means that architecture has to be structurally sound. Walls and bridges shouldn't collapse, roofs shouldn't leak (some architects famously ignore or fail at this), landscapes shouldn't flood, roads shouldn't sink under the weight of vehicles.

"Art" includes the aesthetic or expressive aspects of architecture. This refers to people's efforts to make what they build beautiful, in addition to practical and sound (for instance, the Mark Twain House, place 17). For some, the search for beauty is the defining characteristic that separates architecture from what they consider mere building. But art involves more than aesthetic appeal. It may also include the expression of some emotion or meaning that goes beyond mere usefulness or prettiness. As art, architecture may comment on function, or on the nature or state of society in a broader sense. It may reflect social conditions, or express hopes for changing them. It may seek to articulate something about its users or builders or to evoke an emotional response in its viewers.

For example, the Church of the Good Shepherd in Hartford (1867–1869, Edward Tuckerman Potter) was commissioned by Elizabeth Colt as a memorial to her husband, pistol manufacturer Samuel Colt, and three of their children who all predeceased her. Elizabeth chose many of the church's decorative motifs herself, notably images and scriptural passages related to the theme of

FIGURE 1. Edward Tuckerman Potter, Church of the Good Shepherd, Hartford, 1867–1869. Connecticut Trust for Historic Preservation

God's comfort amid sorrow. The church's south entry presents a different message. Known as "the Armorers' Door," it faces the Colt company housing (figure 1). Around the door, carvings of pistols and pistol parts intertwine with more conventional flowers and crosses in an unparalleled marriage of Gothic and industrial imagery, while a carved motto proclaims, "Whatsoever thou doest, do all to the Glory of God." Clearly addressed to Colt employees, it is an injunction to hard work and a warning that they are answerable not merely to the boss but to God.[1]

Almost never is a work of architecture either purely science or purely art. Instead, function and structure and beauty and expressiveness intertwine to form a whole. Function may determine a structural system, for instance, in factories such as Hockanum Mill (place 33), which had to be strong to support heavy machinery. Structure, in turn, may determine aesthetics, as at Lover's Leap Bridge in New Milford (place 12), or the Temple Street Parking Garage in New Haven (1961; figure 2), where architect Paul Rudolph chose arched forms to express the plastic nature of concrete. Art may enhance function, as the decoration of the Church of the Good Shepherd does. Expressiveness may *be* a function, as at the Groton Battle Monument (place 60), built to commemorate traumatic losses in war.

This leads to the heart of the definition of architecture: "making places." What is a "place"? And what does it mean to "make" a place? As used here, a "place" is not merely some location on earth, but rather one that has some significance. It *means* something. This meaning can reside in the mind of the creator or in the mind of the beholder. For instance, the straightforward design of barns and factories can be meaningful to their owners and users for their functionality and perhaps as expressions of the importance of the work that they house. They also can have an aesthetic appeal that was not consciously intended by their builders, but that present-day viewers readily acknowledge (figure 3).

As a rule, "making" places involves human alteration: shaping, smoothing, digging, assembling, or organizing materials to create something new. But one of the places discussed in this book—Mohegan Hill (place 1)—points to a different approach, arising from a very different, non-European culture. For Native Americans, making a place could entail discovering the meaning inherent in the hill's natural features rather than altering them.

As a definition of architecture, "making places" is very broad. It includes not only buildings (structures big enough for humans to move in), but also the interior design of those buildings, which may be independent of their actual construction and is more easily altered to suit changing tastes or needs. It includes landscapes, both those consciously designed, like parks and gardens and campuses, as well as those that emerge out of the function they serve, such as the Catlin Farm in Litchfield (place 24) or larger regional landscapes as in South Windsor

(top) FIGURE 2. Paul Rudolph, Temple Street Garage, New Haven, 1961. Tom Zetterstrom
(bottom) FIGURE 3. Charles Sheeler, *On a Connecticut Theme #2 (Bucolic Landscape #2)*, 1958. New Britain Museum of American Art; copyright estate of Charles Sheeler

(place 2). Places also can be structures that do not provide shelter, such as bridges or dams or roads (for instance, the Lover's Leap Bridge, place 12). Finally, places include towns or neighborhoods or streets, or any other grouping where the whole is greater than the sum of its parts (for example, downtown Norwich, place 41).

In today's world we divide the work of creating places into a number of separate disciplines—architecture, landscape architecture, engineering, planning, and interior design—but all these really are aspects of this single activity of making places. In practice, it is not always easy to draw firm dividing lines among these disciplines. Architects design landscape settings for their buildings. Landscape architects design habitable buildings or structures like dams or bridges. Engineers create buildings such as sports arenas or aircraft hangars. Interior design affects exteriors. Architects and landscape architects alike plan neighborhoods or large developments, and planners draw up architectural guidelines for buildings in their projects, if not the actual buildings.

Calling all this "architecture" might feel like co-opting the work of interior designers, planners, landscape architects, and engineers in favor of architects. What is needed is a single, straightforward term that encompasses all those fields. "Placemaking" might work, although it seems to have become the property of tourism marketing boards. For the moment, with apologies to the American Society of Landscape Architects, the American Planning Association, the American Society of Interior Designers, and the American Society of Civil Engineers, I'm sticking with "architecture."[2]

Why is architecture important? I'll focus on two brief points that grow out of my definition of architecture as making places: humans are place-based beings, and humans are beings that create.[3]

Humans have bodies, and those bodies occupy space. The nature of that space makes a difference to us: it can be comfortable or uncomfortable, it can further our activities or frustrate them, and it can ennoble us or debase us. How we design and build places, then, can affect the quality of our lives in them—sometimes in ways that are crucial to our well-being. See the description of the Connecticut Hospice (place 67), which was carefully designed to shelter people at a particularly difficult and traumatic time not only for patients but for their friends and families. Similarly, the urban renewal programs of the mid-twentieth century were grounded in the confidence that architecture could solve social ills, a belief that was tragically overstated, to the ongoing distress of cities like Hartford or New Haven (places 46, 99). Even that failure, though, demonstrates the power that places have to affect our lives. How we shape them matters.

Humans also have an innate need to create, to make things. Our reaction to place is not passive; we need to manipulate and alter the environment and materials we find about us. If a place is uncomfortable or hinders a desired activity, people try to make it more comfortable or more conducive to the activity. Or they may just try to make it more attractive.

Creating refers to more than artistic achievements like painting or sculpture. It might mean doing carpentry or setting up a classification system for a library or writing an instruction manual. Whether it involves physical or mental activity, it is still the remaking of one's world. All humans do it, even the toddler who delightedly smears food on a wall and calls it "painting." How we shape the physical world around us, how we create places, says much about what we want our world to be, how we want to live in it, and, in some cases, how we want others to *think* we live in it. Making places lies at the very heart of what it means to be human.

THE LAND

Connecticut architecture begins with the land, the given which its settlers first encountered, beginning with Native Americans who arrived more than ten thousand years ago and, later, the Europeans who started coming at the beginning of the seventeenth century.[4] The land provided materials with which to build. Its topography influenced where people settled and how they communicated between settlements. As far as they were able, the people who lived here shaped the land. Where they have ceased to maintain the land in its altered state, the land has reasserted itself, undoing much of their attempts to dominate nature.

Thrust up by geological upheavals, scraped down by rain and rivers and glaciers, flooded and uncovered by sea

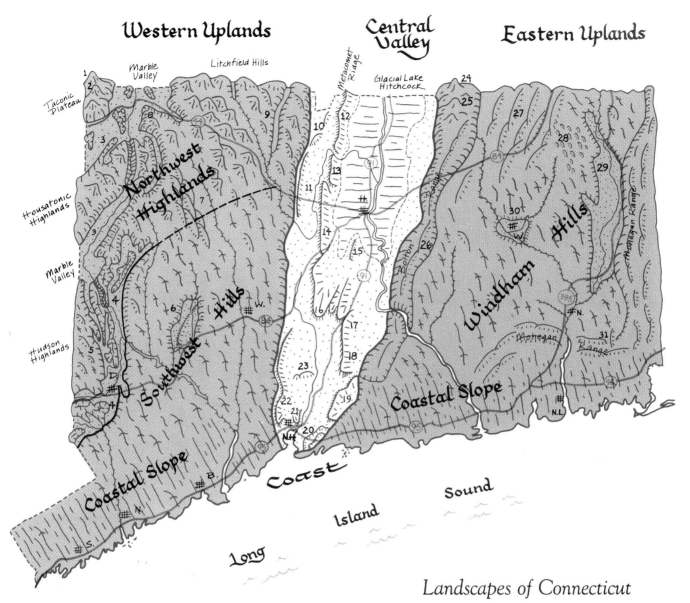

Landscapes of Connecticut

FIGURE 4. Geological regions of Connecticut. Map from Michael Bell, *The Face of Connecticut*, 1985. Connecticut Department of Energy and Environmental Protection

waters, the land of Connecticut as we know it emerged from the ice ages about ten thousand years ago as a gently hilly territory, abundantly watered by rivers and streams draining southward to Long Island Sound, with fertile soil that supported thick forests (figure 4).

Running through the middle of Connecticut is a broad valley that begins in Massachusetts and meets Long Island Sound at New Haven. As far south as Middletown, the Connecticut River runs through this central valley (figure 5), but then the river breaks through the valley wall and turns eastward to finish its run to the Sound through

OVERVIEW

(top) FIGURE 5. Connecticut River, Cromwell.
Connecticut Trust for Historic Preservation
(bottom) FIGURE 6. Highlands hills and valleys, Cornwall.
Connecticut Trust for Historic Preservation

a narrower passage. North of Rocky Hill, the valley was the bed of a prehistoric glacial lake, whose silted deposits of alluvial soil provide fertile farmland. This level land—rich, easily worked, nearly free of stone, and easily built upon—attracted the first Europeans, who built prosperous agricultural communities like South Windsor (place 2). Flourishing farms, along with easy transport, both on the level ground and along the Connecticut River, fostered the rise of cities: Hartford and Middletown on the Connecticut River, plus New Haven at the mouth of the Quinnipiac River on Long Island Sound.

To the east and west of the central valley lie uplands with long, streamlined hills, mostly running north and south, and fertile, if stony, soil (figure 6). The hilly topography influenced development, with early settlers preferring the hilltops for their good drainage and what they considered more healthful air. Transportation and communications follow similar lines; even a modern highway map shows more, and better, roads running north–south than east–west.

As upland forests were cleared, stones deposited by the glaciers worked their way to the surface and had to be removed from fields. In many cases farmers simply tossed stones into piles lining the edges of their fields. A more labor-intensive approach was to build stone walls, which took up less space and could serve as dividers between fields (figure 7). These walls have become a widely recognized feature of the New England landscape, and the varying types of stone and methods of construction highlight regional differences.[5]

Farming was more difficult in the uplands than in the central valley, but it could support families, and even be profitable (Cyrus Wilson Farm, place 25). With the opening of the American West and improvements in transportation that made it possible to import agricultural products from other places, general farming declined, and the land so laboriously cleared of its forests grew up in trees again. In addition to agriculture, the uplands offered stone for building, ores for mining, and timber for building or charcoal making.

The uplands contain two smaller river systems. In the east are the Quinebaug and Shetucket Rivers, which join at Norwich to form the Thames (pronounced with a soft *th* and a long *a*). To the west is the Housatonic, which is joined by the Naugatuck at Derby. Although navigable historically, these streams were narrower and faster than the Connecticut River. Easily and profitably dammed for waterpower, the uplands water systems fostered the industrial development that transformed Connecticut in the nineteenth century. Under the influence of Rhode Island and Massachusetts, the Quinebaug-Shetucket corridor, in the east, concentrated on textiles. In the west, the Housatonic-Naugatuck region became known for metals manufacturing, particularly brass (see the metals factories described in places 35, 36). Dependent on waterpower, new industrial communities grew up in the valleys, creating a layered landscape of older, agricultural hill towns and newer, lowland, mill towns.

Along the state's southern border is Long Island Sound, sheltered from the open ocean by its namesake island. The shoreline's extensive marshes proved valuable for Connecticut's people as well, providing habitat for shellfish and fowl for food, and grasses for a variety of uses (figure 8).

The indented coastline offers many small harbors and river mouths, like Mystic's, which fostered maritime industries including fishing, trade, and shipbuilding (figure 9). Larger harbors at Bridgeport, New Haven, and New London became ports, but these were overshadowed by New York and Boston. It is often forgotten that even inland towns such as Middletown, Hartford, Derby, and Norwich all were busy ports before they became industrial cities, and that steamship travel on the Connecticut River continued through the first third of the twentieth century, bringing traffic and commerce to river towns like Essex (place 52). At the beginning of the twenty-first century, evidence of this water-based economy has largely disappeared, as shipping has shrunk to a fraction of its earlier importance, railroad lines and highways have cut towns off from their waterfronts, and maritime traffic has been mostly reduced to private pleasure craft and oil tankers.

In sum, Connecticut is topographically varied, while modest in scale (figure 10). There are no real mountains, hills and valleys are relatively gentle, and harbors small. There are few sweeping views, and scenery is bucolic

(*top*) FIGURE 7. Stone walls, Connecticut Route 165, Griswold. M. Scott
(*middle*) FIGURE 8. Marsh, Milford. Connecticut Trust for Historic Preservation
(*bottom*) FIGURE 9. Mystic River, Groton. Connecticut Trust for Historic Preservation

FIGURE 10.
Mount Riga, Salisbury.
Connecticut Trust for
Historic Preservation

FIGURE 11. Wigwam, in a display at the Mashantucket Pequot Museum and Research Center. Mashantucket Pequot Museum and Research Center

rather than dramatic. Second-growth forests further restrict the scenery, leaving few wide, distant views or open areas. This gives the state a divided quality, broken (apart from the central valley) into small segments where the inhabitants of one town are isolated from their neighbors in the next. It also gives it an intimate quality, in which humans are rarely overwhelmed, but rather feel at home.

HISTORY

How the people of Connecticut have built is inextricably intertwined with how they lived their lives—economically, socially, politically, culturally. What follows is a brief sketch of the state's historical and architectural development. It is meant to provide a general background for the one hundred places that follow.[6]

Beginnings: Prehistory to 1730

There is no written record for most of human history in what we now call Connecticut.[7] What we know about the period prior to the arrival of Europeans comes to us in fragmentary form through the oral traditions of Native Americans and the discoveries made by archaeologists. Humans arrived here more than ten thousand years ago, and for millennia they moved from place to place by season in search of food. With the introduction of agriculture, particularly the growing of maize, as early as 1000 CE, longer-term settlements began to appear, but Connecticut's Native Americans remained seminomadic.

The oldest structures for which there is physical evidence were rock shelters or pit dwellings dug into hillsides, some dating from as much as ninety-five hundred to ten thousand years ago. For the most part, Connecticut's native inhabitants built light, impermanent shelters of bent saplings covered with slabs of bark. Called weetoos or wigwams, these structures lasted only a few seasons before returning to the earth (figure 11). However, evidence of their design remains in the archaeological record, in Native American cultural traditions, and in drawings or descriptions made by European settlers.

In addition to these structures, Native Americans shaped the land itself. They cleared fields for crops, burned out underbrush to ease hunting, and constructed weirs to aid fishing. The geographical historian William Cronon quotes seventeenth-century Europeans who marveled at the parklike landscape they found. They believed this to be natural, but it was in fact the product of Native American practices. One other way Native Americans shaped the land was by blazing footpaths, some of which were taken over for colonial roads and in turn became the transportation corridors that underlie modern development. Although drawn in 1930, the map shown in figure 12 is still considered accurate.[8] Many of the routes it shows are used by modern roadways, such as the Quinnipiac-Sucklauk Path connecting the sites that would become New Haven and Hartford along present-

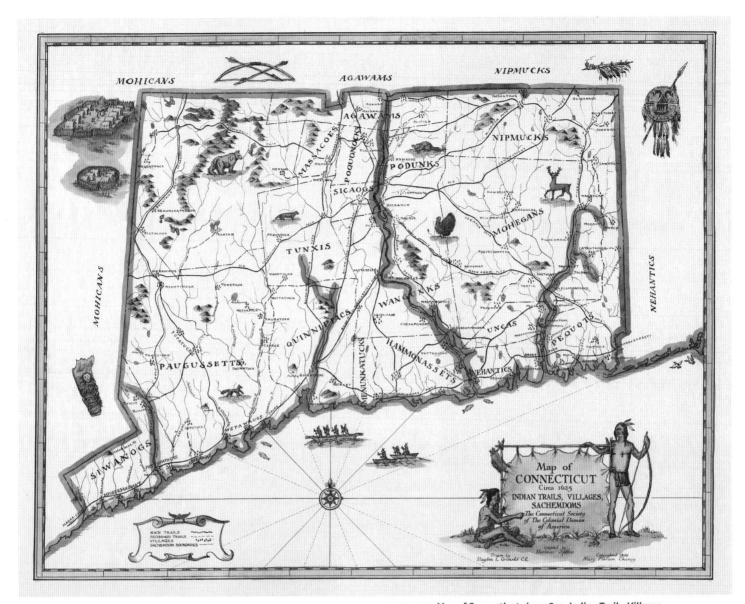

FIGURE 12. *Map of Connecticut circa 1625: Indian Trails, Villages, Sachemdoms.* Compiled by Matthias Spiess, drawn by Hayden L. Griswold, issued by Connecticut Society of the Colonial Dames of America, 1930. The Connecticut Historical Society

day Interstate 91, or the Old Connecticut Path, now Interstate 84.

As European settlers gained dominance, Native American building practices faded into obscurity. Interest in these practices reemerged at the end of the twentieth century, when a resurgence of tribal pride and political action led to federal recognition of tribal nations, and subsequent economic prosperity has made possible a burst of new construction for casinos, museums, and tribal facilities (see place 94, the Mashantucket Pequot Museum and Research Center).

The first European settlement in Connecticut was a Dutch trading post built in 1633 at the present-day site of Hartford. Within a few years, Puritan settlers from England and Massachusetts began establishing permanent settlements that pushed out the Dutch: Windsor, Wethersfield, and Hartford on the Connecticut River, and New Haven and Saybrook on the coast. These settlements soon coalesced into two colonies, Connecticut and New Haven, which were united by the Charter of 1662, obtained from King Charles II of England by John Winthrop Jr. From the fertile central valley and the navigable shoreline, settlers moved inland to less-choice upland areas; by the mid-eighteenth century the entire area that now is Connecticut was occupied.

The colonial settlers' first task was ordering the land—imposing systems of ownership and governance on what they perceived as virgin wilderness. The basic unit of government was the town, a self-governing geographical division that in most cases was founded by a group of proprietors. These were essentially shareholders who jointly acquired rights to a tract in exchange for financing its settlement.[9] The proprietors laid out roads and set aside parcels for public functions such as marketplaces, militia training grounds, and meetinghouses. They might also offer land as an inducement for people with desirable skills, such as a minister, a miller, or a blacksmith, to settle in the town. The remaining land they divided among themselves, to keep or sell to others. By the end of the eighteenth century, almost all commonly held lands had been distributed. Remnants of this system survive in two Connecticut communities, New Haven and Lebanon, where the town greens are still considered to belong to the heirs of the original proprietors. Adjoining property owners still make hay on the Lebanon green (figure 13), while ultimate decision-making power for New Haven's green is vested in the Committee of the Proprietors of the Common and Undivided Lands, a body chartered by the Connecticut General Assembly in 1805 that legally represents those heirs (place 40).[10]

The earliest settlements were compact, with residents living close together and working dispersed fields, sometimes in common. Rather than a contiguous allotment, each proprietor might receive several

FIGURE 13. Town green, Lebanon. Connecticut Trust for Historic Preservation

disconnected parcels, providing some of each type of land in the town: a home lot in the central settlement, fields for crops, pastureland, a woodlot, even marshland for hay. Very quickly, the attraction of working one's own land, and then of living on independent farmsteads, led inhabitants to consolidate their holdings and move out of central villages. Later towns were laid out in larger individual parcels from the start, creating scattered farmsteads, each supplying much of its inhabitants' basic needs.

Each town also had a church. The Puritans who settled Connecticut sought to create a society based on their ideal of a radically purified Christianity, through which God's will permeated every aspect of life. All inhabitants were required by law to attend Sabbath worship. As populations grew and settlements expanded, differences over the location of the meetinghouse often caused disputes. Outlying residents sought permission to form separate religious parishes, or societies, which in many cases became the nuclei of separate villages and eventually split off as separate towns. However it was founded, each congregation functioned as an independent, self-governing entity, subject to no higher authority but God. This governance, by independent individual congregations, led the Puritans' religious descendants to be called "Congregationalists."

The political and religious system of organization devised by the first English settlers created a framework that still determines much of the present-day shape of

Connecticut. The first towns are still occupied, and their boundaries, although subdivided, still can be traced on maps, along with early roads and land divisions, as in South Windsor (place 2).

Another legacy of early land planning is the town green found at the heart of many Connecticut communities (figure 14). Greens actually began as public spaces set aside for a variety of purposes: planned market places, lots for meetinghouses or schools, broad main streets, even leftover space at intersections (see Colebrook and New Haven, places 39 and 40). Whatever their origins, they have merged into a single category that has come to be considered uniquely characteristic of New England towns—landscaped spaces whose civic character distinguishes them from parks.[11]

In addition to these physical characteristics, another legacy of the colonial period is a persistent mind-set that continues to shape how Connecticut builds. Based on their origins as self-governing, primarily agricultural, and both secular and spiritual in nature, Connecticut towns in the colonial period were inward-focused and independent, and they remain so. No matter how small, nearly every town has its own town hall, its own library, and its own fire and rescue service. (More than a dozen regional school systems represent rare examples of inter-town cooperation, as economies of scale have overridden municipal independence.) Each town shapes its built environment through its own zoning and planning regulations and competes to attract (or avoid) commercial development. Reinforcing the small scale of the land, this multiplication of municipalities breaks Connecticut up into a patchwork of small units.

Like colonial settlement patterns, colonial building patterns started with English traditions, which gradually were adapted to local conditions. The only firmly documented structure to survive from the first generation of settlement is the Henry Whitfield House in Guilford, said to have been begun in 1639 (figure 15). Although extensively altered and heavily restored, it resembles, on a modest scale, an English manor house and suggests an intention to transplant English social patterns to the New World. Archival sources indicate that several other early leaders built similarly ambitious dwellings.

FIGURE 14. Town green, Southington.
Connecticut Trust for Historic Preservation

Although the Whitfield House was constructed of stone, wood dominated Connecticut building from the first. Most of the early English settlers came from East Anglia, a region that had a well-developed tradition of timber construction, and Connecticut's forests offered them plenty of raw materials to work with. Timber-framed buildings are essentially cages of hewn wooden posts and beams fitted together with joints suited to the particular stresses of their location in the building (figure 16). Inside, framing members continued to serve decorative as well as structural purposes. They were smoothed and edged with chamfers or moldings, and occasionally further decorated with paint.[12]

Most surviving houses from the seventeenth and early eighteenth centuries follow a common plan, with two rooms flanking a central chimney, often but not always with a second layer of rooms behind them. From these, early twentieth-century historians such as J. Frederick Kelly deduced a linear evolution of house types (figure 17), starting with two-over-two room plans like the Buttolph-Williams House (place 79) and moving on to lean-to ("saltbox") plans like the Deacon Adams House (place 80) and then full two-story plans, all with central chimneys. The sequence culminated in houses like that of Ebenezer Grant (place 87), with center halls and paired chimneys, which Kelly considered the most advanced. Recent researchers have concluded that there was a much greater

FIGURE 15. Henry Whitfield House, Guilford, ca. 1639–1640. Courtesy of Henry Whitfield State Museum, Guilford, Connecticut

variety of plan and construction than Kelly recognized, including one-room houses; long, linear houses; houses with end chimneys; impermanent structures constructed with no proper foundation, just posts set into holes in the ground; and smaller variants of the center-chimney plan such as the Benjamin Hall Jr. House (place 15). And while Kelly got the relative sequence right, many of the types that he placed within a particular period actually continued to be built alongside supposedly later types.[13]

Part of the difficulty in understanding the architecture of Connecticut's early colonial period is due to the difficulty of determining construction dates. Since the 1980s, new research, notably by former professor Abbott Lowell Cummings at Yale University, has begun to change our understandings of the state's colonial building culture.[14] Cummings concluded that Connecticut tended to be more stylistically conservative than Massachusetts and Rhode Island, which makes the earlier practice of dating based

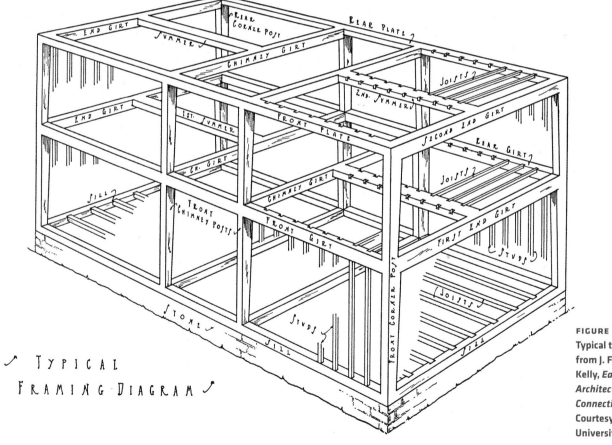

FIGURE 16. Typical timber frame, from J. Frederick Kelly, *Early Domestic Architecture of Connecticut*, 1924. Courtesy of Yale University Press

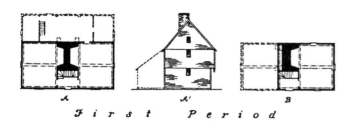

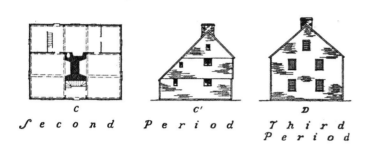

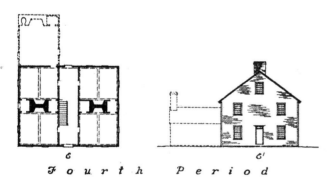

FIGURE 17. Chronology of colonial plan types, from J. Frederick Kelly, *Architectural Guide for Connecticut*, 1935

FIGURE 18. Chidsey-Linsley House, East Haven, ca. 1790. Connecticut Trust for Historic Preservation

on stylistic comparisons across the region less reliable. Based on research by Cummings and others, the dates of structures such as the Buttolph-Williams and Hyland Houses (places 79, 82) have been revised, and further work will doubtless produce other revisions. The result, as Cummings warned, is that almost any seventeenth-century building date needs to be looked at skeptically.

Another recent development has been the recognition of architectural influences from the neighboring New York Colony with its more heterogeneous population and building practices. Differences in framing, the use

of shingles rather than clapboards as a wall covering, and wide, flaring eaves all are features that have been attributed to Dutch or other continental European traditions that reached Connecticut through New York (figure 18).[15]

When it came to public buildings, the colonial settlers relied less on English precedent. The Puritans insisted that the term "church" referred to a congregation of people, never a building, so they rejected traditional church architecture. Instead, they developed a new type of public building that could serve both religious and secular purposes: the meetinghouse.[16] Influenced by Protestant architectural experimentation in Europe, meetinghouses were designed to allow a large body of people to gather and hear a speaker. Early examples were square or nearly square, with a raised pulpit on one wall, a floor tightly packed with seating, and, where needed, additional seating in galleries (figure 19). In new settlements or poorer communities, meetinghouses often were rudimentary structures, poorly built, poorly maintained, and quickly outgrown and replaced. However, in towns like Wethersfield, where circumstances allowed, they could be solidly built and finely ornamented (place 56).

In sum, our understanding of Connecticut architecture in the first century after English settlement is at once less complete and more complicated than previous generations thought. What remains constant is the overall point that its inhabitants transplanted European settlement and

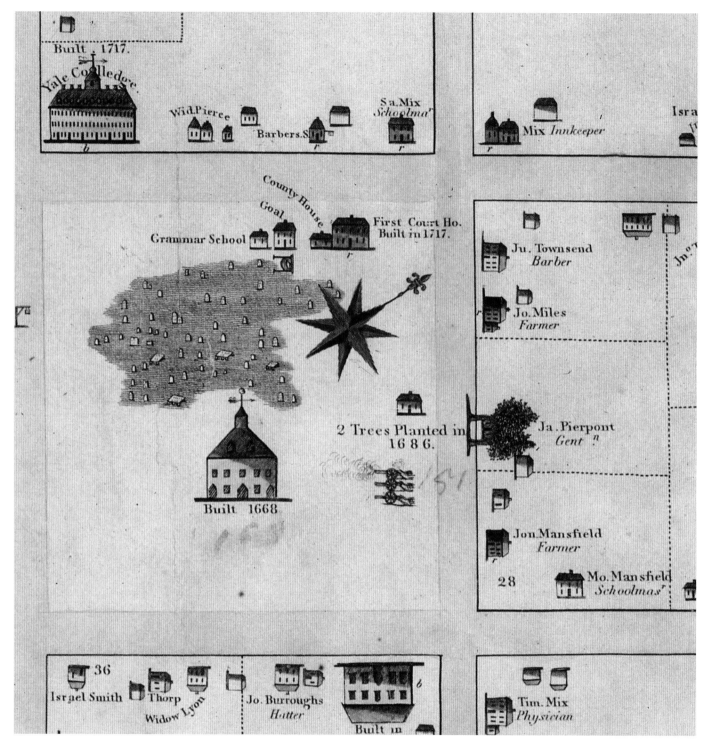

Built 1717.

Yale Colledge.

Wid. Pierce

Barbers.S.

S a. Mix
Schoolma'

Mix Innkeeper

Isr

County House

Goal

Grammar School

First Court Ho.
Built in 1717.

Ju. Townsend
Barber

Jo. Miles
Farmer

2 Trees Planted in
1686.

Ja. Pierpont
Gent.

Built 1668

Jon. Mansfield
Farmer

28

Mo. Mansfield
Schoolmas'

36

Israel Smith

Thorp

Widow Lyon

Jo. Burroughs
Hatter

Built in

Tim. Mix
Physician

FIGURE 19. Second Meeting House, New Haven, 1668; demolished ca. 1757. Detail from James Wadsworth, *A Plan of the Town of New Haven with All the Buildings in 1748*, T. Kensett, engraver, Wm. Lyon for the Connecticut Academy of Arts and Sciences, 1806. Courtesy of the New Haven Museum

building patterns to the new land, then made necessary changes to adapt them to different conditions.

Agricultural Connecticut, 1730–1840

By about 1730, Connecticut was well established and beginning to prosper. Although the colony remained officially Congregational, its uniformly Puritan character changed, as religious fervor rose and sank, and the population became more religiously diverse (although still almost entirely Protestant), including Anglicans, Baptists, and Quakers. Society continued to be dominated by a small, interrelated elite, yet compared to other colonies there were narrower extremes of wealth and poverty.

The economy of the colony, and later the state, remained predominantly agricultural (figure 20). Nearly everyone farmed, including artisans and even professionals who pursued other occupations. Expanding opportunities for trade encouraged the growth of market agriculture, first in the fertile Connecticut Valley, and then in other areas. Specialized crops included tobacco and onions, as well as foodstuffs and livestock exported to the West Indies. However, by the first decades of the nineteenth century, many rural residents were moving to industrial cities or to cheaper, more fertile land on the frontier.

After the Revolution, release from British colonial restrictions opened new possibilities for trade. Increasing prosperity fueled urban growth, and Connecticut's first cities, Hartford, Middletown, New Haven, New London, and Norwich, were incorporated in 1784. At the turn of the nineteenth century, private companies built turnpikes, vastly improving overland travel and commerce in communities like Thompson (place 50). The Farmington and Enfield Falls Canals extended navigation inland (place 51), and the new federal government took over improvements for coastal navigation such as lighthouses (place 49). These improvements further increased trade, and also opened up more of the state to religious, social, and architectural ideas from the outside world. Water remained the easiest way to travel, and this period saw the fullest development of Connecticut's maritime economy.

In light of later history, the most significant development of the late eighteenth and early nineteenth centuries was the emergence of industry. Gristmills and

North view of Pequot Hill, Groton.

Cotton Factory village, Glastenbury.

(*top*) FIGURE 20. *North View of Pequot Hill, Groton,* from John Warner Barber, *Connecticut Historical Collections,* 1836
(*bottom*) FIGURE 21. *Cotton Factory village, Glastenbury* [*sic*], from John Warner Barber, *Connecticut Historical Collections,* 1836

sawmills had been necessary economic components since the beginning of European settlement and continued to be vital to local economies (see Ledyard Up-Down Sawmill, place 30), but now larger-scale manufacturing appeared, employing capital generated by agriculture or trade and taking advantage of the power available from the state's many watercourses. From the first, Connecticut's chief products included armaments and textiles, exemplified respectively by Eli Whitney, who made rifles in Hamden beginning in 1798, and by early woolen and cotton mills in places such as Derby and Glastonbury (figure 21). Little remains of these earliest manufacturing complexes, but

FIGURE 22. Jacobson barn, Storrs, ca. 1870.
Connecticut Trust for Historic Preservation

manufacturers like the Collins Company set patterns of industrial construction and development that others would follow (place 31). Connecticut's growing size and prosperity during this era created a need for more specialized and more imposing architecture. In addition to transportation improvements, the increasingly complex society demanded new types of buildings such as town halls and alms houses (place 58). Private institutions such as colleges and hospitals sought appropriate facilities to accommodate their work. Expanding commerce and new manufacturing enterprises required commercial buildings and factories. Congregations, even in modest towns like Warren, built new meetinghouses that were more overtly religious in nature and began to call them "churches" (place 59).

Farmers improved barn design, adding windows and cupolas for ventilation, and setting barns into banks to provide lower-level space for livestock. They adopted a new type of barn, framed with a series of transverse bents, which could be expanded more easily than the older three-bay English barn type seen at the Catlin Farm (place 24). Nonetheless, both types continued to be built, along with hybrids that combined features of each (figure 22).

One important architectural trend from the middle of the eighteenth century to the middle of the nineteenth was the desire to create an overall environment that reflected the growing prosperity and refinement of Connecticut and its people. As with the laying out of

towns in the early period, this process was first seen in planning and landscape design. Towns began to clean up their streets and their greens by removing tumbledown utilitarian buildings and unkempt burial grounds, and by grading, fencing, and planting trees. New Haven was a leader in this trend, but other towns quickly followed (place 40).

The illustrations in John Warner Barber's *Connecticut Historical Collections*, published in 1836, capture this civic improvement in mid-progress (figures 23, 24). Some show old, unpainted meetinghouses or rough greens like Ashford's, littered with stumps or rocks; others show newly planted trees and stylish buildings, as in Canterbury. Barber depicted Connecticut as a place of tidy farmsteads and bustling towns ornamented with shade trees surrounding peaceful greens, an image that still holds sway nearly two hundred years later.

One trend reinforcing civic improvement was a growing taste for refined buildings that incorporated classical motifs from ancient Greece and Rome. The ways builders translated ancient classicism into current architecture varied over time. In the mid-eighteenth century the intertwined network of elite families that dominated the Connecticut Valley, known as the "River Gods," adopted their own variant of Baroque design, combining big scale and bold effect in works like the Ebenezer Grant House in South Windsor (place 87). In the years before and after the Revolution, Georgian design used classical imagery from pattern books more correctly, but it was still often applied to buildings of vernacular plan and construction, such as the Epaphroditus Champion house in East Haddam (place 68).

At the turn of the nineteenth century, Charles Bulfinch's design for the Old State House in Hartford (place 88) introduced Neoclassicism, an international movement based on recent studies of ancient ruins (still transmitted through books), as well as a taste for clear geometry and slender forms. Known in the United States as the Federal style, this phase of Neoclassicism gave way in the 1830s to a preference for Greek rather than Roman precedents, as well as for the chunkier proportions and more austere geometry seen in the New London Custom House (place 89). But all these designs were united by a conviction that

Southwestern view of Ashford, (central part.)

South view of the central part of Canterbury.

(top) FIGURE 23. *Southwestern View of Ashford (Central Part)*, from John Warner Barber, *Connecticut Historical Collections*, 1836
(bottom) FIGURE 24. *South View of the Central Part of Canterbury*, from John Warner Barber, *Connecticut Historical Collections*, 1836

FIGURE 25. Ralph Earl, *Houses Fronting New Milford Green*, ca. 1796. The Dorothy Clark Archibald and Thomas L. Archibald Fund, the Ella Gallup Sumner and Mary Catlin Sumner Collection Fund, the Krieble Family Fund for American Art, the Gift of James Junius Goodwin and the Douglas Tracy Smith and Dorothy Potter Smith Fund, 1994.16.1. Wadsworth Atheneum Museum of Art, Hartford, Connecticut. Photograph by Allen Phillips

the architecture of the age must be based on classical antiquity.

Although primarily associated with Enlightenment rationalism, early nineteenth-century classicism also appealed to the growing Romanticism that sought to engage the emotions rather than the intellect (see the Samuel Russell House, place 16). In Connecticut, as in other places, Romanticism first appeared in naturalistic landscape designs, such as the garden that painter Ralph Earl depicted behind Elijah Boardman's house in New Milford (figure 25). Shortly thereafter, Episcopal churches began to make tentative explorations of Gothic design, as a way of claiming their denomination's medieval English heritage in order to distinguish themselves from Congregationalists. These earliest Gothic Revival buildings were Neoclassical designs dressed up with a few pointed arches, as seen on the Union Episcopal Church at Riverton, in the town of Barkhamsted (figure 26).

Both classical and Romantic strains of architecture required new kinds of builders. The period saw the rise of a generation of master builders who employed architectural pattern books in addition to orally transmitted building lore. Figures such as Thomas Hayden of Windsor, William Sprats of Litchfield, and Lavius Fillmore of Norwich produced buildings that met their clients' demands for refinement and sophistication (figure 27; Epaphroditus Champion House, place 68).

Even greater change was afoot. Charles Bulfinch, who

designed the Old State House in 1796, later claimed to be
the first professional architect in the country. However, it
was not until the 1830s that any architects set up practice
in Connecticut. Ithiel Town started as a master builder,
executing Asher Benjamin's design for Center Church in
New Haven in 1812 (place 40). He worked as an architect
in New York before moving back to New Haven in 1836.
By that time, both Henry Austin and Sidney Mason Stone
were practicing there. Austin had opened an office in
Hartford in 1839 but didn't stay long; that city didn't get
another resident professional architect until Octavius
Jordan in 1850.

In the meantime, other master builders who were
trained through traditional apprenticeships and relied
on pattern books for inspiration continued to work
throughout the state, among them David Hoadley in
New Haven County (figure 28), John Bishop in New
London, James Jennings in Warren (place 59), and the
Truesdale/Truesdell family in Tolland County. Others
provided engineering expertise needed for factories and
infrastructure projects such as the Farmington and Enfield
Falls Canals (place 51). But the professional lines remained
indistinct; in the course of his career a man might

successively call himself a carpenter, a master builder, and an architect. The distinctions in terminology seem in some cases to have been as much a matter of self-promotion as of training or practice.

The century between about 1730 and 1840 saw Connecticut move beyond its initial, primarily agricultural, economy to become an economically diverse society. This development was reflected in movements to improve its towns and landscapes, to adopt internationally recognized classical standards of architecture, and then to temper that classicism with Romanticism. Economic and social diversification inspired the development of new building types and the emergence of educated, professional architects.

Industrial Connecticut, 1840–1930

By 1840, Connecticut was a vastly different place from what it had been one hundred years before, and it stood on the brink of even greater changes. Over the next century, the processes that had begun after the Revolution completely transformed the state, turning it into an urban, industrialized society whose members traced their lineage to every country of Europe as well as many other places throughout the world. Other states experienced similar changes, but in small, densely settled, overwhelmingly homogeneous Connecticut they were particularly dramatic.

The main factor was industry. Manufacturing came to dominate Connecticut's economy, and mills and factories appeared in nearly every town. Textiles and armaments continued to be principal products, but the state also became known for processed materials such as sheet brass, wire, and thread, as well as a wide range of consumer products, including clocks and watches, tools and hardware, and household goods. Less visible in the marketplace but crucial to continued industrial prominence were the companies that produced industrial machinery; ongoing innovation kept Connecticut at the forefront of the nation's economic development during this period.

Industrial expansion sparked explosive growth in existing cities like Bridgeport and gave birth to new ones such as Shelton (figure 29; place 34). By the 1860s, improvements in steam power freed manufacturers from the need to locate where there was waterpower. Increasingly, they clustered in cities with their better transportation connections and ready labor supply. There, the need for infrastructure and services to support the industrial population fueled additional growth: transportation networks to move raw materials and finished goods, housing for workers and their families, stores to sell them the goods they needed for daily life, and schools, churches, and other community institutions.

Even in the countryside, industrial development prompted changes. Most rural towns lost population as residents moved to cities to find work. Those who remained behind concentrated on providing city markets with foods that could not be transported long distances, or on cash crops such as tobacco (place 26). Nearly every rural community also had some small-scale manufacturing enterprise. Some of these served local needs; others eventually fostered the growth of a new industrial center or else moved to a larger existing community with better access to labor or transportation or suppliers.

The need for labor and the promise of economic opportunity drew immigrants from abroad. In 1840, Connecticut's population still traced its roots primarily to the British Isles. In 1850, immigrants made up approximately 10 percent of the state's population; by 1870, the number was 25 percent, and by 1900 Connecticut had one of the largest percentages of foreign-born residents in the country.[17] The newcomers came in waves from different areas: Irish and Germans in the antebellum years, French Canadians beginning in the 1860s; Southern and Eastern Europeans from the 1880s. They brought new religions, new social patterns, and new faces to the state.

The growth in size and complexity of Connecticut society affected architectural development. First of all, there was simply more of everything, and everything was bigger: cities, factories, schools, commercial buildings— even houses for the prospering middle and upper classes and multifamily dwellings for urban workers. Prosperity and economies of scale thanks to mass production encouraged growth and elaboration. No building embodied the new scale and lavishness of Connecticut architecture better than the State Capitol, completed in 1879 (place 91).

FIGURE 29. View of Bridgeport, Ct. O. H. Bailey & Co., 1875 (detail). Library of Congress

Industrial architecture was dominated by multipurpose loft buildings suitable for many types of manufacturing, such as the Hockanum Mill (place 33). But as processes and products diversified, many manufacturers, particularly those such as the Clark Brothers Bolt Company who worked in metals, needed more-specialized structures (place 35). Whatever the type, structures had to withstand the weight and stresses of ever-bigger and ever-faster machinery. By the early twentieth century, the introduction of electric lighting and power meant

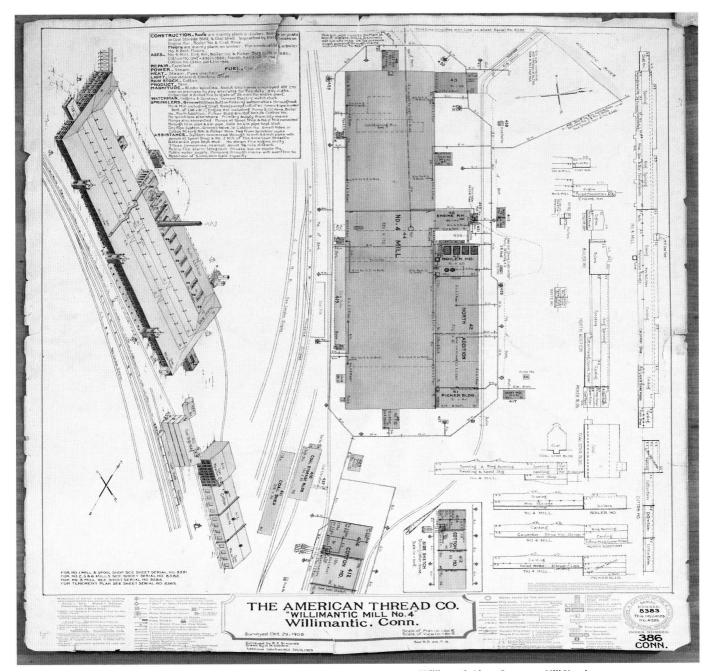

FIGURE 30. Willimantic Linen Company, Mill Number 4, Willimantic, 1884, destroyed 1995. Insurance map, 1909. The Windham Textile and History Museum

that it no longer was necessary to have workers close to windows for illumination, or to keep machinery in the straight lines dictated by shaft-and-belt power transmission systems. With electricity, buildings could spread out, like the Willimantic Linen Company's Mill Number 4 (1884; demolished; figure 30), claimed as the first industrial building in the country specifically designed for electric lighting. Insurance companies, many of them headquartered in Hartford, influenced industrial buildings as well. They pushed for fire-safety efforts such as eliminating attics, where flammable materials often accumulated, and building separate towers to isolate stairs. Beyond functional changes, owners often asked for ornamentation to proclaim their prosperity and stability to potential customers. At the Meriden Curtain Fixture Company's plant, in Meriden, two powerhouses—one with an eye-catching arched roof—supplemented loft buildings, and bands of decorative brick ornamented the entire complex (figure 31). This ornament could benefit the bottom line as companies used images of attractive facilities like this in marketing materials.

Industrial architecture was not limited to factory or mill buildings. Factory complexes also needed auxiliary structures to house specialized processes, as well as warehouses, power plants, rail sidings, bridges, and dams and canals for waterpower systems (place 34). Companies continued to develop or expand factory towns and neighborhoods offering housing, stores, and community buildings for their workers. In the early twentieth century the Progressive and Garden City movements inspired efforts to improve working-class housing (see Seaside Village, place 44). A privately built example is Connecticut Gables (1917, W. H. Cox; figure 32), a multifamily structure erected by the Connecticut Mills Company in the Danielson section of Killingly. Its fourteen apartments each comprised three to five rooms, plus modern kitchens and bathrooms. The building, which resembled an English country inn, bore a plaque proclaiming it "A Forward Step in Good Housing for Working People."

Companies were less likely to get involved in neighborhood building in the cities, where private investors were active. However, industrial expansion still drove rapid growth in Connecticut cities from the mid-nineteenth to the mid-twentieth centuries. During this period the two- or three-family house emerged as the most common urban residential type. These narrow buildings with units stacked one on top of the other gave each unit windows on all four sides, providing more light and air than the older row houses or side-by-side double houses (figure 33). Multifamily buildings like the Perfect Sixes

(*top*) FIGURE 31. Meriden Curtain Fixture Company, Meriden, 1891 and later. Connecticut Trust for Historic Preservation
(*bottom*) FIGURE 32. W. H. Cox, Connecticut Gables, Danielson, 1917. Connecticut Trust for Historic Preservation

of Hartford (place 19), or bigger apartment blocks could accommodate larger numbers of people. Fire laws required brick construction in inner neighborhoods, changing the texture and visual weight of buildings.

Immigrants faced challenges fitting into the built environment in the late nineteenth and early twentieth centuries. In the cities they generally lived and worked in buildings constructed and owned by the Yankee upper classes. In the countryside, they moved into farms abandoned by their Yankee owners. The newcomers' most visible effect on the built environment was in houses of worship: synagogues and Catholic and Orthodox churches brought new forms to Connecticut communities. Catholic

FIGURE 33. 50 Francis Street, Ansonia, ca. 1900. Robert Egleston

(*top*) FIGURE 34. Main Street, New Hartford.
Connecticut Trust for Historic Preservation
(*bottom*) FIGURE 35. Travelers Insurance Company, Hartford,
1906–1918. Connecticut Trust for Historic Preservation

churches, convents, and schools formed complexes that served as a religious centers for the Irish, Germans, Italians, Eastern Europeans, and French Canadians who worked the state's mills or farms (see Catholic churches in Baltic and Ashford, places 61, 75). Jewish immigrants built synagogues with onion domes and other Moorish Revival design motifs that expressed the Middle Eastern roots of their faith and distinguished the buildings from their Christian counterparts (place 97). Eventually members of some immigrant groups went into the building trades and contributed to the construction of many character-defining structures in the state (Villa Friuli, place 93).

Downtowns became ever more densely developed, as commercial buildings pressed to the sides and rears of their lots and grew taller. In Bridgeport, the Bishop brothers adopted an uncommon building type, the arcade, to use one property more fully (place 43). Even in small towns a few multistory "blocks" (as commercial buildings were called) proclaimed modernity and prosperity (figure 34). Very tall buildings remained rare, but each of the state's large cities has at least one structure that might qualify as a skyscraper, relatively speaking. A city's tallest building might become a local landmark, like the Travelers

Insurance Company's tower in Hartford (1906–1918, Donn Barber; figure 35).

In transportation, railroads broadened their coverage to create a statewide network of rails and stations, as well as engineering wonders like the Rapallo Viaduct in East Hampton (figure 36). Built in 1873 for the Air Line Railroad, it spans an eight-hundred-foot valley on slender wrought-iron trestles sixty feet high (eventually filled in with sand and compacted cinders to support heavier loads). Many a town's fate—whether it prospered or withered away—depended on whether or not it gained a railroad connection.

FIGURE 36. Rapallo Viaduct, East Hampton, 1873, altered 1912–1913. Archives and Special Collections at the Thomas J. Dodd Research Center, University of Connecticut Libraries. Accession number UC17-0264, IMG0028-1015

FIGURE 37. Railroad station (1886) and concrete highway bridge (1930), Cornwall. Connecticut Trust for Historic Preservation

The Connecticut Highway Department, established in 1895, improved roads and bridges, an effort that gained momentum after 1900 as automobiles proliferated. By the 1930s, the statewide network of roads and highways had become a prominent feature of the landscape (figure 37). Meanwhile, the growing cities' need for water and electricity prompted the construction of reservoirs that flooded vast portions of rural towns such as Barkhamsted (place 6).

While progress was often celebrated, the sweeping changes wrought by industrialization and urbanization also prompted reaction. The beauty of the natural world provided the central theme, expressed in picturesque, Romantic, or eclectic buildings designed to harmonize with their landscape settings and to hark back to seemingly simpler eras. In planning it expressed itself in the building of naturalistic parks and the proliferation of suburbs (figure 38). Almost every Connecticut city established one or more parks during this period, a number of them designed by Hartford native Frederick Law Olmsted (1822–1903). Vacationers escaping the heat and dirt of the cities also flocked to Connecticut's countryside and coasts, creating resorts at every level from farmstead boardinghouses (Orchard Mansion, place 28) to grand country estates (Eolia, place 3).

To guide growth, cities turned to more intensive planning from the 1890s on. Allied with the reformist goals of Progressivism, the City Beautiful movement advocated carefully considered transportation networks, systems of parks to provide recreation and literal breathing space, and construction of public buildings as civic amenities— many the gifts of wealthy industrialists like Timothy Beach Blackstone of Branford (place 92). Both Hartford and New Haven commissioned wide-ranging city plans by nationally known firms in the 1910s. Only fragments of these City Beautiful ideas were executed—a new bridge and approaches in Hartford, a new railroad station and a couple of parks in New Haven—but they remained on the books as ideals. On a smaller scale, in 1921 the city of Bristol opened Memorial Boulevard, a landscaped gateway to the city and a monument to its World War I dead (figure 39).

Aesthetically, late nineteenth- and early twentieth-century designers focused on the concept of "style" and cycled through an ever-changing assortment of architectural fashions. Almost all of them sought to harmonize with nature through rambling footprints, picturesque outlines, and muted color schemes, as seen

(*top*) FIGURE 38. Olmsted, Vaux, and Co., Walnut Hill Park, New Britain, 1870 and later. TO Design, LLC
(*bottom*) FIGURE 39. Memorial Boulevard, Bristol, 1921. Connecticut Trust for Historic Preservation

FIGURE 40. A. J. Davis, Harral-Wheeler House, Bridgeport, 1846–1850, demolished 1958. Smithsonian Institution Archives. Image #MAH-61190

in the Harral-Wheeler House in Bridgeport, designed by Alexander Jackson Davis (1846; figure 40). By the 1870s the mixing of styles and materials and encrustations of ornament were becoming more and more complex, usually combining elements from a number of periods and places in a single composition. In newly developed upper-middle-class neighborhoods, like Prospect Hill in Willimantic, the array of ornament and color can be dizzying (figure 41).

Beginning in the 1890s a reaction set in, in the form of a trend toward more disciplined design. It still remained possible to choose from among a variety of sources, including Old English, the French Beaux-Arts, Italian, and others. But instead of mixing historical sources in a single building, architects replicated designs of the past more precisely, as seen in suburban streets such as those of New Haven's Beaver Hills neighborhood (place 21).

In the hands of a skilled designer, the combination of modern planning and historic imagery could produce a masterpiece. Nowhere in Connecticut is this better seen than in Yale University's great rebuilding of the 1920s and '30s. In order to convert to a system of residential colleges,

FIGURE 41. Prospect Hill, Willimantic.
Connecticut Trust for Historic Preservation

FIGURE 42. James Gamble Rogers, Harkness Tower, Yale University, New Haven, 1917–1921. Robert W. Grzywacz

Yale demolished entire blocks for new construction (figure 42). Most of this was the work of architect James Gamble Rogers, who gave his designs careful craftsmanship and details, as well as an illusion of development over centuries that evoked Britain's Oxford and Cambridge universities. Rogers skillfully and subtly wove the new Yale into the city, following existing street patterns and aligning gates or towers to focus views from all parts of New Haven. By the mid-1930s Yale had established an architectural image of a quality and consistency that few American universities could match, though many tried.[18]

One historic style came to define Connecticut, both in its own eyes and in those of outsiders: the Colonial Revival, which drew on the state's own heritage and consciousness of its history. As early as the 1850s, members of Hartford's Fourth Congregational Church found inspiration in colonial buildings (place 81), but widespread enthusiasm for the movement began in the 1870s, when celebrations of the centennial of the American Revolution focused attention on the nation's history and architecture. Elements of "Colonial" design (the term could cover anything built from the seventeenth century up to, and sometimes including, Greek Revival) first appeared as part of the late nineteenth-century eclectic mix, but by the twentieth century, designs more faithfully resembled colonial buildings, reinterpreted to suit modern lifestyles (figure 43).

Paralleling the use of period styles was a strain of nonhistorical design, beginning with the Arts and Crafts movement. In reaction to industrialization, Arts and Crafts promoters stressed hand-craftsmanship as an antidote to impersonal mass production. While its principles could be applied to historic styles, the American branch of the movement is chiefly associated with rustic buildings characterized by chunky forms and materials left in their natural state (see the Nathaniel R. Bronson House, place 20).

In the 1920s and '30s, nonhistorical design took another form in the stylized motifs of the closely related Art Deco and Art Moderne, as seen in the Warner Theatre (place 45), or in streamlined interpretations of historical styles, as seen in New London's Post Office (figure 44) with its abstracted pilasters and low-relief carvings. More radical was European Modernism, which eschewed ornament altogether and promoted rationalism in planning. Introduced to Connecticut in the 1930s through such buildings as Ansonia High School (place 66), Modernism did not become a major design force in the state until after World War II.

Underlying stylistic changes, advances in materials and technology moved along in a parallel path. Here

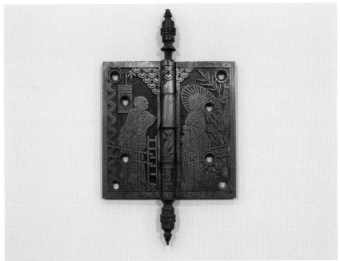

industry played a direct role, with Connecticut's factories developing and making materials and products that changed American architecture (figure 45). Russell & Erwin in New Britain and Sargent in New Haven manufactured hardware, and Bigelow Boiler, also in New Haven, made giant boilers for central heating. Wire screening came from Gilbert & Bennett in the Georgetown section of Redding, Lincrusta embossed wall coverings from Stamford, and brick from Windsor and North Haven. Lumber mills in nearly every city supplied the mass-produced trim that both reflected the taste for ornamentation and by reducing costs made it possible to indulge that taste. One Connecticut product found all across the country was iron-truss bridges from the Berlin Iron Bridge Company (place 12).

Architecture became professionalized during this period. In 1840 Connecticut had only a handful of professional architects. Self-proclaimed and self-qualified, they learned construction through apprenticeship with a master builder and design from pattern books, producing works like the Indian-inspired Willis Bristol House (place 70).[19] By 1900, architects in every city in the state were producing designs for institutional and commercial buildings and fashionable houses. Less well known was that they also designed factories and even the double-decker houses and tenements of working-class

(top) **FIGURE 43.** 44 Center Street, Windsor Locks, 1929. Connecticut Trust for Historic Preservation
(bottom) **FIGURE 44.** Payne & Keefe, United States Post Office, New London, 1933. Connecticut Trust for Historic Preservation

FIGURE 46. Fletcher-Thompson Inc., Bridgeport. Drafting room, ca. 1955. Fletcher-Thompson Inc.

neighborhoods. Many were professionally trained—Yale established its architecture department in 1916—although many others still learned through apprenticeship.

By 1930, the increasing size and complexity of construction meant that some architectural firms, such as the offices of Douglas Orr in New Haven or Fletcher-Thompson in Bridgeport, now had dozens of employees (figure 46). Firms from nearby New York and Boston also worked in Connecticut, exposing local clients and builders to big-city influences.

The second half of the nineteenth century also saw the emergence of other building-related professions. Connecticut native Frederick Law Olmsted is well known as the father of landscape architecture in the United States. His firm, although based in Massachusetts, worked extensively in the state, designing parks in Bridgeport, Hartford, Waterbury, and New Britain, as well as campuses and estates. Landscape architecture provided opportunities to women, and Connecticut has works by national leaders such as Beatrix Farrand (notably at Eolia, place 3), as well as by local designers, including Marian Coffin of New Haven. Not surprisingly, industrial design and construction became a needed specialty for some

architectural and engineering firms in the Northeast. The most prominent, such as Boston's Lockwood Greene, were located outside Connecticut, but in-state firms such as Fletcher-Thompson of Bridgeport also developed industrial expertise.

Connecticut's third century—its industrial era—created the urbanized, industrialized, diverse state that we know today. Despite the state's colonial image and the overwhelming development of the post–World War II period, a large proportion of Connecticut's architecture dates from this era. It reflects a people and a time that were dynamic, prosperous, and confident.

Modern Connecticut, 1930 to present

An industrial giant in the early twentieth century, Connecticut saw its economic base weakened in the Great Depression of the 1930s, as companies closed or moved elsewhere in search of cheaper labor. In fact, the roots of the decline go back even farther, to a slowing of innovation and investment in new machinery and facilities that began in the 1920s or even earlier.[20] World War II briefly revived the state's industries, but since the war Connecticut's economic history has largely been one of industrial loss. Nonetheless, manufacturing continues to contribute to the economy, with companies producing jet engines and parts, electronics, helicopters, and submarines.

As industry shrank, other economic sectors gained importance. Connecticut became home to large corporate headquarters, particularly in Fairfield County, where major companies such as General Electric, American Can, Pitney Bowes, and Union Carbide (place 38) settled after moving out of New York City. (Nearness to top executives' suburban residences often was an unstated factor driving the relocations.) Hartford continued to be a center of the nation's insurance industry, with some companies remaining in the city while others, like their New York counterparts, moved to the suburbs. An influential pioneer was the Connecticut General Life Insurance Company, which built a new headquarters in Bloomfield in 1957 (figure 47). Designed by the corporate architectural firm Skidmore, Owings & Merrill, with art and landscaping by sculptor Isamu Noguchi and interiors by the design firm Knoll Associates, Connecticut General's new headquarters

FIGURE 48. Amenta / Emma Architects, Advanced Manufacturing Technology Center, Naugatuck Valley Community College, Waterbury, 2007–2009. Robert Egleston

FIGURE 47. Skidmore, Owings & Merrill, Connecticut General Life Insurance Company headquarters, Bloomfield, 1957. National Register of Historic Places

received nationwide attention as a model of Modernist design and planning. However, by the end of the century, mergers and offshoring were weakening the corporate presence, and companies that remained found it more advantageous to occupy rented quarters rather than invest in imposing headquarters that future reorganization might render redundant.

Education, always important in Connecticut, came to the forefront as other sectors declined. This is most dramatically seen in New Haven, once known primarily as a manufacturing city. As factories closed, Yale University became the city's biggest and richest employer and played an increasingly influential role in the city's overall development. Trinity College has played a similar role in its neighborhood of Hartford, where it has promoted redevelopment projects to benefit the city while enhancing its own surroundings. In addition, the state college and university system grew rapidly. The flagship University of Connecticut exploded from thirty-five hundred students in 1945 to more than twenty-five thousand today, and regional normal schools established to train teachers have been upgraded to universities (figure 48). Private education also continues to draw national and even international student bodies, and prestigious secondary schools like

Avon Old Farms are prominent presences in a number of communities (place 73).

Despite the economic changes, Connecticut continued to attract new residents. African Americans from the South and Puerto Ricans came to the cities in the 1940s and '50s, ironically as the industries that attracted them were beginning to fail (see New Haven's Dixwell neighborhood, place 99). After changes to immigration law in the 1960s, Asian immigrants increasingly came to the state. These newcomers shaped the places where they lived, worked, and worshipped in a variety of ways, both subtle and overt. In Montville, for example, recent Chinese immigrants are making their mark on the suburban landscape (place 48).

As the period from 1840 to 1930 was dominated by the growth of industry and cities, the time since then could be characterized as the age of suburbanization and regulation. No doubt the most significant development of the past seventy years has been the growth of the suburbs. While suburbanization in Connecticut had roots as far back as the early nineteenth century, and by the 1920s was becoming a significant factor in the state's development, after World War II it intensified dramatically. Part of a sweeping change in settlement patterns that affect the whole country, suburbanization in Connecticut reversed the centralizing forces of the industrial era, spreading the state's urban population back across the countryside. New planning types, such as residential subdivisions (Broadview Lane, place 77), shopping centers, and

FIGURE 49. 2 Arnold Street, Havemeyer Park, Greenwich, 1950. Greenwich Historical Society

FIGURE 50. John H. Duncan, "Walhall," residence of Jacob Langeloth, Greenwich, 1912–1914. Greenwich Historical Society

industrial parks (Medway Business Park, place 37), along with new versions of older building types such as schools, factories, and corporate offices (Union Carbide, place 38), took their places in a landscape of widely scattered construction linked by new roads.

While suburbanization has well-known social and environmental problems, it represented a broadening of the housing market. Subdivisions like Havemeyer Park in Greenwich (1946; figure 49), intended largely for returning veterans of World War II, or individual houses like that of Axel Nelson (place 22), offered convenient, spacious, and affordable housing to a larger share of the population than ever before.[21]

Connecticut is best known nationally for the Fairfield County communities linked to New York City. Featured in books such as *Mr. Blandings Builds His Dream House* (published in 1946 and made into a movie in 1948) and in television shows of the 1950s such as *I Love Lucy*, Connecticut gained a national reputation as a retreat for New Yorkers weary of city stresses and crowding.[22] Commuters had been traveling to New York from Fairfield County towns as early as the mid-nineteenth century, first by steamship and, after 1848, by railroad. By the 1860s developers were laying out middle-class neighborhoods close to railroad stations, such as Prospect Avenue in

Darien, built by Melville Mead in 1865. In the meantime, the very rich were building opulent estates in the countryside (figure 50).

Automobiles greatly increased the rate of growth in Fairfield County. In addition to providing a bypass to the chaotic Boston Post Road, the Merritt Parkway (place 54) was promoted for its potential to open new territory in the county's backcountry to development. Always keeping one eye on New York, Fairfield County's suburban towns can seem a world apart from the rest of the state. Nonetheless, the dominance of the Colonial Revival continued to provide cultural linkage to New England.

Outside New York's sphere of influence, suburbs also grew up around Connecticut's own cities. Some, like Norwich or Torrington, had space for suburban development within their own boundaries. In other cases, towns like West Hartford or Hamden connect almost seamlessly with a neighboring city. Perhaps most characteristic of Connecticut suburbanization are the places that, while primarily bedroom communities, manage to maintain the appearance and atmosphere of independent municipalities. Among these are places like Glastonbury, Guilford, and Ridgefield, which have functioning small-town downtowns even though much of their citizenry works elsewhere (figure 51). Despite the overlaying of suburban development on colonial agricultural towns, these communities jealously guard their independence.

FIGURE 51. Main Street, Ridgefield.
Connecticut Trust for Historic Preservation

FIGURE 52. Planned route of Interstate 84, Hartford, 1960.
Hartford History Center, Hartford Public Library

Since the 1930s, government at every level—federal, state, and local—played an increasingly visible role in shaping the physical environment. The federal government led the way. During the Depression, it funded public works projects that provided infrastructure improvements, public buildings, and park buildings like the People's State Forest Museum (place 76). After World War II, federal financing for homebuyers favored suburban development (see Broadview Lane, place 77), while urban renewal programs demolished and rebuilt the state's cities. New Haven was a national leader in urban renewal, receiving more federal money per capita than any other city in the country, but nearly every Connecticut city embarked on major redevelopment efforts (see, for instance, Constitution Plaza and the Phoenix Building, Hartford, place 46, and Dixwell Plaza, New Haven, place 99). Federal highway programs had an even greater impact, affecting both cities and countryside (figure 52). Conceived to ease travel *to* cities, new highways also encouraged movement *from* them, further dispersing the state's population.

State and local governments followed the federal lead (in many cases they administered federal programs). The result was that, in the second half of the twentieth century and the beginning years of the twenty-first, planning emerged as a dominant force. Town planning and economic development efforts often determine what is built where, and increasingly detailed building codes determine how it is built. The near-universal adoption of zoning has driven the separation of activities by use and contributed to suburban sprawl. In many communities, zoning regulations intended to preserve rural character have in fact created a very different landscape, one in which widely spaced single-family houses sit on uniformly sized lots served by shopping centers along busy connector roads. Changes in zoning also made possible new types of development such as large condominium complexes, like Heritage Village in Southbury (place 23).

Toward the end of the twentieth century, a regional planning movement began to attempt to overcome the fragmented growth patterns created by Connecticut's patchwork of towns, but with only limited success. At the same time, new regulations protecting clean air, water, and natural features complicated large-scale infrastructure works like dams and roadways, while fostering greater attention to the natural and physical environment and the social consequences of new construction.

The overarching architectural movement since the mid-twentieth century has been Modernism. For its proponents, Modernism was not a style but rather an entirely new way of building. To Modernists, "style" meant decoration unrelated to the structure or function of a building, merely pasted on after the real work of determining layout and construction was completed, which made it inauthentic. They wanted to get away from that approach and build "truthfully" with the latest materials and planning methods, experimenting with new plans for buildings like Ansonia High School (place 66) or with new technologies like prefabrication, seen in two early examples in New London (place 13).

Connecticut was well situated to take part in the spread of Modernism after World War II. The western part of the state had easy access to the international cultural center of New York. Its wealthy, educated populace eagerly called on leading New York architects, as the state's elite had regularly done for more than a century, only now the architects were Modernists such as Wallace K. Harrison, who designed the First Presbyterian Church in Stamford (place 14). Yale's architecture program was training many of them, and bringing nationally and internationally known practitioners to teach or lecture—and get commissions. To a lesser degree, Boston and Providence played a similar role for eastern Connecticut. In New Haven, both the urban renewal program and Yale's postwar expansion projects deliberately included up-to-date Modernist architecture by prominent leaders of the architectural profession, a model followed by other cities and institutions. These policies brought cutting-edge design to users who otherwise might not have chosen it, such as the Dixwell Avenue Congregational United Church of Christ, an African American congregation that had been considering a Colonial Revival edifice before the Redevelopment Agency assigned the Modernist architect John Johansen to it (place 99).

While New Haven was uniquely located at the intersection of academia and aggressive urban renewal, Connecticut had other, if smaller, centers of Modernism. Enclaves for like-minded pioneers popped up, often around other colleges or universities or in suburbs like Guilford or Farmington. Village Creek, in Norwalk, was founded in 1949 as a multiracial community based on equality and nondiscrimination; Modernist architecture reflected its progressive social goals (figure 53). An important circle of patronage operated in Litchfield, in contrast to that community's well-known self-image as the ideal colonial town (place 78).

One of the nation's most publicized Modernist hotbeds

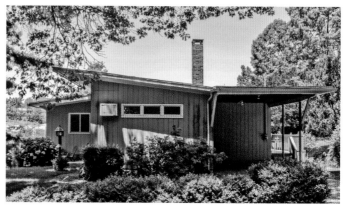

FIGURE 53. 12 Split Rock Road, Village Creek, Norwalk, 1964. Tod Bryant

was New Canaan, where five architects formerly associated with Harvard University settled in the late 1940s (place 5). Known as the "Harvard Five," Marcel Breuer, John Johansen, Philip Johnson, Eliot Noyes, and Victor Christ-Janer led a flowering of Modernist architecture in the town. Seeking prestige and a progressive image, corporations and schools also enthusiastically adopted Modernism. Almost any American architectural journal printed between about 1945 and 1970 will include at least one Connecticut building, whether a school, office building, or residence.

Amid Connecticut's well-publicized Modernist activity, it is easy to forget that a significant segment of the population resisted Modernism. Suburban residential building in particular continued to be dominated by the Colonial Revival (see the Axel Nelson House, place 22). A large portion of this was the work of speculative builders and non-architect designers, although some architects continued to produce traditional designs. They were resolutely ignored by the mainstream architectural press, so it can be difficult to find information about them and their work (figure 54).

In the 1960s and '70s the dividing lines softened somewhat as architects dissatisfied with the rigidity of Modernism explored ways of reincorporating traditional design into their work. Among the leaders of this Postmodernism were Charles Moore, dean of the Yale School of Architecture from 1965 to 1970, and Robert Venturi, a Philadelphia architect who occasionally taught at Yale. Venturi's firm, Venturi, Rauch and Scott Brown,

FIGURE 54. Russell & Gibson Architects, Bakerville Methodist Church, New Hartford, 1958–1960. Connecticut Trust for Historic Preservation

FIGURE 55. Steven Izenour of Venturi, Rauch & Scott Brown, George Izenour House, Stony Creek, 1980. Tom Bernard, Courtesy of Venturi, Scott Brown and Associates Inc.

designed the widely publicized Izenour House in Stony Creek in the town of Branford (figure 55). As built, the house featured a porch with supports in the form of cutout silhouettes of Doric columns with exaggerated chunky proportions, plus a window like a huge ship's wheel—cartoonish features typical of many Postmodernist works. This game-playing opened the way for the revival of more conventionally traditional designs, although an ongoing legacy of Postmodernism was an attitude that historical styles no longer were subject to the compositional rules that previously had governed them (see Salisbury Town Hall, place 86).

Whatever clients' attitudes toward Modernism and tradition, new technologies and materials strongly influenced planning and construction. Although most new houses were built of traditional brick and clapboards and featured pedimented front doors and small-paned windows flanked by shutters, their split-level forms, open plans, and picture windows all reflected trends introduced by Modernists. And even the most conservative buyers insisted on up-to-date mechanical systems.

Resistance to Modernism also fed the rise of historic preservation. Like the Colonial Revival, preservation had roots in the late nineteenth-century rediscovery of American history and architecture. Early preservationists had concentrated on restoring colonial buildings as private homes or museums like the Hyland House in Guilford (place 82). But reaction to the widespread demolition of urban renewal and the unfamiliar forms of Modernism brought preservation to public consciousness, and a broader movement emerged.

In spite of its active Modernists, Connecticut with its long history actively took to preservation. As early as 1955 the state established the Connecticut Historical Commission to promote its historic heritage. Two developments in 1959 indicated the growing influence and changing face of the preservation movement. First,

Before | Proposal | After

FIGURE 56. 87–93 Lyon Street, New Haven. Renovation images from the New Haven Redevelopment Agency, from Mary Hommann, ed., *Wooster Square Design*, 1965. Courtesy of the New Haven Redevelopment Agency

the town of Litchfield established a local historic district, which required that a town historical commission approve any alterations to the exterior of buildings or any new construction within the district (place 84). Passed under special enabling legislation from the General Assembly, Litchfield's was the first of what now are more than one hundred such districts across the state. The second development was the adoption of an urban renewal plan for New Haven's Wooster Square neighborhood (figure 56). This was one of the first projects in the nation to take advantage of a change in urban renewal regulations allowing federal funding to be used for renovation in addition to demolition and new construction. The Wooster Square plan also demonstrated the broadening of the preservation movement in its acceptance of Victorian-era buildings.[23]

These two developments epitomized the new face of preservation. It is publicly administered and uses public funds to supplement and encourage private investment. Its targets are entire communities and neighborhoods, places of many types and from many eras. No longer focused primarily on commemorating the past, preservation is seen as a tool for planning and revitalization, and reusing significant buildings such as the abandoned Cheney Yarn Dye House (place 100). To accomplish this, it employs feasibility studies and marketing analyses alongside architectural and historical research. One such

FIGURE 57. Peter Robinson Fur-Cutting Factory, Danbury, 1884, 1895; converted to apartments, 1983. Connecticut Trust for Historic Preservation

study, completed by the Connecticut Trust for Historic Preservation, led to the conversion of the Peter Robinson Fur-Cutting Factory in Danbury to apartments in 1983 (figure 57). Over the years, specific programs have come and gone, funding has risen and fallen, but preservation itself has increasingly influenced the shape of Connecticut.

The most recent architectural trend to affect Connecticut is sustainability, which emerged at the turn of the twenty-first century. The need to conserve fuels first became a significant issue during the oil shortages of the early 1970s. In Connecticut, which relied heavily on oil for heating, builders and homeowners eagerly sought to

FIGURE 58. Thomas Lamb, Capitol Building, Hartford, 1926; converted to the Hollander Foundation Center, 2008–2010, Crosskey Architects. Crosskey Architects, LLC

orientation for passive warming and natural lighting, while also adding new features like the green roof installed on the Capitol Building in Hartford (figure 58).

These are, briefly put, some of the historical developments and architectural trends that have shaped Connecticut's evolution over more than four hundred years. Keeping them in mind, let us now look at one hundred places whose stories will flesh out this overview.

reduce energy consumption. But as shortages eased, the search for efficiency lost its urgency. It reappeared in the 1990s along with growing awareness of the toxic effects of some building materials and concerns about climate change caused by the use of fossil fuels.

To many, "sustainability" still primarily means efficiency in the use of energy for lighting, heating, and cooling—the main concerns of the 1970s. New buildings have more insulation, and increasingly are designed to use solar, wind, or geothermal power for at least part of their operation. In its current sense, though, sustainability addresses other considerations as well, as the Yale School of Forestry has demonstrated in building Kroon Hall (place 8). Materials are evaluated for the environmental effects of extracting, processing, and transporting them. Planners and developers favor higher densities, to avoid the high costs and disruptions of building new infrastructure systems, and locations easily served by public transportation, to reduce automobile use. Landscape designers incorporate hardy native plants to reduce the need for irrigation or mechanized maintenance such as lawn mowing. Preservationists promote recycling existing buildings as a way of conserving the materials and energy used in their initial construction. They also highlight traditional, low-tech ways of keeping buildings comfortable, such as solar

NOTES

1. William Hosley, *Colt: The Making of an American Legend* (Amherst: University of Massachusetts Press in association with the Wadsworth Atheneum, Hartford, 1996).

2. For more on what architecture is see James F. O'Gorman, *ABC of Architecture* (Philadelphia: University of Pennsylvania Press, 1998).

3. For more on why architecture is important see Paul Goldberger, *Why Architecture Matters* (New Haven, Conn.: Yale University Press, 2009).

4. Michael Bell, *The Face of Connecticut: People, Geology, and the Land* (Hartford: Connecticut Geological and Natural History Survey, 1985).

5. Robert M. Thorson, *Stone by Stone: The Magnificent History of New England's Stone Walls* (New York: Walker Books, 2002).

6. For a short summary of Connecticut history see Bruce Fraser, *The Land of Steady Habits: A Brief History of Connecticut* (Hartford: Connecticut Historical Commission, 1988). Regional histories with architectural summaries are found in the Connecticut Historical Commission's six-volume Historic Context series, *Historic Preservation in Connecticut*: volume 1, *Western Coastal Slope*, by Janice P. Cunningham (1992); volume 2, *Eastern Uplands*, by Linda S. Spencer (1993); volume 3, *Central Valley*, by Janice P. Cunningham (1995); volume 4, *Western Uplands*, by Geoffrey L. Rossano (1996); volume 5, *Eastern Coastal Slope*, by John Herzan (1997); and volume 6, *Northwest Highlands*, by Geoffrey L. Rossano (1997).

7. Lucianne Lavin, *Connecticut's Indigenous Peoples: What Archaeology, History, and Oral Traditions Teach Us about Their Communities and Cultures* (New Haven, Conn.: Yale University Press, 2013); William Cronon, *Changes in the Land: Indians, Colonists, and the Ecology of Early New England* (New York: Hill & Wang, 1983).

8. I am grateful to Laurie Pasteryak Lamarre, former executive director of the Institute of American Indian Studies and currently curator of exhibitions for the Fairfield Museum; and to Katherine Grandjean, assistant professor of history specializing in early American and Native American history at Wellesley College, who both recommended this map.

9. In Connecticut, as in the rest of New England, the term "town" refers first to a geographical/political division, not necessarily a built-up settlement. In other regions, the less-confusing term "township" is used. Built-up settlements within a town may be called villages (although that term has no legal meaning) or, more vaguely, sections or areas, with the principal one referred to as the town center. In the nineteenth century, boroughs and cities were established as legally incorporated areas within a town that have special taxing privileges in order to supply services not required in less densely settled areas. Today, a few towns still have boroughs (Litchfield and Stonington, for example), while most cities have been expanded to have coterminous boundaries with their towns. For settlement history see Anthony N. B. Garvan, *Architecture and Town Planning in Colonial Connecticut* (New Haven, Conn.: Yale University Press, 1951).

10. James Sexton, "Not a Park or Mere Pleasure Ground: A Case Study of the New Haven Green," documents, www.towngreens.com.

11. For more on town greens in general, as well as specific Connecticut greens, see www.towngreens.com.

12. For English timber framing and its adaptation in Massachusetts see Abbott Lowell Cummings, *Framed Houses of Massachusetts Bay* (Cambridge, Mass.: Belknap Press of Harvard University Press, 1979). Note, however, that Massachusetts information does not always apply to Connecticut.

13. Ross K. Harper et al., *Highways to History: The Archaeology of Connecticut's 18th-Century Lifeways* (Connecticut Department of Transportation, 2013); Ann Y. Smith, "A New Look at the Early Domestic Architecture of Connecticut," *Connecticut History* 46, no. 1 (Spring 2007): 16–44.

14. Abbott Lowell Cummings, "Connecticut and Its First Period Houses," *Connecticut Preservation News* 16, no. 1 (January/February 1993): 1, 8–10.

15. Abbott Lowell Cummings, "Connecticut and Its Building Traditions," *Connecticut History* 35, no. 1 (Spring 1994): 192–233.

16. Peter Benes, *Meetinghouses of Early New England* (Amherst: University of Massachusetts Press, 2012).

17. "Late 19th-Century Immigration in Connecticut," ConnecticutHistory.org; "Early 20th-Century Immigration in Connecticut," ConnecticutHistory.org; Bruce Clouette, "'Getting Their Share': Irish and Italian Immigrants in Hartford, Connecticut, 1850–1940" (PhD diss., University of Connecticut, 1992).

18. Vincent Scully et al., *Yale in New Haven: Architecture and Urbanism* (New Haven, Conn.: Yale University Press, 2004), especially Paul Goldberger's chapter, "James Gamble Rogers & the Shaping of Yale in the Twentieth Century." See also Patrick Pinnell, *Yale University: An Architectural Tour* (New York: Princeton Architectural Press, 1999) and Elizabeth Mills Brown, *New Haven: A Guide to Architecture and Urban Design* (New Haven, Conn.: Yale University Press, 1976).

19. James F. O'Gorman, *Henry Austin: In Every Variety of Architectural Style* (Middletown, Conn.: Wesleyan University Press, 2008), 7–8, 179–186.

20. Douglas W. Rae, *City: Urbanism and Its End* (New Haven, Conn.: Yale University Press, 2005).

21. Richard Longstreth, *Looking beyond the Icons: Midcentury Architecture, Landscape, and Urbanism* (Charlottesville: University of Virginia Press, 2015), chap. 5, "The Extraordinary Postwar Suburb."

22. In later seasons of *I Love Lucy*, the Ricardos moved to Westport. Eric Hodgins's *Mr. Blandings Builds His Dream House* (New York: Simon & Schuster, 1946) spoofs his own experience in building a house in New Milford.

23. Christopher Wigren, "Keeping History on the Map," *Hartford Courant*, September 13, 2009, page C5. See also Mary Hommann, *Wooster Square Design: A Report on the Background, Experience, and Design Procedures in Redevelopment and Rehabilitation in an Urban Renewal Project* (New Haven, Conn.: New Haven Redevelopment Agency, 1965).

Part One

SHAPING THE LANDSCAPE

All architecture begins with the land. Historically, the shape of the land determined where people settled, how they made their living, what materials they had to build with. In Connecticut, the fertile soils and open meadows of the Connecticut River Valley supported farming, while the swift-flowing streams of the Quinebaug-Shetucket and Naugatuck-Housatonic river systems powered mills and factories. Cities grew up on harbors or rivers at points where navigation was promising, and agricultural towns on hilltops away from the dangers of flooding or what settlers believed was unhealthy lowland air. At the same time, Connecticut builders haven't merely built *on* the land. They altered the land itself to meet their needs and desires, to ease their work or give pleasure. They divided it into fields and towns, dammed streams and rivers, excavated hillsides, filled valleys, created parks and gardens: asserting, for better or worse, their mastery over their environment. But nature has ways of reasserting itself.

I

THE FIRST BUILDERS

MOHEGAN HILL, UNCASVILLE

The common image of Native American building in the Northeast is of temporary structures such as the wigwams recorded by English colonists: ephemeral structures of bent saplings covered with bark. However, the modern environmental historian William Cronon has shown that native peoples also shaped the landscape in more wide-ranging ways. They cleared fields for crops, managed woodlands to attract game and make hunting easier, and built weirs to catch fish. Some of the rock piles and stone cellars hidden in Connecticut forests are believed to be Indian structures.

How can traces of the first builders be located today? The Mohegan Congregational Church, on Mohegan Hill in Uncasville, part of the town of Montville, is one starting point. It was established in 1831, at a time when governmental agencies were forcing Indians from their ancestral lands. Building a Christian church demonstrated that the Mohegans had been "civilized" and posed no threat to their white neighbors. The strategy worked. After the Mohegan reservation was broken up in the 1860s, the church was the only property still owned by the tribe and became a focus for Mohegan identity.

The site for the church was chosen for specific, significant reasons. Mohegan Hill had been meaningful to Mohegans long before 1831. All around the church are features important to the tribe, including Moshup's Rock, bearing an indentation identified as a giant's footprint; formations where the Makiawisug, or "little people," lived; and Uncas's spring, associated with the man who was the leader of the Mohegans when they split from the Pequot tribe in the early 1600s.

In the 1860s Mohegan Hill became the site of the Mohegans' annual Green Corn festival, an event of spiritual significance revived to cement tribal identity. The festival is a thanksgiving for the harvest and an expression of hospitality to the Mohegans' neighbors. Tribal members build a large brush arbor, known as the Wigwam (derived from a word meaning "welcome"), in which to serve food and display crafts. This structure gave the celebration its alternate name, the Wigwam Festival. Since 2003 the festival has taken place at Fort Shantok in Montville, another sacred Mohegan site, but Mohegan Hill remains central to the life of the tribe.

Also on the hill is the Tantaquidgeon Indian Museum, established in 1931 by John Tantaquidgeon and his children Harold and Gladys. The small building is constructed of local fieldstone, with arrowheads and stone mortars and pestles embedded in its walls and a diamond-shaped protective symbol on the chimney. Outdoor displays include examples of traditional wigwams and longhouses. The versions of these on view in 2017 were erected in 2011 and reflect current research in historic materials and construction methods.

Remembered, visited, celebrated, and sometimes reinterpreted, Mohegan Hill is central to the tribe's identity. But although the Mohegans have constructed buildings on the hill and shaped its landscape, its significance is rooted in a different, non-European, concept of place that arises not from human actions but rather from discovering the significance inherent in its natural features. The identification and continued use of places like Mohegan Hill are among the ways in which Native Americans shaped their environment, and should be considered as the first Connecticut architecture.

THE PLACE
MOHEGAN CONGREGATIONAL CHURCH
1831. 1873, remodeled. 1997–2002, restored.
27 Church Lane, Uncasville
TANTAQUIDGEON INDIAN MUSEUM
www.mohegan.nsn.us/heritage
1931, John and Harold Tantaquidgeon. 1957, 1962, additions.
1819 Norwich–New London Turnpike (Connecticut Route 32), Uncasville. Open to the public.

FURTHER READING
Cronon, William. *Changes in the Land: Indians, Colonists, and the Ecology of New England.* New York: Hill & Wang, 1983.
Fawcett, Melissa Jayne. *Medicine Trail: The Life and Lessons of Gladys Tantaquidgeon.* Tucson: University of Arizona Press, 2000.
Lavin, Lucianne. *Connecticut's Indigenous Peoples: What Archaeology, History, and Oral Traditions Teach Us about Their Communities and Cultures.* New Haven, Conn.: Yale University Press, 2013.

FIGURE 59.
Wigwam, Green Corn Festival, Mohegan Congregational Church, ca. 1935.
Courtesy of the Mohegan Tribe

FIGURE 60.
Mohegan Congregational Church.
Connecticut Trust for Historic
Preservation

2

COLONIAL FRAMEWORK
MAIN STREET, SOUTH WINDSOR

Blessed with some of the most fertile soil in New England, the Connecticut River Valley developed into a flourishing agricultural region by the eighteenth century. Prosperous farming towns lined the river from Connecticut through Massachusetts and into Vermont and New Hampshire. One piece of this world survives in South Windsor, on the east side of the river. Here, Main Street, the old riverside road, has been bypassed by modern-day U.S. Route 5, leaving a historic landscape that extends for nearly five miles.

South Windsor was settled by inhabitants from Windsor on the west bank in the late seventeenth century. The southern part of the Main Street corridor eventually became a community called Windsor Farms. To the north, separated from Windsor Farms only by a gully and a dip in the road, East Windsor Hill grew up around a ferry landing where merchants shipped agricultural products to New York and the West Indies and received imported goods to sell to the local population. Some of these businessmen made fortunes and built splendid mansions like that of Ebenezer Grant (place 87).

Windsor Farms didn't produce mansion-level wealth until well into the nineteenth century, when tobacco became the Connecticut Valley's most important agricultural product (see the tobacco farms in place 26). Tobacco money made possible a building boom that began in the 1840s and continued well into the twentieth century. Consequently, the grandest houses in Windsor Farms date to that period and are noticeably more fashionable than farmhouses built at the same time in many other parts of Connecticut, where most agriculture was less lucrative after the mid-1800s.

Impressive as they are, the great houses are only a part of a bigger picture. Also of note are the rows of trees that line the street, the barns and other outbuildings (particularly tobacco sheds), the warehouses and stores, and the workers' homes and boardinghouses. Suburban infill is on the increase but for the moment remains largely unobtrusive.

Most important to note is the land itself, stepping up and back from the river in a series of terraces. The first is alluvial plain, containing fertile sediment and devoted almost entirely to cropland, now as it was three hundred years ago. A steep bank leads to the second tier where the street runs, safe from flooding, and where most of the buildings are concentrated. Beyond them are more fields and then another rise, up to the level of Route 5.

This topography determined the shape of the settlement. The inhabitants divided the land into narrow strips, running east from the river, which gave each property owner a bit of each type of land: fields for crops, a home lot on the street, and pasture and woodland farther in. The pattern is still visible from the air in the parallel field divisions and roads running back from the river. Older than surviving structures, this agricultural landscape still provides the framework for South Windsor's present-day life and development—a living inheritance from colonial days.

THE PLACE
WINDSOR FARMS AND EAST WINDSOR HILL
1630s–present
Main Street from North King Street to Ferry Lane, South
    Windsor

FURTHER READING

Cunningham, Jan. "East Windsor Hill Historic District." National Register of Historic Places, reference number 86001208, listed May 30, 1986.

———. "Windsor Farms Historic District." National Register of Historic Places, reference number 86000723, listed April 11, 1986.

Ward, Gerald W. R., and William N. Hosley Jr., eds. *The Great River: Art & Society of the Connecticut Valley, 1635–1820.* Meriden, Conn.: Stinehour Press for the Wadsworth Atheneum, Hartford, 1985.

(*top*) FIGURE 61. Main Street, South Windsor, aerial view, ca. 1985. National Register of Historic Places

(*bottom*) FIGURE 62. 1146 Main Street, South Windsor, ca. 1850 (demolished). Connecticut Trust for Historic Preservation

3

GARDEN BY THE SEA
EOLIA (HARKNESS MEMORIAL STATE PARK), WATERFORD

The summer home of Edward Harkness and his wife, Mary, Eolia was one of the last and grandest estates built on the Connecticut shore between the Civil War and World War I. The mansion, surrounded by elaborate gardens, sits on 235 sprawling acres. Despite this splendor and despite their wealth (Harkness's father was a silent partner of John D. Rockefeller), local lore maintains that the Harknesses were modest and unassuming people, more interested in philanthropy than display.

Although the buildings are grand, the real reason to see Eolia is its landscape. Parklike grounds surround the house, and the original entry drive winds through stone-walled fields, orchards, and pastures dotted with barns, greenhouses, stables, and other estate buildings. All this makes it clear that Eolia was not only a summer retreat but also a working farm that supplied food for the Harknesses both when in residence here and at their home in New York City.

At the heart of the landscape are extensive gardens, which Mary Harkness closely supervised. The original plan, by the Boston landscape firm of Brett and Hall (with contributions by Lord and Hewlett, who designed the house, and later modifications by James Gamble Rogers, who remodeled it), was strongly symmetrical and relied heavily on architectural features such as walls and pergolas. Plantings, equally formal, consisted of rows of annuals in bright colors.

After 1919, Mary Harkness turned to Beatrix Farrand to redesign the gardens. Farrand (1872–1959) was one of a number of women who broke into landscape architecture by designing gardens for the wealthy. Her first work at Eolia was the Asian-inspired East Garden, intended to display statuary that the Harknesses collected on their travels. In the West Garden, she replaced the rigid rows of annuals with drifts of perennials in softer colors. The use of billowing, informal plantings in a formal, geometric framework is typical of Farrand's work, and can be traced back to the influential English garden designer Gertrude Jekyll. Farrand also added a naturalistic rock garden that wraps around the West Garden, as well as a secluded box parterre.

Since Eolia was a summer home, Farrand had the luxury of not worrying about what the gardens would look like off-season. But a winter visit reveals the bones of the landscape. Without the mitigating softness of the plantings, one can more easily perceive the formality of the layout, divided into roomlike spaces with different characters but tied together by axial views. One can note the transitions from one space to another, marked by gates or flights of steps. And one can experience the contrast between the sheltered parterre and the sunny, exposed rock garden open to the ocean breezes. This underlying structure gives the garden its strength as a place.

THE PLACE
EOLIA, EDWARD S. HARKNESS ESTATE
(Harkness Memorial State Park)
www.harkness.org

Buildings: 1902–1907, Lord and Hewlett. 1909–ca. 1924, additions and alterations, James Gamble Rogers. 1996–1998, restoration, Roger Clarke.

Landscape: ca. 1910, Brett and Hall. 1919–ca. 1935, Beatrix Farrand. 1992 and later, restoration.

275 Great Neck Road, Waterford. Open to the public.

FURTHER READING

Clouette, Bruce. "Eolia—Harkness Estate." National Register of Historic Places, reference number 86003331, listed November 20, 1986.

Emmett, Alan. *So Fine a Prospect: Historic New England Gardens.* Hanover, N.H.: University Press of New England, 1996.

FIGURE 63. Eolia, Waterford. Connecticut Trust for Historic Preservation

RESHAPING THE LANDSCAPE
ROCKY RIVER HYDROELECTRIC STATION, NEW MILFORD

In the twentieth century, humans developed the ability to reshape their environment on an unprecedented scale. Road-building filled valleys and cut through mountains. Reclamation projects turned wetlands into dry ground. Irrigation transformed deserts into lush suburban lawns. Mighty rivers were dammed to create reservoirs to satisfy ever-increasing demands, particularly from growing cities, for water and electricity.

Around 1900, engineers found that electrical current could be transmitted for greater distances than had previously been considered feasible. Based on this discovery, businessman J. Henry Roraback consolidated a number of smaller electric companies into the Connecticut Light and Power Company (CL&P), which constructed a system of reservoirs and power plants to provide power to Connecticut cities.

The Housatonic River offered great potential for power generation, but seasonal fluctuations made it an unreliable resource. To address this problem, CL&P built the first major pumped-storage hydroelectric facility in the United States. Beginning in 1926, the company constructed a dam, 100 feet high and 952 feet long, across the Rocky River, a tributary of the Housatonic, to create Candlewood Lake. When the river is high, water is pumped up two hundred feet to the lake. When the river is low or demand is high, water is released from the lake and runs back down to turn turbines and generate power. Pumping water up actually uses more power than is produced on the return trip, but ensuring a reliable supply was worth it.

The powerhouse is a lofty brick structure, tall enough that the turbines can be lifted out of their housings for servicing. Full-length steel-sash windows emphasize the building's height and provide natural light for monitoring the machinery within. Across the road the penstock, a giant tube fifteen feet in diameter, carries water up the hillside to the lake or allows it to flow back down to the power plant when needed. A seventy-six-foot vertical standpipe provides an escape in case of water surges.

Candlewood Lake flooded more than eight square miles in the towns of Danbury, Brookfield, New Fairfield, New Milford, and Sherman. It is eleven miles long and has more than sixty miles of shoreline. This was change on a massive scale. CL&P not only built an electric plant; it created a new landscape many miles long that has attracted development in the form of vacation cottages and year-round homes.

The lake also attracted a different mix of plants and animals and fish and birds, forming an ecosystem that in the following decades achieved its own stability. Yet the existence of this ecosystem depends on the human-made facility. For as solid as the dam seems to be, it also is fragile. Without ongoing human intervention in the form of maintenance, the water behind the dam, always seeking to run downhill, eventually will break through or flow around it. It will flood the towns downstream, leave lakefront property high and dry, and wipe out the Candlewood ecosystem. It is a useful reminder that whatever people build, they build in opposition to the laws of nature. In the end nature will win out.

THE PLACE
ROCKY RIVER HYDROELECTRIC STATION
1926–1929, UGI Contracting Company
200 Kent Road (U.S. Route 7), New Milford

FURTHER READING
American Society of Mechanical Engineers. "Rocky River Pumped-Storage Hydroelectric Station, New Milford, Connecticut." National Historic Mechanical Engineering Landmark documentation, September 13, 1980.

FIGURE 64. Rocky River Hydroelectric Station. Connecticut Trust for Historic Preservation

5

MODERNISM IN THE GARDEN
THE GLASS HOUSE, NEW CANAAN

One of the most famous buildings in the world, the Glass House is a poster child for the Modernist vision of a revolutionary new architecture that would dispense with all the inefficiencies and stylistic folderol of the past. Its designer and owner, Philip Johnson (1906–2005), was a leading evangelist of the new faith. Johnson was the curator, with Henry-Russell Hitchcock, of the *Modern Architecture: International Exhibition* at the Museum of Modern Art in New York City in 1932, which introduced European Modernism to the United States. For his own house in New Canaan, Johnson took Modernist design to its logical extreme. He used modern industrial materials — steel and glass — in simple geometric forms, and created a universal space with no partitions save for the bathroom.

The Glass House doesn't stand alone. It was built with a companion, the Brick (or Guest) House, and Johnson added other structures to his estate over the years. (Confusingly, "Glass House" can mean either the house or the estate as a whole.) He and his partner, David Whitney, would move from one to another, depending on what they were doing or what the weather was like. Together, these other buildings present a timeline of Johnson's ever-changing enthusiasms: New Formalism in the pond pavilion, architecture as procession in the Sculpture Gallery, Postmodernism in the gate, Deconstructivism in the Visitors' Center, and so on. Unlike the Glass House, they tend to have solid walls, small windows, and tightly controlled views to the outside.

The key to the relationship between the other buildings and the Glass House is the landscape that they occupy. As much as Johnson loved building, he loved shaping the land. Over the years he cleared much of the second-growth woods on the site to reveal the contours of the land, which slopes down from the road to the shelf on which the Glass House perches, then plunges to the pond while stretching north and south into more fields, divided by stone walls and dotted with trees. With its transparent walls, the Glass House looks out on this landscape. Despite common comments about how the glass blurs the line between the inside and outside, the effect is not to make occupants feel as though they are outdoors. Rather, it brings the outside in. As Johnson himself put it, the views act as wallpaper.

Within this landscape, the other buildings punctuate

views and terminate vistas. Like temples or fake ruins in an English landscape garden, they are follies, built more for appearance than practicality, and frequently playing games with form or scale or structure. The miniature pond pavilion misleads viewers about its size and distance from the hilltop. Beams supporting a bridge look impossibly thin—will it hold? The Glass House itself is the ultimate folly. Freezing in winter, broiling in summer, totally lacking in privacy, triumphantly unlivable, it is an idea rather than a home.

At the same time, the distinction between the buildings and their setting remains sharp and strong. With few exceptions (the half-buried Art Gallery or the vine-covered Ghost House, perhaps), there is no effort to blend the architecture into the landscape. Through all his stylistic experimentations, Johnson remains true to one aspect of the European Modernism he championed in the 1930s: the aesthetic celebration of machine-made materials. The relation between building and landscape remains one of harmony through contrast.

THE PLACE
THE GLASS HOUSE

theglasshouse.org

1949, Glass House and Brick House; 1962, Pavilion; 1965, Art Gallery; 1970, Sculpture Gallery; 1980, Study; 1984, Ghost House; 1985, Kirstein Tower; 1995, Visitors' Center: all by Philip Johnson

798–856 Ponus Ridge Road, New Canaan. Open to the public.

FURTHER READING

Clouette, Bruce, and Hoang Tinh. "Philip Johnson's Glass House." National Historic Landmark. National Register of Historic Places, reference number 97000341, designated February 18, 1997.

Whitney, David, and Jeffrey Kipnis, eds. *Philip Johnson: The Glass House*. New York: Pantheon Books, 1993.

(*top*) FIGURE 65. Glass House, New Canaan. Robert Gregson
(*bottom*) FIGURE 66. Glass House, pond pavilion, and Lincoln Kirstein Tower. Connecticut Trust for Historic Preservation

6

LANDSCAPE ON A GRAND SCALE

SAVILLE DAM AND BARKHAMSTED RESERVOIR, BARKHAMSTED

In the early years of the twentieth century, public works projects changed the landscape of Connecticut. The state bought up wide tracts of land for parks and forests. At the same time, utility companies built dams and reservoirs to supply water and power to the rapidly growing cities. One of these enterprises was the Hartford Metropolitan District Commission (MDC). Between the 1910s and the 1940s, the MDC bought thousands of acres of land in Connecticut's northwestern highlands, cleared it, and flooded the valleys for a system of reservoirs to provide water to Hartford and its rapidly growing suburbs. Barkhamsted Reservoir, built between 1936 and 1940, is a part of that regional water-supply system. To create the reservoir, the MDC built the Saville Dam, an earthen structure 135 feet high and 1,950 feet long. It was named for its designer, chief engineer Caleb Mills Saville.

Curving gently and carrying a state road (Connecticut Route 318, Saville Dam Road) along its top, the dam is a massive presence. But it's not just big; it is also handsomely designed. The 1930s were an age that demanded that civic infrastructure be attractive as well as functional. Just as the Civilian Conservation Corps provided well-designed facilities to enhance state parks, and the Connecticut Highway Department built the Merritt Parkway for enjoyable travel, the MDC planned the Saville Dam to enhance the aesthetics of its new reservoir. To accomplish this, the MDC hired one of the nation's most distinguished landscape architects, Arthur A. Shurcliff (1870–1957). Best known for his re-creations of colonial gardens at sites like Colonial Williamsburg, Shurcliff also designed many parks, dams, and reservoirs.

For the Saville Dam, Shurcliff lined the side of the road toward the reservoir with a stone wall punctuated by clumps of cedar trees. At each end, the wall turns in to form a gateway. At the dam's midpoint stands a gatehouse containing the mechanical equipment. The small, circular building of stone with its tall conical roof and stone-arch bridge looks as though it had been lifted from a French chateau.

But the walls and the plantings and the gatehouse aren't the point. Visitors aren't supposed to say, "What a lovely road," or "What a lovely gatehouse." These features provide a human-scaled place from which to view the eight-mile-long reservoir, to experience the vast expanse of water under a broad stretch of sky that creates a sense of openness—rare in the steep, wooded valleys of northwestern Connecticut—without feeling lost in it. The designed elements create a frame for the picture in front of the viewer, intended to increase appreciation of the picture without capturing too much attention. It's a good designer who knows how to stay in the background, and Shurcliff did just that.

THE PLACE

SAVILLE DAM AND BARKHAMSTED RESERVOIR

1936–1940, Caleb Mills Saville, chief engineer; Arthur A. Shurcliff, landscape

Saville Dam Road (Connecticut Route 318), approximately two miles east of Pleasant Valley, Barkhamsted

FURTHER READING

Murphy, Kevin. "A Valley Flooded to Slake the Capital Region's Thirst." *Hog River Journal* 4, no. 1 (Winter 2005–2006): 20–25.

FIGURE 67. Powerhouse, Barkhamsted Reservoir, Barkhamsted. Patrick L. Pinnell

SHAPING THE LANDSCAPE

7

THE ROAR OF THE LANDSCAPE
LIME ROCK PARK, SALISBURY

As soon as automobiles were invented, drivers began racing them. As with horses, some raced on enclosed oval tracks, while others preferred open country roads with their more challenging configurations and better scenery. By the 1950s, however, the dangers of this latter practice led to the development of tracks that evoked the experience of open road racing in a controlled environment.

One of the first of these was built at Lime Rock, a rural village in the town of Salisbury that had been the headquarters of the Litchfield County iron industry (place 32). There, sports car enthusiast Jim Vaill had taken to driving in the gravel pit he operated on his father's land. Deciding to build a proper track, Vaill enlisted John Fitch, a race car driver who had witnessed terrible crashes and was committed to making racing safer. Fitch in turn asked engineers from the Cornell Aeronautical Engineering Laboratory to review the layout and recommend safety improvements to protect both drivers and spectators. (The lab's director, Bill Milliken, was a racing fan.)

The resulting racetrack is a mile and a half long and has seven curves in varying shapes and combinations to test drivers' skill. The design takes into account the engineers' recommendations for curvature, banking, and elevation. The engineers also called for recovery and deceleration lanes wide and long enough to give drivers a chance to regain control or slow down so that collisions wouldn't cause serious injury to drivers or damage to cars. Barriers were designed to stop cars safely, to be portable and replaceable, and to allow emergency access to disabled vehicles.

The involvement of the Cornell lab at Lime Rock was a first in racetrack design and a reflection of the founders' broader ambitions in shaping the still-new sport of automobile racing. As Fitch told a local newspaper, "We plan to make Lime Rock an outdoor laboratory for highway safety and the automotive industry. We're confident that some of the safety features which we are now working on will be perfected so that they will be applicable to our public highways."

Along with its safety features, the landscape defines Lime Rock Park. Unlike other racetracks, it has no grandstands. Instead, spectators sit on grassy slopes dotted with maples and oaks, screened by rows of pines. There are views to a church steeple in the village and, beyond that, to rolling hills in the distance.

The parklike setting makes going to the races an informal, festive event. There is space to arrange picnic blankets and chairs in the shade or sun. Children can sleep or play while grownups watch the races. Spectators can easily move about to watch the action from different vantage points.

Much thought went into making Lime Rock Park. In addition to engineering the racetrack to balance safety with thrills, all the practical needs of drainage, screening, parking, and crowd control were satisfied. Most important was integrating the practical necessities with the beauty of the natural surroundings to create an inviting setting for the fun of watching the races. The crowds that flock to Lime Rock on summer afternoons attest to the success of its creators.

THE PLACE
LIME ROCK PARK

www.limerock.com

1955–1957, Jim Vaill, Bill Milliken, and Cornell University Aeronautical Engineering Laboratory

497 Lime Rock Road (Connecticut Route 112), Salisbury. Open to the public.

FURTHER READING

Mascia, Sara. "Lime Rock Park." National Register of Historic Places, reference number 08001380, listed October 16, 2009.

Taylor, Rich. *Lime Rock Park: 35 Years of Racing.* Sharon, Conn.: Sharon Mountain Press, 1992.

FIGURE 68. Lime Rock Park, Salisbury. Lime Rock Park, photograph by Casey Keel

SHAPING THE LANDSCAPE

ARCHITECTURE FOR
THE ENVIRONMENT
KROON HALL, YALE UNIVERSITY,
NEW HAVEN

With its pale sandstone walls, Kroon Hall stands out among the darker buildings of Yale University's Science Hill. One suspects that this was a conscious choice, calling attention to a building intended as a prototype for sustainable design. The building's occupant, the Yale School of Forestry and Environmental Science, has as its mission the care and wise use of the natural environment. So when the school needed more space, it was logical for it to build in a way that would further that mission and to choose a design firm, Hopkins Architects, that put a high priority on sustainability.

Sustainable design is emerging as a defining characteristic of twenty-first-century architecture. It can be understood as planning building construction and operation to conserve resources, minimize impacts on the environment, and provide healthy surroundings for building users.

For Kroon Hall, the construction side of the equation involved using renewable or sustainably produced materials—ones that didn't generate pollution or require excessive energy for processing. These include timber from Yale's own forests, stone from quarries not more than five hundred miles away (to minimize the energy used to transport it), and materials with recycled content, such as the insulation. Wherever possible, construction waste was recycled.

Sustainable operation involved many strategies for conserving energy. The building turns a broad side toward the south for natural light and solar warmth. The heavy concrete frame and well-insulated walls soak up heat and release it gradually for warmth in winter; in summer, they slow the absorption of heat, keeping the building cool. The narrow footprint and numerous windows bring sunlight into all parts of the building, and lights are equipped with sensors to turn them on when needed and off when spaces are unoccupied. Operable windows allow natural ventilation, with a colored-light signaling system to tell occupants whether or not it is appropriate to open them, based on outside temperature. A geothermal system provides heat. Solar panels on the roof can supply 24 percent of the building's electricity. Rainwater from the roof and grounds is collected and reused.

In recognition of these measures, the building received

a LEED (Leadership in Energy and Environmental Design) Platinum rating from the U.S. Green Building Council, an organization devoted to helping building designers, builders, owners, and operators be environmentally sensitive. Since the mid-1990s, LEED certification has increasingly been specified by building clients as a measure of environmental stewardship, as well as a marketing tool to promote an institution's or business's ecological sensitivity.

Apart from these technical strategies, the Forestry School also wanted to demonstrate that attractive design contributes to sustainability, since a building that is appreciated is more likely to be cared for and used well. The natural stone and oak give the building a warmth, while abundant natural light makes it bright and cheerful. Outside, courtyards provide inviting outdoor spaces that had been lacking on Science Hill. Stephen Kellert, the chair of the building committee, saw the courtyards as addressing another aspect of sustainability: reducing the separation and alienation of people from the natural environment.

THE PLACE
KROON HALL

http://environment.yale.edu/kroon

2007–2009, Hopkins Architects with Centerbrook
    Architects and Planners

195 Prospect Street, New Haven

FURTHER READING

Crosbie, Michael J. *Green Architecture: A Guide to Sustainable Design*. Washington, D.C.: American Institute of Architects Press, 1994.

Yale University School of Forestry and Environmental Studies. http://environment.yale.edu.

FIGURE 69. Kroon Hall, New Haven. Derek Hayn / Centerbrook

Part Two

MATERIALS AND TECHNOLOGIES

Architecture is a physical art. The qualities of its works cannot be separated from the qualities of the materials that make them up and the technologies employed to assemble those materials. Connecticut's first European settlers established a tradition of building in wood based on the customs they brought with them, and wood continues to play a central role in the state's building culture, despite the abundance of stone suitable for construction. This includes granite, marble, and the brownstone that, shipped to cities across the nation, became one of the state's most important exports in the nineteenth century. In addition to these materials from the land, Connecticut builders also have developed and produced human-made materials, such as bricks, millwork, and wall coverings, and parts, such as hardware, boilers, and lighting fixtures, to name just a few. During the industrial age of the nineteenth and twentieth centuries the number of manufactured products grew rapidly. Manufacturing processes also altered building techniques, inspiring mass-production not only of materials but of entire structures.

9

WOOD FOR STONE

NEW LONDON COUNTY
COURTHOUSE, NEW LONDON

After the American Revolution, the people of New London built a new courthouse to replace one burned by a British invasion force in 1781. An ambitious composition of classical elements on a gambrel-roofed body, the courthouse endears itself to modern eyes by its provincial awkwardness. Monster keystones bristle above the windows, second-story pilasters don't quite align with their first-story counterparts, and a Palladian window is kicked up a notch with arches on all three openings, rather than only the center one. Instead of the Georgian ideal of classical correctness, the effect is of enthusiastic, if naive, vigor.

Part of the courthouse's provincial character is that it is built of wood worked to imitate stone. The keystones, for instance, are patently boards nailed onto the window surrounds. The first-floor pilasters have similar boards suggesting blocks of stone, but the resemblance is undercut by the foundation, which doesn't step out to support the pilasters, so they're left dangling. The windows sit in the plane of the wall, revealing its thinness.

Since antiquity, European builders valued stone or brick for their permanence. They developed building forms, from ancient temples to Gothic cathedrals, based on the characteristics of those materials. In England, timber continued to be used, but by the 1600s centuries of forest cutting led to shortages of suitable wood, forcing framers to use smaller pieces of wood and contributing to a new preference for masonry there.

In New England, traditional timber-framing continued to flourish. Even where stone or clay to make bricks was available, wood remained the material of choice, thanks in part to the plentiful supply of trees and in part to the preference for timber construction that the Puritan settlers brought with them from England. Only in cities, where the spread of fire from one closely packed building to the next was a danger, did masonry construction become common.

For a nation of migrants who often didn't expect to remain long in one place, the cost and time of building in brick or stone in many cases seemed unnecessary. Wood was cheaper and quicker, and lent itself to elaborate but inexpensive ornamentation. But while building in wood, Americans freely employed motifs created for stone, as the builders of the courthouse did. George Washington clad his Mount Vernon in wooden siding beveled to imitate masonry. Nineteenth-century builders erected imitation Grecian temples of wood, Italianate villas with smooth flush-board siding to suggest stuccoed walls, and Gothic Revival cottages and churches with wooden tracery and pinnacles.

To foreign visitors, America's wooden buildings could seem dangerously flimsy. In his *American Notes*, published in 1842 following his first visit to the United States, Charles Dickens remarked, "The white wooden houses … are so sprinkled and dropped about in all directions, without seeming to have any root at all in the ground; and the small churches and chapels are so prim, and bright, and highly varnished … that I almost believed the whole affair could be taken up piecemeal like a child's toy, and crammed into a little box."

For all its lightness and naiveté, the New London courthouse was, and still is, an imposing presence. The use of wood instead of stone contributes to that. Wood made possible the profusion of classical ornament, and also the bold scale that allows the courthouse to command even the later and bigger buildings that now surround it.

THE PLACE
NEW LONDON COUNTY COURTHOUSE
1784, Isaac Fitch. 1909, remodeled, Dudley St. Clair
    Donnelly. 1985, addition, Hirsch Associates.
70 Huntington Street, New London. Open to the public.

FURTHER READING
Luyster, Constance. "New London County Courthouse." National
    Register of Historic Places, reference number 70000705, listed
    October 15, 1970.
Warren, William L. *Isaac Fitch of Lebanon, Connecticut: Master
    Joiner, 1734–1791.* Hartford: Antiquarian & Landmarks Society,
    Inc., of Connecticut, 1978.

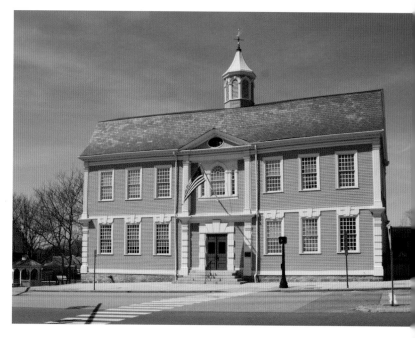

FIGURES 70 AND 71. New London County Courthouse, New London.
Connecticut Trust for Historic Preservation

IO

SOMETHING OLD, SOMETHING NEW

NOROTON PRESBYTERIAN CHURCH, DARIEN

Living in a time of rapid growth and technological innovation, Victorians enthusiastically adopted new building techniques and materials. But they often preferred to clothe them in traditional forms. This was especially the case with such solemn structures as churches. Noroton Presbyterian Church, designed by Henry Hudson Holly (1834–1892) and built in 1865–1866, is just such a combination of old and new. At first glance, it seems conventional enough, patterned as many of its contemporaries were after medieval English parish churches. Buttresses, pointed arches, a tower, and a graceful timber porch provide just enough ornament to establish its dignity as God's house.

However, these tradition-based walls were built of a new, experimental material. At the time it was called "artificial stone," but today it would be considered a sort of concrete block. Unlike modern concrete, however, these blocks are composed of nearly dry sand and lime, molded under pressure in a system patented by Ambrose Foster of Portland, Wisconsin, in 1855.

Holly had already used Foster block in a house in Danbury (since torn down) and written about it in his *Holly's Country Seats*, published in 1863. For the Noroton church, he employed an improved version of Foster block manufactured by the Washington Building Block Company of New York. In a letter to the owner of the company, the architect praised the blocks' "durability, beauty and cheapness." He mentioned that the company also had molded ornamental blocks for the church, which demonstrated that the material would be "peculiarly valuable for church buildings and other like purposes."

Alas, not all experiments succeed. Foster blocks soon demonstrated a tendency to erode, particularly when made of low-quality materials or by inexperienced workers. A building in Washington, D.C., disintegrated while it was still under construction. By the mid-1870s the Washington Building Block Company was out of business, and other types of building blocks were capturing its market.

At Noroton, the Foster blocks held fairly firm for more than a century. However, by the 1980s the blocks had eroded by as much as a half inch in spots. In 1990 the church (now the chapel of an expanded church complex) was restored under the guidance of Richard Bergmann Architects of New Canaan. To prevent further weathering, they applied a coat of specially prepared mortar, carefully matching the color and texture of the original blocks. The mortar was incised to preserve the appearance of blocks. On the interior, the blocks are now simply painted. Despite their imperfect performance, they remain to tell a story of technological innovation.

THE PLACE
NOROTON PRESBYTERIAN CHURCH

1865–1866, Henry Hudson Holly. 1990, Richard Bergmann
    Architects.

2011 Post Road, Darien

FURTHER READING

Bergmann, Richard, and Karen Donnelley. "Building Blocks:
    The Origins of CMUs." Unpublished typescript, 1992.

Holly, Henry Hudson. *Church Architecture*. Hartford, Conn.:
    M. H. Mallory, 1871.

FIGURE 72. Noroton Presbyterian Church, Darien. Connecticut Trust for Historic Preservation

II

CONNECTICUT STONE

PORTLAND BROWNSTONE
QUARRIES, PORTLAND

Locally available materials can shape the character of a place. Prominent examples are red brick in Virginia, redwood in California, and mud adobe in the desert Southwest. Connecticut builders have long favored wood, a legacy of the forests that covered the land when the first settlers arrived. But the state's rocky hillsides contain stone suitable for building, and its complex geology results in a variety of types of stone. As early as 1639, Guilford's minister, the Reverend Henry Whitfield, built a solid stone house (figure 15). Connecticut stones include granite from Branford, Guilford, and Waterford, marble from Milford, Washington, and Canaan, and traprock from the central valley. But the chocolate-brown sandstone from Portland, known as brownstone, ranks as one of Connecticut's most significant contributions to nineteenth-century American building.

The Portland brownstone was formed during the early Jurassic period, when rivers eroded the eastern highlands and deposited silt in lakes dotting the floor of a rift valley. The fine, even grain makes the stone easy to work, and hematite gives it a warm, reddish-brown color. As early as 1665 the town of Middletown (of which Portland originally was a part) began to regulate the taking of this stone. James Stancliff, a mason and gravestone carver, began quarrying in about 1690. Operations remained small until 1788, when Nathan Shaler and Joel Hall opened the first large-scale commercial quarry. The Brainerd quarry followed in 1812, and the Middlesex Quarry in 1841. By the 1850s, these three employed more than one thousand men. Later in the century, even with the introduction of steam-powered equipment, employment grew to fifteen hundred, mostly immigrants from Ireland or Sweden.

Before the 1840s the stone was used primarily for foundations and trim. But Romantic taste came to prize it for its rich color and ease of carving. Portland brownstone soon became a favorite building material in the rapidly growing cities of the nineteenth century, not only in Connecticut, but up and down the East Coast, and as far away as Chicago and San Francisco. In 1880 it was estimated that 78 percent of the stone buildings in New York City were built of brownstone. So dominant was the material that the term "brownstone" came to refer to any urban row house, whatever it was made of.

Not surprisingly, when the Town of Portland in 1871 erected a monument to its Civil War dead, brownstone was the material of choice. The description of this monument in an 1884 county history expressed the popularity of brownstone, grounded in the taste for buildings and structures that blended with natural settings: "While many might prefer the dazzling whiteness of marble, there is something in the soft, quiet tint of brownstone which makes it harmonious to all surroundings, while its durability renders it particularly appropriate for the decoration of parks and pleasure grounds, in statues and fountains." In fact, not all brownstone is durable; it frequently suffers erosion or flaking. For its own monument, though, Portland obtained stone of the highest quality, which has weathered well.

Use of brownstone declined after the 1890s as taste turned to lighter colors, and new machinery made it possible to work harder stones. The Portland quarries continued to operate until two big floods, in 1936 and 1938, made pumping out the pits economically impractical. Quarrying resumed in 1993, only to cease again in 2012.

The Town of Portland bought the quarries in 1997 and leases a portion for recreational uses. A public overlook on Brownstone Avenue provides views of the pits, where one can still see the squared-off "peninsulas" where derricks once stood. Those who want brownstone for construction now get it from India.

THE PLACE
PORTLAND BROWNSTONE QUARRIES
ca. 1690–2012
Brownstone Avenue at Silver Street, Portland
PORTLAND SOLDIERS' MONUMENT
1871, James G. Batterson Company, fabricator; George
    Keller, designer (attributed)
Intersection of Main and Bartlett Streets, Portland

FURTHER READING
Kleussendorf, Joanne. "Portland Brownstone Quarries." National
    Historic Landmark. National Register of Historic Places,
    reference number 00000703, designated May 16, 2000.

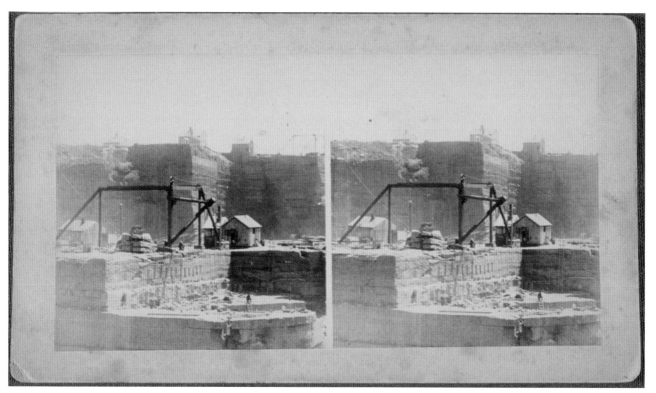

FIGURE 73. Portland Brownstone Quarries and quarrying machinery, stereographic slide, ca. 1910. The Connecticut Historical Society

12

ENGINEERING BEAUTY
LOVER'S LEAP BRIDGE, NEW MILFORD

Springing daintily across a deep gorge, the Lover's Leap Bridge is the second-longest (at 173 feet) and the best preserved of the Berlin Iron Bridge Company's few surviving lenticular truss bridges in Connecticut. More durable than wood, less expensive than masonry, and quickly assembled on site from factory-produced components, iron trusses came to dominate bridge-building in the late nineteenth century.

As early as 1877, the Corrugated Metal Company of East Berlin began producing bridges in addition to the trusses it already made to support its metal roofing. The company developed a signature lens-shaped, or "lenticular," truss that used less material, and therefore cost less, than other designs. In truth, the savings were small, but the distinctive appearance was an effective marketing tool that distinguished the Berlin bridges from those of its competitors. By 1883, bridges had become the company's main product, and it changed its name to the Berlin Iron Bridge Company.

Lover's Leap was one of the last lenticular trusses built, as bridge design moved to greater uniformity, and steel supplanted iron. It was in some ways an unfortunate development. The lacy net of wrought- and cast-iron members and the eye-catching lens-shaped truss give the bridge a springy appeal that is at one with its construction. One might wonder at the Victorians' need to dress it up with extraneous decoration like the urns and cresting. But the National Register of Historic Places nomination for another of the company's bridges, in Canton, Connecticut, says that the ornament was "intended to supplement, rather than distract from, the considerable aesthetic impact of the bridge itself; to Victorians, iron bridges were light and graceful compared with their wooden predecessors and were viewed as signs of progress." The decoration can be thought of as highlighting the innate elegance of the structure.

After being closed for years, the Lover's Leap Bridge was renovated in 2007 for pedestrian use. The work has been criticized for removing original material such as the railings and some structural connections. Despite these changes, the bridge retains the strength and lightness made possible by iron construction.

THE PLACE
LOVER'S LEAP BRIDGE

1895, Berlin Iron Bridge Company. 2007, renovated.
Pumpkin Hill Road at Lover's Leap Road, New Milford

FURTHER READING
Clouette, Bruce. "Lover's Leap Bridge." National Register of
    Historic Places, reference number 76001982, listed May 13,
    1976.
Clouette, Bruce, and Matthew Roth. *Connecticut's Historic
    Highway Bridges.* Newington: Connecticut Department of
    Transportation, 1991.

FIGURE 74. Lover's Leap Bridge, New Milford. Robert Egleston

CONNECTICUT ARCHITECTURE

13

BUILDINGS FROM
THE ASSEMBLY LINE
WINSLOW AMES AND
STEEL HOUSES, NEW LONDON

During the Depression, progressive architects dreamed of houses that could be prefabricated inexpensively on assembly lines and then put together on site. Mass production, they believed, would bring homeownership to ordinary workers just as it had brought them automobile ownership. In the early 1930s, a number of companies vied to produce the housing equivalent of Henry Ford's revolutionary Model T. Among them were American Houses, of New York, which called its product the "Moto Home," and General Houses, of Chicago. After seeing models of their products displayed at the Century of Progress Exposition in Chicago in 1933, Winslow Ames, director of the Lyman Allyn Art Museum in New London, erected one of each in that city.

These houses broke with traditional house-building in both design and construction. The Moto Home has a frame of welded steel, generally used at the time only for commercial or industrial construction. Panels of asbestos cement clad the house, with aluminum battens covering the joints between them. The windows are steel casements originally developed for factories. Inside, services were economically grouped in a central core called the "Moto Unit." Visual features such as the flat roof, corner windows, and exposed bolt heads underline the machine-made character.

Like the Moto Home, the General Houses house—commonly called the Steel House—uses steel for framing and walls. But it also has enameled steel panels as cladding for exterior and interior walls. Also like the Moto Home, it has corner windows, a roof deck, an attached garage, and built-in storage units. Ames chose the company's lowest-priced model, which cost $4,500 and had an open plan that combined living room, dining room, and kitchen into a single space.

Unfortunately, the assembly-line houses of the 1930s were never produced in the numbers needed to be economically viable. No doubt, their uncompromising Modernism, along with the ongoing Depression, played a large part in the failure of both American Houses and General Houses. But the hope lived on. Another spurt of experiments in prefabrication took place just after World War II. The Lustron Corporation produced houses for several years, although architects deprecated its middlebrow designs. Architect Carl Koch's Techbuilt was even more successful and more Modernist in character, in a low-key, Scandinavian manner that used wood framing and siding. However, Techbuilt's products did not achieve wide popularity or truly affordable prices. Traditionally designed dwellings like Hodgson Houses, developed by Massachusetts innovator E. F. Hodgson, did better. Experiments continue, but the goal of attaining both architectural sophistication and affordability remains elusive.

In 1949 Winslow Ames sold his two houses to Connecticut College, which used them for many years as faculty housing. The college restored the Moto Home in 1992 as a new Center for Art and Technology, an apt marriage of the two themes that the house itself embodies. The Steel House also has been restored, and now is home to a center for sustainability. Together, they evoke an age when architects looked to modern technology and design to solve housing problems.

THE PLACES
MOTO HOME
(Winslow Ames House)

1933, Robert W. McLaughlin Jr., American Houses. 1992, restored, Russell E. Sargeant and Michael Pray Associates.

132 Mohegan Avenue, New London

STEEL HOUSE

1933, Howard T. Fisher, General Houses. 2007–2014, restored, Barun Basu Associates.

130 Mohegan Avenue, New London

FURTHER READING

Clouette, Bruce, and Maura Cronin. "Winslow Ames House." National Register of Historic Places, reference number 95000283, listed March 23, 1995.

Royalty, Douglas. "House at 130 Mohegan Avenue." National Register of Historic Places, reference number 8001379, listed October 28, 2009.

FIGURES 75 AND 76. Winslow Ames (*top*) and Steel (*bottom*) Houses, New London. Douglas Royalty

14

INSIDE THE SAPPHIRE

FIRST PRESBYTERIAN CHURCH, STAMFORD

"Have you ever thought what it would be like to live inside a giant sapphire?" So asked architect Wallace K. Harrison (1895–1981) when presenting his design to the building committee at Stamford's First Presbyterian Church. What he was proposing was a modern version of medieval Gothic churches, particularly the Sainte-Chapelle in Paris (1248), which is a lantern of stained glass with barely visible supports holding up the roof.

In Chartres, France, Harrison had discovered twentieth-century stained-glass artist Gabriel Loire's technique of embedding rough chunks of single-colored pot-metal glass in concrete, called *dalle de verre* (glass slab). Harrison came up with a plan to set the glass in pierced panels of precast concrete, which were tilted up to form sloping walls. (Unfortunately, the caulking around the glass is failing, causing leaks that the church struggles to correct.)

The long, tapered shape of the building was intended as a giant megaphone, so the minister could be heard easily in every part of the sanctuary. The resulting shape gave the church its famous nickname, the "Fish Church," but the fishlike appearance was a by-product of acoustical requirements and Harrison's desire to merge walls and roof into a single envelope. That it resembled the ancient Christian symbol for Jesus Christ was a happy accident.

From the outside, in fact, the church seems to be not just any fish, but an origami fish, pleated and folded along its flanks, its head and tail covered with slate scales. The midsection and the tail are ornamented with geometric patterns that turn out to be chunks of glass. The entrance is at the point where the tail joins the end of the body. The walls are solid there, but from the left comes a soft, multicolored glow. If Jonah had been swallowed by a fish like this, he never would have wanted to escape.

From the inside the image is not of a fish but rather a jewel box—that is, a box *made of* jewels: amber, ruby, emerald, amethyst, and, especially, intense, piercing sapphire. The glass chunks have chipped edges that reflect the light like the facets of a jewel, bringing the interior to life. The light dances, spangling the pews, the floor, and the people with shimmering spotlights of brilliant color. As in a medieval cathedral, the glass contains images. Literature provided by the church explains that the side walls depict the Crucifixion and the Resurrection, and the rear shows symbols of Christ's teachings. Without the guide, a visitor is unlikely to decipher the abstracted symbols but will be happy just to drink in the colors.

With its roots in medieval forms and its long, narrow footprint, First Presbyterian actually stood outside the liturgical renewal movement of the postwar years. The most forward-looking new churches of the period were being designed to encourage congregational participation in worship by bringing the people close to the chancel, typically in broad, short footprints rather than long, narrow ones. But Harrison's interest was in Gothic forms, and his Presbyterian clients focused their worship on sermons and prayers rather than ritual. It's all about the blend of technology and mysticism: the enfolding walls that reach in to become the roof (or is it the roof that leans down to form the walls?), the dancing colors, the sense of being inside the sapphire.

THE PLACE
FIRST PRESBYTERIAN CHURCH

www.fishchurch.org

1953–1958, Wallace K. Harrison, Harrison and
 Abramovitz; stained glass, Gabriel Loire; office/
 educational building, Sherwood, Mills, and Smith.
 Carillon, 1967–1968, Wallace K. Harrison.
1101 Bedford Street, Stamford. Open to the public.

FURTHER READING

Fish Church Conservancy. http://fishchurchconservancy.org.
Newhouse, Victoria. *Wallace K. Harrison, Architect.* New York:
 Rizzoli, 1989.

FIGURES 77 AND 78. First Presbyterian Church, Stamford. Robert Gregson

Part Three

WHERE WE LIVE

The most basic role of architecture is to provide a place to live: shelter from the elements where occupants can sleep, eat, and work. Meeting those elemental needs lies at the root of how people shape their environment, with builders developing new and (they hope) better technologies for supplying this protection and comfort.

But once those practical needs are met, the urge for self-expression quickly emerges. How do people live? How do they want to live? How do they want to be seen as living? Any or all of these questions can influence how dwellings are built.

15

FOR THE MIDDLING SORT

BENJAMIN HALL JR. HOUSE, GUILFORD

One of Connecticut's oldest towns, Guilford boasts a fine array of comfortable houses dating from the eighteenth to the twentieth centuries. So the smaller and simpler Benjamin Hall Jr. House seems to be an anomaly. What's it doing here?

Surviving eighteenth-century houses in Connecticut average about twenty-four hundred square feet in size, and Guilford fits that pattern. But historians estimate that, at the turn of the nineteenth century, one in four families in central and southern New England lived in houses of less than six hundred square feet. That is precisely the footprint of the original part of the Hall House. In many towns, one-story cottages of this sort were the dominant form of housing.

Known as "the middling sort," the inhabitants of these small houses weren't poor. They owned land, houses, livestock, and often one or two luxury items such as a book or pieces of silver or porcelain. All practiced some craft or trade, but also depended on farming to meet day-to-day needs. On the whole they worked hard and lived modestly, and their houses were modest, too. There are several such houses in Guilford, and in communities less prosperous or settled later than Guilford they make up a larger proportion of the building stock.

Although the Hall House appears at first to follow the typical New England center-chimney plan, its chimney is visibly off-center, signifying something different inside. The door opens directly into the main front room, which would have served as general living space. The space in front of the chimney, which might be the entry hall in a larger house, serves as a room. This layout provided more living space within the small footprint, but reduced the family's privacy.

The framing of the Hall House is less elaborate than that of bigger houses, with smaller members and simplified joints. The floor, for instance, is framed with planks rather than joists. Partly because of its small size and simple construction, the house was long believed to date from the 1660s. However, recent research has determined that it was constructed about one hundred years later.

Simpler and often less soundly constructed than the houses of the elite, these middling dwellings were less likely to survive. Where they have survived, it often has been because they were enlarged in ways that conceal their original appearance. To rediscover them requires a bit of digging—into existing buildings for evidence of expansion, into the ground for foundations of structures that have disappeared, and into documents for contemporary references.

Like the Deacon Adams House (place 80), the Hall House challenges the typical picture of colonial Connecticut as an egalitarian society that produced relatively uniform buildings. Reevaluating the place of buildings like the Hall House in the landscape suggests that, although Connecticut may not have had the extremes of wealth and poverty found in other places, its society actually was more economically diverse than was previously thought.

THE PLACE
BENJAMIN HALL JR. HOUSE

1778
223 State Street, Guilford. Private residence.

FURTHER READING

Harper, Ross K., Mary G. Harper, and Bruce Clouette. *Highways to History: The Archaeology of Connecticut's Eighteenth-Century Lifeways*. Connecticut Department of Transportation in cooperation with the Federal Highway Administration, 2013.

McCulloch, Sarah Brown. *Guilford: A Walking Guide; The Green & Neighboring Streets*. Guilford, Conn.: Guilford Preservation Alliance, 2006.

Raiche, Stephen J. "Guilford Historic Town Center." National Register of Historic Places, reference number 76001988, listed July 6, 1976.

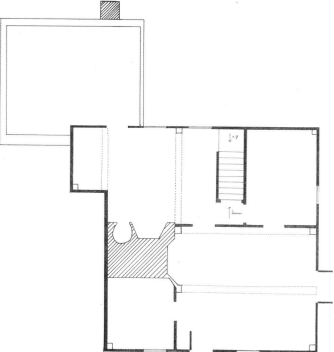

FIGURES 79 AND 80. Connecticut Trust for Historic Preservation (photograph); Bryan Clark Green (plan)

16

TEMPLE MANIA

SAMUEL RUSSELL AND WILLIAM TRENCH HOUSES, MIDDLETOWN

In 1842 the architectural tastemaker Andrew Jackson Downing complained that the American mania for Grecian temples made everything look alike. In some towns, he wrote, it would be difficult for a stranger "to distinguish with accuracy between a church, a bank, and a hall of justice."

Downing was right. Buildings inspired by those of ancient Greece became fashionable around 1830 and dominated America for more than twenty years—even longer in some rural areas. Some designers contended that because Greek architecture was older than Roman it was stylistically purer. Others argued that, because the ancient Greeks invented democracy, their architecture was an appropriate model for the United States. But above all, people liked the way Greek architecture looked.

Connecticut is fortunate to have the Samuel Russell House in Middletown, one of the earliest and most accurate temple-form buildings. Imposing, finely proportioned, and detailed with scholarly exactitude, the Russell House could almost be taken for one of the temples on the Acropolis, if it weren't for its windows and chimneys. A side wing, added in 1855, detracts somewhat from the house's geometric purity, but otherwise it survives intact, well preserved by the Russell family and the current owner, Wesleyan University.

Befitting its wealthy and sophisticated owner, who had made a fortune in the China trade, the Russell House is spacious and elegant, solidly built of brick stuccoed and painted white to look like marble. Its crowning glory is the portico, held up by six mighty Corinthian columns. The Corinthian order, with its leafy column capitals and rich entablature, was the most lavish ornamental motif the ancient Greeks developed, one they used only rarely because it was so extravagant. The imposing portico achieves a monumentality rarely seen before in an American dwelling.

Of course, the full temple treatment, with its expensive columns and carvings, was beyond the reach of most homeowners. But there were other ways of achieving the same effect. Just a few blocks from the Russell House stands the home of William Trench, built in 1839. Trench's house is much smaller than Russell's, is built of wood instead of brick, and lacks a portico. But it has a pediment, which says "temple" in a shorthand way that an educated person of the time could understand. That message is reinforced by the front doorway, which is framed by a pair of handsome pilasters bearing a simple entablature. This model was chosen by hundreds of Connecticut building clients in the years before the Civil War.

The elegance of the Russell House and the simpler version in the Trench House make the fascination with Greek temples understandable. In their purity of form and faithful adherence to ancient models, both buildings are resolutely classical, yet Romantic in their evocation of a past civilization. Their simple geometry is easily grasped by the viewer, yet lightened and humanized by sensitively selected details. The result is a combination of monumental effect and straightforward design that helped the Grecian style to remain popular for so long.

THE PLACES
SAMUEL RUSSELL HOUSE
1828, Ithiel Town; Hoadley and Curtis, builder
350 High Street, Middletown
WILLIAM TRENCH HOUSE
1839
31 Broad Street, Middletown

FURTHER READING
Cunningham, Jan. "Broad Street Historic District." National Register of Historic Places, reference number 88001319, listed August 25, 1988.
———. "Samuel Russell House." National Historic Landmark. National Register of Historic Places, reference number 70000688, designated August 7, 2001.

FIGURES 81 AND 82. Samuel Russell (*top*) and William Trench (*bottom*) Houses, Middletown. Patrick L. Pinnell (Russell House); Connecticut Trust for Historic Preservation (Trench House)

17

ARTISTIC DESIGN

MARK TWAIN HOUSE, HARTFORD

Although the author known as Mark Twain cultivated his image as an innocent abroad or a no-nonsense westerner, his alter ego, Samuel Clemens, lived in a house that epitomized advanced artistic taste of the 1870s and 1880s. While the house is often characterized as an expression of his exuberant personality, there is no historical basis for the assertion that it was intended to resemble a Mississippi River steamboat. In fact, Samuel Clemens's wife, Olivia, who was well-read in the works of John Ruskin and other Victorian theorists, played a significant role in shaping the house to reflect current fashions.

The architect, Edward Tuckerman Potter (1831–1904), was an early American adopter of the multicolored masonry of French seaside resorts. He used banded brick to highlight the house's picturesque bays and nooks. From these vantage points the Clemens family could enjoy views of the peaceful Nook Farm neighborhood where their neighbors included fellow writers Harriet Beecher Stowe and Charles Dudley Warner.

A few years after moving in, the Clemenses hired Associated Artists, the firm founded by Louis Comfort Tiffany in collaboration with Lockwood DeForest, Samuel Colman, and Candace Wheeler, to redecorate the first floor. Insisting on total control over colors, materials, and furnishings, the firm aimed to create a sense of color harmony, adapt foreign designs to American uses, and express room function and individuality.

In the entry hall, stenciled American Indian–inspired motifs in black and silver overlay the red walls and walnut woodwork, reflecting Candace Wheeler's recommendation that entry halls be painted red and "be treated in such a way as to lead up to and prepare the mind for whatever of inner luxury there may be in the house." The drawing room, dedicated to entertaining guests, has pale salmon-pink walls and ecru woodwork stenciled with East Indian designs in shimmering silver. The Clemenses' daughter Clara remembered the room as giving "an impression of hospitable *light*."

The dining room has a color scheme of red, gold, and brown (recommended for its cold northern exposure), with embossed wallpaper imitating tooled leather and woodwork stenciled in gold with Japanese-inspired designs. The less formal library (the equivalent of today's family room) has peacock-blue walls stenciled in gold with a pattern reminiscent of Scottish plaid, supposedly to complement the baronial chimneypiece the Clemenses brought from Scotland.

The overall effect is rich but restrained. Twain wrote of the house, "How ugly, tasteless, repulsive, are all the domestic interiors I have seen in Europe compared with the perfect taste of this ground floor, with its delicious dream of harmonious color, and its all-pervading spirit of peace and serenity and deep contentments." But there was more to the design than peace and serenity. Above all, it was Artistic, with a capital *A*. It was no mistake that Tiffany and his colleagues called their company Associated *Artists*. Art was the aim: art for art's sake, but also art to assert Twain's position as a major figure in American culture.

THE PLACE
MARK TWAIN HOUSE

www.marktwainhouse.org

1873–1874, Edward Tuckerman Potter. 1881, interior decoration, Associated Artists. 1955–1974, restored.

351 Farmington Avenue, Hartford. Open to the public.

FURTHER READING

Faude, Wilson. "Associated Artists and the American Renaissance in the Decorative Arts." *Winterthur Portfolio* 10 (1975): 101–130.

Schroer, Blanche Higgins. "Mark Twain House." National Historic Landmark. National Register of Historic Places, reference number 66000884, designated December 29, 1962.

Wheeler, Candace. "The Philosophy of Beauty Applied to House Interiors." In *Household Art*. edited by Candace Wheeler, 3–34. New York: Harper Brothers, 1893.

FIGURE 83. Mark Twain House, Hartford, dining room. Mark Twain House & Museum, Hartford, Connecticut. Photograph by John Groo

CONNECTICUT ARCHITECTURE

18

BEHIND THE SCENES
WALLACE T. FENN HOUSE, WETHERSFIELD

If our homes are the stages on which people live their lives, what happens backstage? Architectural history, at least the popular version, is full of styles and influences and famous architects, but it frequently skips over the heating ducts, cisterns, laundry facilities, and other backstairs unmentionables that keep households running. In the closing decades of the nineteenth century, these unseen elements played a growing role in shaping houses.

Wallace T. Fenn, an executive with the Hartford lithography company Kellogg & Bulkeley, took advantage of new technological developments when he built a house in Wethersfield around 1895. A description of the house, published in 1897, pays relatively little attention to its style and decoration but focuses instead on its modern materials and conveniences.

The primary construction material is lumber in standardized sizes, enumerated in a very long paragraph in the article. The availability of such lumber made possible the spread of the balloon frame, which reduced construction costs and made it easier to construct complex forms. What the description didn't mention was that the door and window trim, stair railings, mantels, and paneling that gave the house an individual character were also made by machine. By the 1890s, such mass-produced millwork probably was too common to merit noting.

Discussed next were the polished French plate glass, beveled in the sidelights of the front door, and the "rolled cathedral" (i.e., stained) glass in the tall staircase window. Other modern materials are tin and canvas roofs on the porches and bay windows, iron posts to support the porches, and a cement (i.e., concrete) cellar floor.

Modern technology is apparent in the cellar. In addition to the cement floor, it contains the furnace and an ash pit, with drains from the sinks, toilets, and outside gutters connected to pipes under the floor that run toward the street. Upstairs, the kitchen contains a range and sink, as well as laundry tubs, although, the 1897 description noted, "some owners prefer to have the tubs in the cellar." The icebox is located in the rear hall, "convenient for the iceman and general use." The plans also show a boiler in the kitchen, a second sink in the pantry, and gaslight fixtures in most of the rooms and hallways. The plumbing fixtures are "modern in every respect."

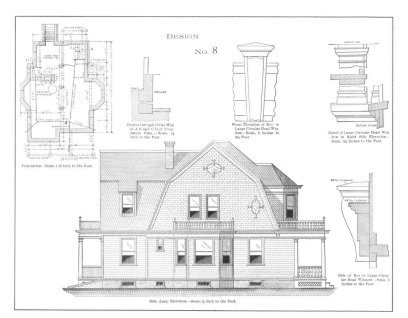

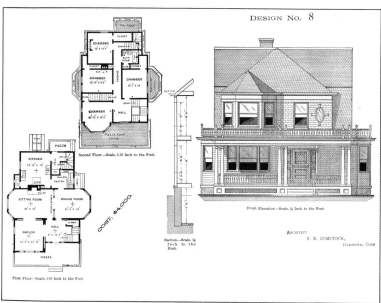

FIGURES 84 AND 85. Wallace T. Fenn House, Wethersfield, plans. From *Modern American Dwellings by Numerous Architects*, 1897

Mechanical equipment like this changed the way people lived. With improved lighting, the main meal of the day migrated from afternoon to evening, making the nine-to-five workday more feasible. Labor-saving devices simplified housekeeping and made it possible to maintain a middle-class lifestyle with fewer servants, or none at all. Plumbing and drains improved sanitation, decreasing the likelihood of disease.

But these advances came with costs. Building clients found a growing proportion of their outlay going to equipment that previously had little or no presence in the budget. Maintaining and operating the new systems had to be accounted for, too. As money that once had gone to square footage and ornament shifted to pipes and wires and gas and electric bills, houses began to be smaller and simpler. Of course, other factors also fed this trend, including changing tastes and a growing market for houses at lower levels of the economic ladder, thanks to rising wages and the lower cost of mass-produced building products. But the never-ending search for greater comfort and less work continued to shape American living.

THE PLACE
WALLACE T. FENN HOUSE
ca. 1895, F. R. Comstock
84 Broad Street, Wethersfield. Private residence.

FURTHER READING

Berg, Donald J., ed. *Modern American Dwellings*. David Williams Co., 1897. Reprint, Rockville Center, N.Y.: Antiquity Reprints, 1982.

Luyster, Constance. "Old Wethersfield Historic District." National Register of Historic Places, reference number 70000719, listed December 29, 1970.

19

LOCAL SPECIALTY
PERFECT SIXES, HARTFORD

Throughout New England, two- and three-family houses, known as double-deckers and triple-deckers, form the backbone of industrial cities. Built by the thousands during the peak industrial years from the 1890s to the 1920s, the compact buildings fit perfectly into the rapidly growing communities. Unlike earlier row houses or side-by-side double houses, they have units stacked one atop another, so that each apartment has exterior exposure on all four sides. This provided a bright and airy environment that addressed health concerns and provided a good fit for the emerging middle class. Many were occupied by their owners, with the additional units accommodating extended families or providing rental income to supplement wages.

Hartford builders developed a variant on the triple-decker, essentially joining two of them to create a building known locally as a "Perfect Six." Unlike most double- and triple-deckers, Perfect Sixes were almost universally built of brick, with bows or bays flanking the entry porch and a heavy classical cornice at the roofline. With their larger size and big cornices they brought a monumental scale to middle-class neighborhoods where investors often constructed them in rows. Putnam Heights and Mortson Street are two single-block streets lined with red-brick Perfect Sixes. Some have decorative shaped gables, and some have Queen Anne porches, examples of the ways developers varied the form.

Inside, the apartments typically contain two or three bedrooms, plus a living room, a kitchen, and perhaps a dining room. In larger buildings, everything opened off a long hallway; in smaller ones rooms opened directly to one another. A back porch with a stair provided secondary access and a place to hang laundry.

By the 1910s, reformers were criticizing stacked housing like Perfect Sixes and double- and triple-deckers for overcrowding (which wasn't necessarily caused by the architecture) or, in the case of wooden buildings, vulnerability to fire. The reformers proposed housing like Seaside Village (place 44), designed with more architectural variety and, where possible, located in self-contained enclaves rather than in rows along city streets. Nonetheless, the stacked multifamily buildings continued to be constructed well into the 1920s, and in many Connecticut neighborhoods they still provide comfortable housing at

FIGURE 86. Perfect Sixes, Park Terrace, Hartford. Connecticut Trust for Historic Preservation

affordable prices. With falling urban populations, a recent trend has been to reduce the number of units. The Mortson Street and Putnam Heights Perfect Sixes were renovated as two- and four-family buildings in the early 2000s.

THE PLACES
PERFECT SIXES

ca. 1905–1910
Mortson Street, Putnam Heights, Park Terrace, Hartford

FURTHER READING

Andrews, Gregory E., and David F. Ransom. *Structures and Styles: Guided Tours of Hartford Architecture*. Hartford: Connecticut Historical Society and Connecticut Architecture Foundation, 1988.

Ransom, David F. "Frog Hollow Historic District." National Register of Historic Places, reference number 79002635, listed April 11, 1979.

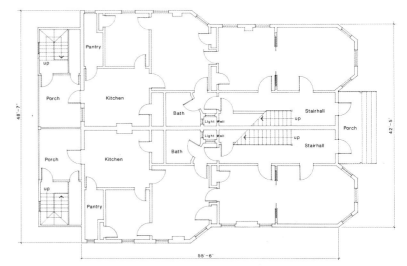

FIGURE 87. Perfect Six, plan. Richard K. Charney, AIA, and Joel Raphael, AIA

20

ART VERSUS THE MACHINE

NATHANIEL R. BRONSON HOUSE, MIDDLEBURY

This bungalow is securely anchored to the landscape by its horizontal lines and overhanging roof, its sturdy stone piers and soft colors. The deep porch and wide banks of windows provide a connection with nature, as do the rough stone and dark wood, touched only lightly by the builder's hand. Although a close look shows that the house is actually quite large, the first impression it makes is not of size or expense, but rather of solidity and comfort.

The word "bungalow" refers not to the house's style but to its *form*—low and spreading, with a big sheltering roof and a deep porch. The name comes from Bengal, India, where the colonial British encountered one-story houses with good ventilation and generous porches. The bungalow's connotations of coziness appealed to the suburban middle class, first in England and then in the United States, where in the opening years of the twentieth century bungalows became so fashionable that the word was applied to almost any informal dwelling, from rustic cabin to mansion.

The bungalow's popularization was part of the Arts and Crafts movement, an international phenomenon that began in the mid-nineteenth century in reaction to the impersonal assembly-line production of the Industrial Revolution. Arts and Crafts leaders advocated a return to soul-satisfying hand craftsmanship, simple design (in contrast to machine-made elaboration), and respect for the inherent characteristics of materials.

The American leader of the Arts and Crafts movement was Gustav Stickley (1858–1942), a furniture maker who started a magazine called the *Craftsman*. At first a vehicle to publicize Stickley's products, the magazine quickly became the American voice of the movement. It offered articles on artistic theory, instructions for do-it-yourself projects ranging from furniture making to embroidery, pottery to metalworking to gardening—and plans for houses by Stickley's team of in-house architects. In addition to designs for the magazine, the Craftsman Architects also undertook private commissions for well-to-do clients such as Nathaniel R. Bronson, a Waterbury lawyer.

Buildings featured in the *Craftsman* tend to be blocky in outline and detail, with materials left as much as possible in their natural state: unpainted shingles or stucco, rough brick, stained wood, unfinished stone. Framing is often exposed, and open plans and built-in furnishings increase the sense of spaciousness inside. Almost all these traits are seen in the Bronson house. The emphasis is on good craftsmanship and simple design, rather than luxurious materials or elaborate ornament. Long after the *Craftsman* ceased publication in 1916, its influence continued to be strong. In suburban towns and rural communities, bungalows were constructed by local builders or by customers who bought kits from companies such as Sears, Roebuck.

Although the term "Craftsman" has come to denote rustic-looking design like that of the Bronson house, the magazine also published Colonial Revival, Japanese, and Old English designs, among others. For Stickley, style was less important than its effect; he wrote that he hoped "the Craftsman house may be instrumental in helping

establish in America a higher ideal, not only of beautiful architecture, but of home life." Countless well-loved Craftsman houses across the country bear witness that he realized his wish.

THE PLACE
NATHANIEL R. BRONSON HOUSE
1914, Craftsman Architects
19 Richardson Drive, Middlebury. Private residence.

FURTHER READING

Smith, Mary Ann. *Gustav Stickley: The Craftsman*. Syracuse, N.Y.: Syracuse University Press, 1983.

Stickley, Gustav. *Craftsman Homes*. New York: Craftsman, 1909. Reprinted as *Craftsman Homes: Architecture and Furnishings of the American Arts and Crafts Movement*. New York: Dover, 1979.

FIGURE 88. Nathaniel R. Bronson House, Middlebury. Deb Cohen

21

COMFORTABLE HOUSES
BEAVER HILLS, NEW HAVEN

Throughout the nineteenth and early twentieth centuries American architects endlessly debated what style to build in. Some wanted to invent a new style. Others wanted to adapt historical styles to American needs, sometimes picking a single "best style," sometimes advocating different styles to suit different purposes or to match clients' personalities. One result of this fixation was that, to this day, the first question many people ask when they look at a building is, "What style is it?"

With no agreement on which style to use, clients and architects were free to choose from a wide selection. A good deal of energy was put into researching and executing details correctly, and it was common for architects to visit historic buildings, sketchbook in hand, to collect ideas for their work. Every Connecticut city has at least one neighborhood where the results of this eclectic approach are visible. One is Beaver Hills in New Haven, built largely between 1910 and 1940. In a practice typical for the time, the developers laid out lots and sold them to buyers who built their houses individually, producing a more varied streetscape than the mass-produced subdivisions constructed after World War II.

In Beaver Hills we see the popular styles of the day. There are bungalows and other products of the Arts and Crafts movement, with shaggy shingles, wide eaves, and chunky brackets. There are Old English houses, with irregular outlines and half-timbering or wildly random masonry, built at scales ranging from Cotswold cottage to Elizabethan manor house. There are different kinds of Colonial Revival, from Dutch (with gambrel roofs) to New England farmhouses (with overhangs and decorative pendants) to Georgian mansions (built of brick with columns and pediments). There are even stuccoed villas with arched loggias and tile roofs, labeled "Italian" or "Spanish" or simply "Mediterranean." (An unexpected sight in snowy New England, these probably owed their popularity to the allure of Hollywood, where the style was popular for its evocation of California's Spanish origins.) Architectural historian Elizabeth Mills Brown comments that with all this variety, "you get the feeling that you are riffling through the pages of a magazine" (see further reading).

Indeed, magazines and books of plans helped spread

this architecture, educating readers in the nuances of the various "models." But these styles are only skin deep. Behind their porticoes or loggias or half-timbering, the houses are remarkably similar. They are built to the same scale, and with a rather narrow range of materials: wood, brick, stucco, and a little stone. Inside, the houses have many of the same plans, and certainly the same selection of rooms, to accommodate a middle-class lifestyle. And all have the same amenities: kitchens with built-in counters and cupboards, fireplaces in the living rooms, porches for summer evenings, up-to-date plumbing and heating and wiring, and garages for the cars.

In light of their similarities, rather than the incidental differences of exterior decoration, these houses are all expressions of what the historian Alan Gowans called the "Comfortable House"—homes that offered physical comfort and expressed the middle-class values of stability, security, and cultured living. Perhaps Comfortable Houses, rather than Colonials or Tudors or Italian villas, is what they really should be called.

FIGURE 89. Beaver Hills, New Haven. Connecticut Trust for Historic Preservation

THE PLACE
BEAVER HILLS

1908–1938, Beaver Hills Company
Bounded by Goffe Terrace, Crescent Street, and Ella
 Grasso Boulevard, New Haven

FURTHER READING

Brown, Elizabeth Mills. *New Haven: A Guide to Architecture and Urban Design*. New Haven, Conn.: Yale University Press, 1976.

Gowans, Alan. *The Comfortable House: North American Suburban Architecture, 1890–1930*. Cambridge, Mass.: MIT Press, 1986.

Loether, J. Paul. "Beaver Hills Historic District." National Register of Historic Places, reference number 86002108, listed July 31, 1986.

FIGURE 90. Beaver Hills, New Haven. Connecticut Trust for Historic Preservation

FIGURE 91. Beaver Hills, New Haven. Connecticut Trust for Historic Preservation

22

FROM CAPE COD TO CONNECTICUT
AXEL NELSON HOUSE, WATERFORD

In 1942, Axel Nelson, a foreman at the nearby Millstone granite quarry, built a house for himself of local stone, a surprisingly rare choice in this quarrying community. Since the seventeenth century, wood has been the default material for Connecticut houses, with cost probably being the deciding factor in most cases. As if to compensate for this departure from the norm, Nelson employed the full range of granites available at Millstone, using a warm palette of pinks, golds, and coppers, as well as a pinkish gray that functions as a neutral color to highlight the others. Amid a street full of more conventional houses, Nelson's lively patchwork stands out.

Apart from his choice of material, Nelson's house was typical for the Connecticut suburbs in the 1930s, '40s, and '50s. One-story houses with big chimneys and steep roofs had been built in New England almost since the first Europeans arrived, and by the late eighteenth century they dominated certain areas. During a tour of Cape Cod in 1810, Yale's president Timothy Dwight was so struck by their numbers that he referred to the type as "Cape Cod houses," a term still used.

The Cape Cod came to the forefront nationally during the Great Depression of the 1930s, when economic hardship inspired new interest in small, inexpensive houses. During World War II, private construction was strictly limited, and little was built outside of projects needed for the war effort. But where housing construction did take place, small Capes were a good choice, and rows of them filled developments for war-industry workers in cities like New Haven and Willimantic. After the war, pent-up housing demand, along with policies that favored new construction in the suburbs, led to the widespread development of suburban subdivisions.

From the 1930s to the '50s and beyond, the Cape appealed to middle-class suburbanites on several levels. It represented history and tradition, thanks to the Colonial Williamsburg restoration and publications like the photography books of Samuel Chamberlain, which maintained public interest in the eighteenth century as the font of American democracy. At the same time, the simple geometry of the Cape struck a chord in mid-century taste. Although more directly associated with Modernism, such simplification appealed to traditionalists of the period, too, as seen in the streamlined classical design used on post offices and other government buildings in the 1930s (see figure 44).

Finally, the Cape economically and efficiently satisfied middle-class housing needs. Compact and inexpensive to build, it was a good starter house for first-time homeowners like Axel Nelson, a Swedish immigrant who previously lived in rented quarters. The Cape also could be expanded as families grew or prospered, or personalized as Nelson did with his multicolored granite. For the more adventurous, the basic form could be reworked in a mildly Modernist style while still retaining the familiar shape, like some houses in Levittown, the groundbreaking suburban development on Long Island.

"Unpretentious." "Cozy." "Modest." "Charming."

"Practical." "Simple." These are words used to describe Cape Cod houses in the literature of the mid-twentieth century. From the Great Depression to the Cold War, they offered an achievable ideal of home: affordable houses rooted in tradition.

THE PLACE
AXEL NELSON HOUSE
1942, Axel Nelson
19 Locust Court, Waterford. Private residence.

FURTHER READING
Gebhard, David. "Royal Barry Wills and the American Colonial Revival." *Winterthur Portfolio* 27, no. 1 (Spring 1992): 45–74.

FIGURE 92. Axel Nelson House, Waterford. Connecticut Trust for Historic Preservation

23

REDESIGNING THE SUBURBS
HERITAGE VILLAGE, SOUTHBURY

In the 1960s, changes in state law that legalized condominium ownership and planned-unit development altered the face of many Connecticut towns. These new provisions allowed more flexibility in design that resulted in a greater variety of housing options. Planned-unit development (PUD) allowed developers to cluster housing units and preserve large areas of public open space, to reduce or eliminate property-line setbacks, and to mix single-family and multifamily dwellings. One of the earliest, biggest, and most influential PUDS in Connecticut is Heritage Village in Southbury. Built by the Paparazzo Development Corporation as a planned community for "active adults" over fifty-five years old, Heritage Village attracted nationwide attention for its architecture and plan.

The architect, California-based Charles Callister (1917–2008), worked with the developers to site the buildings, selecting locations while walking the ground in a process that he called "architecture on the spot." One of his aims was to minimize disturbance to the land; grading was done to provide screening or visual interest rather than to even out the terrain. Another goal was to minimize the impact of automobiles; garages and carports were located slightly apart from the housing units, roads were kept narrow, and footpaths connect the clusters. Nonetheless, since it is located in the countryside, Heritage Village is not a place where one could live easily without a car.

The bulk of Heritage Village consists of buildings containing two to six units, arranged in clusters separated by open space. The clusters contain a limited number of models, unified by a basic vocabulary of barnlike forms, vertical cedar siding in muted colors, and standardized details. The rambling, informal layout and woodsy architecture were inspired by California developments such as Rossmoor Leisure World, in Walnut Grove, California (1963), an earlier age-restricted retirement community for which Callister had won acclaim. The informality and environmental consciousness of these West Coast developments inspired "California-style" imitations in Connecticut and elsewhere through the 1970s and into the '80s, with widely varying degrees of faithfulness and success.

The first section at Heritage Village, containing 119

FIGURE 93. Heritage Village, Southbury. Patrick L. Pinnell

units, opened in 1966. The development now comprises 2,850 units on one thousand acres and makes up nearly one-fourth of Southbury's population. Later sections have included apartments in addition to townhouses, although these larger buildings have not always been sited with the same environmental sensitivity.

Part of the concept of Heritage Village was the provision of community facilities, including tennis courts and a golf course, a library, meeting and party spaces (some in historic buildings on the property), and a small commercial center on Heritage Road, with shops, offices, and an inn. Unfortunately, its centerpiece, the Heritage Bazaar, a "haute hippie" indoor mall that resembled a Middle Eastern souk, has been demolished.

The historian Gwendolyn Wright observes that PUDS like Heritage Village offered a middle ground between suburban sprawl and urban high-rises, providing access to nature but also accommodations for households other than stereotypical nuclear families. However, Heritage Village, with its age restriction and relatively narrow range of unit types, remains a single-category development, just for a different category. More diverse suburban development would have to come elsewhere.

THE PLACE
HERITAGE VILLAGE
1965 and later, Charles Warren Callister of Callister and Payne
Heritage Road, Southbury. Private residences.

FURTHER READING
Wright, Gwendolyn. *Building the American Dream: A Social History of Housing in America*. Cambridge, Mass.: MIT Press, 1981.
"Improvised Siting for Planned Community." *Progressive Architecture* 48, no. 12 (December 1967): 114–119.

Part Four

WORKING THE LAND

At first, everyone in Connecticut farmed—if not as a primary occupation, then at least to supplement other pursuits. Whether for sustenance or profit, agriculture was central to the colony's and state's economy, and farms were perhaps the most common feature of its landscape.

By the time of the Civil War, Connecticut agriculture was changing in response to competition from larger farms with richer soils in other parts of the country. General farming declined, as well as large-scale grain and livestock production. Dairy and poultry farming grew in significance, and providing produce to local markets remained important. Immigrants took over many of the state's farms, while gentlemen hobbyists introduced new techniques and technologies, with assistance from agricultural scientists at the Connecticut Agricultural Experiment Station and the University of Connecticut.

24

THE BUSINESS OF FARMING

THOMAS CATLIN JR. FARM, LITCHFIELD

By the last quarter of the eighteenth century, well-to-do farmers in northwestern Connecticut were building large, comfortable, stylish houses nearly as imposing as the in-town residences of the great merchants. One of these farmers was Thomas Catlin Jr., who owed his prosperity not only to farming but to business dealings as well. In addition to raising crops and livestock, he sold or bartered his own and his neighbors' surpluses, and hired out his draft animals and wagons to haul timber or farm products.

In 1786 Catlin bought land from his father on East Chestnut Hill, a long glacial ridge of the sort favored in colonial Connecticut for good drainage, fertile soils, and elevation above what was considered unhealthful lowland air. Litchfield's soil was noted in the early nineteenth century as good for grazing, and staple products included cheese, butter, and pork.

On East Chestnut Hill, Catlin built a residence that rivaled in size and finish those in major population centers. It still stands at the heart of a nearly intact farm complex with three surviving eighteenth-century outbuildings. The larger two are identified as a hay barn and a horse barn. Both are of a type called an "English barn" that had been built from the colony's earliest days.

Originally developed for grain storage and processing, the English barn has three structural bays with doors on the broad, eave sides. Doors on both sides allowed wagons to drive through the central bay without turning around or backing up. The doors also allowed the center to be used for threshing and winnowing grain, as cross breezes blew away the chaff. The side bays were for storing hay or grain; on farms with only one barn they came to house animals as well. A third, smaller outbuilding, located behind Catlin's house, may have been used for ice or storage. A bigger barn was moved to the property in the 1950s.

While arrangements varied, many eighteenth-century farmers located their barns close to the road—for convenience but also, perhaps, for display. Hay barns, with their flammable contents, were set a bit apart from other structures, to lessen the risk of fire spreading. Catlin's hay and horse barns follow this pattern: the former stands to the north of the house, while the latter sits across the road. Standing amid the fields (now largely grown up into woods), they created a clearly defined farm complex.

Farming was a business. Some farmers produced just enough to get by, while others like Catlin diversified and expanded. His farmstead functioned as a small commercial center. It may have presented an air of self-sufficiency, but its success depended on Catlin's relations with neighboring farmers and attention to the demands of markets farther away.

THE PLACE
THOMAS CATLIN JR. HOUSE AND FARM
ca. 1786
125 East Chestnut Hill Road, Litchfield. Private.

FURTHER READING

Carley, Rachel D. "Litchfield Farms, Parts I and II." Litchfield Historical Society, 2006–2007.

———. *Litchfield: The Making of a New England Town*. Litchfield, Conn.: Litchfield Historical Society, 2011.

Historic Barns of Connecticut. http://connecticutbarns.org.

Visser, Thomas Durant. *Field Guide to New England Barns and Farm Buildings*. Hanover, N.H.: University Press of New England, 1997.

FIGURE 94. *The Catlin Homestead* (Thomas Catlin Jr. Farm), Litchfield, oil on canvas by Annie Bidwell Catlin, 1898. Collection of the Litchfield Historical Society, Litchfield, Connecticut

25

MODEST FARM

CYRUS WILSON FARM, HARWINTON

The Cyrus Wilson Farm in Harwinton is a good example of the small family farms that dominated the Connecticut countryside until well into the twentieth century, when keeping them running became increasingly difficult financially. Cyrus Wilson owned about two hundred acres, one of the largest farms in Harwinton, on which he transitioned in the late nineteenth century from generalized to more market-oriented agriculture. By the 1880s, he was concentrating on potatoes, butter, and eggs; in the 1900s his daughter and son-in-law went even more heavily into egg production.

The Wilson house, built to replace an earlier dwelling, turns a formal face to the road, but its entry is from the south side, along the drive that leads to the barn behind, probably built at the same time and extended with an attached shed. Together, the house's rear ell, the barn, and the shed define a sheltered work yard open to the south to capture light and warmth from the sun.

Across the road is the main barn, built in three parts in the late nineteenth and twentieth centuries. Two sections are of wood, banked into the hillside to allow direct access to the lower level (the cattle stalls) from the downhill side, and to the upper level (the hayloft) from the uphill side. A later addition was constructed of concrete block and has a gambrel roof. Although the gambrel form is popularly identified with barns, it didn't actually come into widespread use until the twentieth century, when dimensional lumber made it easier to construct. There are three silos, used to store fermented green feed considered more nutritious than hay. Their wood-stave construction was most common from the 1890s to the 1930s.

In the 1930s, J. Henry Roraback—president of the Connecticut Light and Power Company (see place 4) and a powerful politician—bought the Wilson farm along with numerous other local properties for farming and also to serve as a vast hunting preserve. The most prominent structure on the farm, the seventy-three-foot-tall windmill with its shingled tower, was built in 1936 under Roraback. The windmill pumped water from a well up to a holding tank from which it flowed by gravity to farmstead uses. The slanting walls of the lower section provide buttressing to support the weight of the water tank, while the decorative

railings probably reflect Roraback's status as a gentleman farmer, even though he didn't live here.

The Wilson farm remained in operation until the property was sold to the state in 1982. It now houses the regional offices of the Department of Energy and Environmental Protection. This pattern—from general farming to a big private landowner to public ownership—is a common one in rural Connecticut.

THE PLACE
CYRUS WILSON FARM
(Connecticut Department of Energy and Environmental
    Protection Western District headquarters)
1878–1950s
230 Plymouth Road, Harwinton

FURTHER READING
Clouette, Bruce, and Matthew Roth. "Cyrus Wilson Farm."
    National Register of Historic Places nomination, reference
    number 85003699, 1985 (not listed on register).

FIGURES 95 AND 96. Cyrus Wilson Farm, Harwinton. Patrick L. Pinnell (farm); Connecticut Trust for Historic Preservation (barn)

26

THE RHYTHM OF THE SEASONS
TOBACCO FARMS, WINDSOR

Tobacco, suited to the well-drained, fertile soil of the Connecticut River Valley, has been grown in Connecticut since the seventeenth century. But it didn't become a major cash crop until the nineteenth century, when tobacco for cigars became the valley's most important agricultural product. At the height of production in the 1920s, thirty thousand acres of tobacco were under cultivation in the state. Even with the sharp decline in smoking, the high cost of labor needed to tend and harvest the plants, and the pressures of suburbanization, tobacco farming still survives in some corners of the valley.

The most obvious evidence of tobacco growing is the distinctive barns—called sheds—used for curing the leaves. The New England tobacco shed is a readily identifiable regional type developed in the mid-nineteenth century and different from tobacco barns in other parts of the country. It is long and narrow, between 24 and 40 feet wide, and up to 240 feet long. Board siding covers the timber frame, with vents that can be opened and closed to regulate ventilation. Openings can be either vertical, hinged on the sides like doors, or at the top to swing out, or horizontal, swinging up like louvers. Some sheds also have ridge vents to increase airflow.

Big tobacco farms can have dozens of sheds, scattered throughout the fields for easy storing of the harvested leaves but still grouped for ease of loading the cured leaves for shipment. To catch the prevailing breezes, they are often built in parallel rows, like herds of cattle all facing into the wind. Other groupings, like the O. J. Thrall Company sheds at Kennedy Road, appear more random.

But there is more to tobacco farms than the sheds. Since about 1900, Connecticut farmers have specialized in thin-leafed tobacco used for cigar wrappers. This strain needs a humid environment and filtered sunlight to replicate conditions in Sumatra, where it originated. The Connecticut Agricultural Experiment Station developed the method of growing this tobacco under gauze tents, which shelter the plants from the sun and maintain humidity.

Together, sheds, fields, and tents form a complete tobacco-related landscape. During the course of a year, plants are set out and grow, eventually becoming taller than a person. The tenting is stretched out on wires

FIGURES 97, 98, AND 99. Tobacco farms, Windsor. Lowell Fewster

FIGURE 100. Tobacco farms, Windsor. Lowell Fewster

running between poles, turning the summertime fields white. When harvest time comes, the side curtains of the tents are folded back, providing access for workers to pick the big leaves. The leaves are sewn into bundles and hung in the sheds to be cured. Depending on the breeze and the temperature and humidity, the ventilators are opened or closed. When they are open, the solid, windowless sheds become skeletal frames, hung with bundles of leaves that change color from green to gold.

Like the natural landscape, the human-made tobacco landscape is constantly in flux—as the plants grow and develop, as the tenting is extended to enclose them or opened for harvesting, as the shed ventilators are opened or closed. This sequence echoes the rhythm of the growing year, an unending cycle of growth and change.

THE PLACES
TOBACCO FARMS
Twentieth century
Pierson Lane, Kennedy Road at Joseph Lane, and Day Hill and Old Iron Ore Roads, Windsor
LUDDY/TAYLOR CONNECTICUT TOBACCO VALLEY MUSEUM
www.tobaccohistsoc.org
135 Lang Road, Windsor. Open to the public.

FURTHER READING
O'Gorman, James F. *Connecticut Valley Vernacular: The Vanishing Landscape and Architecture of the New England Tobacco Fields.* Philadelphia: University of Pennsylvania Press, 2002.

27

AGRICULTURAL SHOWPLACE
HILLTOP FARM, SUFFIELD

Beginning in 1913, George M. Hendee, a Springfield industrialist whose company developed the Indian Motorcycle, built an extensive estate on the banks of the Connecticut River. The house (now demolished) was designed by Max Westhoff, a New York architect known for country estates and Adirondack camps. For the grounds, Hendee hired Carl Rust Parker (1882–1966), a former member of the Olmsted firm who mostly designed parks, subdivisions, and estates. Parker planned formal gardens with views to the river, and laid out winding drives and an extensive drainage and water-supply system.

Unlike J. Henry Roraback, who lived in Hartford, far from his Harwinton landholdings, Hendee remained closely involved in the operation of Hilltop as a working farm, where he raised prize Guernsey cattle and white leghorn chickens. In the late nineteenth and early twentieth centuries such "gentlemen's farms" were popular with the rich. Although farming was a hobby for these men, many pursued it seriously, closely following the latest developments in techniques and equipment.

The agricultural trends of the day emphasized industrialization and sanitation. The farmstead as a whole was organized for efficiency in handling materials. To inhibit the spread of diseases, functions such as storing manure and processing milk were separated into different structures. Buildings were made of modern materials that facilitated operations; concrete floors, for example, could be hosed off.

A gentleman's farm was usually identifiable by the specialization and stylishness of its buildings. At Hilltop, Hendee built chicken houses, a hen emporium, an incubator house, calf and bull barns, tobacco sheds, a root cellar, and a carriage house. There were also living quarters for farmworkers and managers, some of them older farmhouses acquired with the property. While fancy architecture and new gadgetry were usually beyond the means of ordinary farmers, hobbyists like Hendee did provide a means of introducing improvements to their neighbors.

The centerpiece of Hilltop Farm is the monumental dairy barn, like Hendee's mansion probably designed by Westhoff. Sited for maximum visual impact, the barn sits at the top of a hill, clearly visible from the road. The lower level contains milking stanchions, separated by iron pipe railings, with concrete floors and feed trough. A waste gutter and a manure trolley suspended from a ceiling track aided in removing manure. The upper level was a vast open hayloft, with equipment and shafts for moving hay. The tile-lined silos represented an early use of a material that would become common in the 1920s and '30s.

In spite of the barn's Colonial Revival white clapboards, green trim, and classical columns and pediments, the predominant image is medieval: a castlelike entry across a bridge over a moatlike driveway and between two fat round towers (the silos). Inside, it is a cathedral of agriculture: a lofty nave and aisles dim and dusty with shafts of light.

THE PLACE
HILLTOP FARM
www.hilltopfarmsuffield.org
1913 and later, Max Westhoff; Carl Rust Parker, landscape architect
1550 Mapleton Avenue (Connecticut Route 190), Suffield

FURTHER READING
Historic Barns of Connecticut. http://connecticutbarns.org.
Olausen, Stephen, and Jeffrey Emidy. "Hilltop Farm." National Register of Historic Places, reference number 04001463, listed January 12, 2005.

FIGURES 101 AND 102. Dairy barn, Hilltop Farm, Suffield. Photographs by Ray Pioggia (exterior) and John G. Smith (interior), courtesy of the Friends of the Farm at Hilltop Inc.

28

CONNECTICUT CATSKILLS
ORCHARD MANSION, MOODUS

In the middle of the twentieth century, the area around the towns of East Haddam and Colchester was called the "Connecticut Catskills." This nickname recognized the many summer resorts in the area that, like their better-known counterparts in upstate New York, catered to a predominantly Jewish clientele.

These resorts grew out of earlier efforts to help Jewish immigrants from Eastern Europe settle as farmers, away from big-city crowding and squalor. Two organizations, the Baron de Hirsch Fund, established in 1890 by a prominent German Jewish philanthropist, and the Jewish Agriculture Society (JAS), founded in 1900, provided agricultural training as well as mortgages to support the new farmers. Thanks to their efforts, by 1920 several eastern Connecticut towns, such as Colchester, Lebanon, and East Haddam, had thriving Jewish populations.

To supplement their income, many farmers took in summer boarders seeking temporary escape from the cities. While this practice crossed ethnic lines, it was particularly advantageous for Jews, since it ensured access to synagogues and kosher food, and avoided anti-Semitism. Over the years, some farms grew into full-fledged resorts that offered accommodations in larger hotels or separate cottages, meals in dining halls (farm boarders often cooked for themselves), more elaborate recreational facilities, and entertainment. Although the resorts varied in elaborateness and price, they mostly catered to a middle- and working-class clientele from the Northeast.

One of the larger resorts was Orchard Mansion near Moodus, a village in the town of East Haddam. Its story dated to 1926 when Morris Mager took out a mortgage from the JAS to buy Clovermead Farm, a forty-six-acre property that included a big Greek Revival farmhouse, a twentieth-century barn, and an apple orchard. It is not clear when Mager began taking in guests, but by the mid-1930s the farm had become a resort. The barn was converted to a social center, a rambling one-story building was built to house dining rooms and a kitchen, and rows of small cabins lined the edges of open lawns. The property, expanded to sixty-two acres, also offered a swimming pool, play equipment, and later, a television room.

As one vacationer described Orchard Mansion, "The

rooms were simple; the beds were hardly firm; and hot showers were at a premium. But people were not there for the amenities. They were working-class Jews who needed a break and stumbled upon a good deal. For my parents—small business owners—it was heaven: fresh country air, a big swimming pool, camp for the kids, and some quiet time that they couldn't get in the city. Time was spent outdoors mostly at the pool and often, in a matter of hours, complete strangers who had randomly chosen lounge chairs were chatting away like lifelong friends."

Mager's daughter and son-in-law, Rose and Morris Kabatznick, continued operating Orchard Mansion until 1972. After sitting vacant for twelve years it reopened in 1984 as My Father's House, a Catholic retreat center.

Orchard Mansion is still little changed, and its agricultural origins remain obvious. The old farmhouse and the gambrel-roofed barn are the most prominent structures on the property, and the other buildings, loosely clustered around them, look like farm sheds or outbuildings. Most of the property remains as open fields, now used for camp activities instead of crops or grazing. The informality and farmlike character serve as reminders of the attractions that Orchard Mansion and resorts like it offered: fresh air, fresh food, sociability, and the simple life.

THE PLACE
ORCHARD MANSION

(Now My Father's House, www.myfathershousect.org)
ca. 1840; ca. 1920–1950
39 North Moodus Road, Moodus

FURTHER READING

Cunningham, Janice P., and David F. Ransom. *Back to the Land: Jewish Farms and Resorts in Connecticut, 1890–1945*. Hartford: Connecticut Historical Commission, 1998.

Donohue, Mary M., and Briann G. Greenfield. "A Life on the Land: Connecticut's Jewish Farmers." *Connecticut Jewish History* 4 (Fall 2010).

Simon Pure Productions. "The Resorts That Put the Mood in Moodus." http://www.simonpure.com/resorts.htm.

CABINS AT ORCHARD MANSION, MOODUS, CONN.

FIGURES 103 AND 104. Orchard Mansion, Moodus, postcard views. Courtesy of Ken Simon, simonpure.com

29

SCIENTIFIC FARMING

WENGLOSKI POULTRY HOUSE, LEBANON

In the twentieth century, agricultural specialists produced improved designs for farm buildings. Their goals were to ease farmers' labor, to prevent the spread of disease, and to provide better facilities for storing agricultural products or housing livestock.

Chicken farming was particularly prevalent in eastern Connecticut. Egg production emerged as a major pursuit early in the century. At first, farmers kept chickens in open lots or adapted existing barns to house their flocks. Increasingly, however, they shifted to purpose-built poultry houses, such as a prototype exhibited by the Connecticut Agricultural Experiment Station in 1918. In the 1950s poultry production shifted from eggs to meat, particularly broilers, thanks to new feed that speeded chicks' growth, antibiotics to halt the spread of diseases, and the introduction of heated poultry houses that allowed farmers to raise birds year-round.

Since poultry farming didn't require a big investment in land, it appealed to immigrants and part-time farmers. Among the latter was Isadore Wengloski, whose father, originally from Poland, had a dairy farm nearby. An employee at Pratt & Whitney, the younger Wengloski also raised broilers to sell in Willimantic. About 1955, Wengloski built a poultry house: a long, narrow building, two stories tall and with a simple shed roof. Ribbons of windows line the south wall. According to family members, the building was designed by a professor from the nearby University of Connecticut. Founded in 1881 as an agricultural college, the university was designated Connecticut's land-grant college in 1893, which made it the recipient of federal funding for the study and improvement of agriculture.

Wengloski's poultry house strongly resembles a design published by the United States Department of Agriculture (USDA) in *Plans of Farm Buildings for Northeastern States* (1950). A catalog of plans for sale that listed the University of Connecticut School of Agriculture as a contributor, the booklet boasted that the plans all incorporated "the latest research findings and the best available information."

The USDA drawing—perhaps drawn up by the same UConn professor—shows a poultry house very like Wengloski's. Two stories high and measuring 24 by 108 feet, the poultry house was divided inside into four pens

FIGURE 105.
Wengloski Poultry
House, Lebanon.
Barbara Wengloski

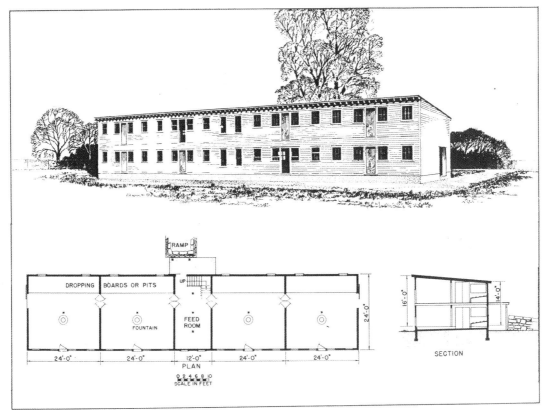

DRAWING No.
5652
(4 sheets)

DROPPING BOARDS OR PITS

RAMP

UP

FEED ROOM

FOUNTAIN

24'-0"

24'-0"   24'-0"   12'-0"   24'-0"   24'-0"

PLAN

0 2 4 6 8 10
SCALE IN FEET

16'-0"   14'-0"

SECTION

Two-story poultry house; 24 feet wide.—Because of climatic variations within the region, no ventilating system is shown. The county agricultural agent or State agricultural engineer should be consulted about ventilation. Capacity: 160 small birds or 140 large birds per pen.

FIGURE 106. Poultry house, from U.S. Department of Agriculture, *Plans of Farm Buildings for Northeastern States*, 1950

on each level, with a capacity of 160 small birds per pen, or 140 large ones—in all, more than one thousand birds. In keeping with the booklet's goal of planning for local conditions, the caption notes, "Because of climatic variations within the region, no ventilating system is shown. The county agricultural agent or State agricultural engineer should be consulted about ventilation."

On larger farms, poultry houses could be much bigger, as many as four stories high. As Thomas Visser observes in his *Field Guide to New England Barns and Farm Buildings*, such structures, containing mechanized systems for ventilation and for the provision of food and water to thousands of birds, could become agricultural factories. But even the smaller versions, like Wengloski's, brought more scientific farming to rural Connecticut.

THE PLACE
WENGLOSKI POULTRY HOUSE
ca. 1955
Lebanon Avenue, Lebanon, 0.1 mile north of Goshen Hill Road

FURTHER READING
Cunningham, Janice P. "Connecticut's Agricultural Heritage: An Architectural and Historical Overview." Connecticut Trust for Historic Preservation, 2012.
United States Department of Agriculture. *Plans of Farm Buildings for Northeastern States*. Washington, D.C., 1950.
Visser, Thomas Durant. *Field Guide to New England Barns and Farm Buildings*. Hanover, N.H.: University Press of New England, 1997.

Part Five

MEANS OF PRODUCTION

The Industrial Revolution came early to Connecticut. Along with Massachusetts and Rhode Island, the state was the site of some of the nation's first manufacturing enterprises, and as the nineteenth century progressed, industry increasingly dominated Connecticut's economy and its built environment.

Change was constant, as industrialists continually improved manufacturing machinery and processes and developed new products to meet the changing demands of the marketplace. Keeping up with this continual growth and improvement challenged the builders of mills and factories. General-purpose and specialized manufacturing and subsidiary buildings, waterpower installations, even housing and community facilities all formed Connecticut's industrial landscape. These places not only accommodated industrial needs, but also became expressions of industrial power and pride.

30

INDUSTRIAL BEGINNINGS

LEDYARD UP-DOWN SAWMILL, LEDYARD

Thanks to the Town of Ledyard and volunteers from the Ledyard Historical Society, one water-powered sawmill continues to operate in Connecticut. Sawmills reduced the human labor needed to cut logs into usable timbers for construction. Along with gristmills, which ground grain into flour, they were ubiquitous and necessary parts of the rural economy, as early as the seventeenth century.

The Ledyard sawmill uses an up-down saw, an early technology that mimics the action of a hand-operated pit saw. The long, straight blade, clamped into a wooden frame called a sash, cycles up and down while a carriage pushes the log along. After the mid-nineteenth century, more efficient circular saws almost entirely superseded up-down saws, but the older equipment survived in remote locations like Ledyard, where demand was low and thrifty operators saw no need to replace machinery that still worked. The present mill, the third on a site that was in active use from the 1790s to the 1930s, was constructed around 1877 by Israel Brown, who installed a turbine in place of the less-efficient waterwheel but kept the old saw. The turbine is housed on the lower level of the barnlike building, along with shafts and belts for power transmission, while the saw proper is on the upper level.

As Connecticut's first mechanized industries, sawmills and gristmills used waterpower technology developed in antiquity and brought to America by European settlers. The mechanical know-how needed to operate them provided a basic body of expertise that aided the development of larger-scale manufacturing in the nineteenth century. Many of Connecticut's most important manufacturers got their start in small shops no bigger than the Ledyard sawmill. Sometimes, after a company had grown and achieved a level of success, it would include images of its first building in advertising materials.

These early factories looked like rural mills; often they actually were mills adapted for new purposes. Like mills, they required integrated waterpower systems with a dam to hold back the water, gates and canals to deliver it where needed, the wheel or turbine to generate power, and belts, gears, and shafts to transmit the power to the machinery. The timber-framed building had to be sturdily built, both to support the weight of the machinery and to withstand the vibrations when in operation. One notable feature of the Ledyard sawmill is the use of some of the machinery supports as part of the building's structure. Through the nineteenth century, industrial engineers continued to incorporate machinery into factories in this way; at the Colt Armory in Hartford, steam-engine cylinders still serve double duty as load-bearing columns.

At Ledyard and countless other small mills that dotted the Connecticut countryside, early operators learned to harness waterpower and use machinery to produce building materials. They also determined how to construct buildings suited for industrial activity.

THE PLACE
LEDYARD UP-DOWN SAWMILL
(Main Sawmill)
www.ledyardsawmill.org
ca. 1877. 1970, restored.
172 Iron Street (Connecticut Route 214), Ledyard. Open seasonally.

FURTHER READING
Babbitt, Susan. "Main Sawmill." National Register of Historic Places, reference number 72001332, listed April 26, 1972.

FIGURE 107. Up-down sawmill, Ledyard. Connecticut Trust for Historic Preservation

31

THE COMPANY TOWN
COLLINSVILLE

One of Connecticut's earliest mill villages, and still one of its most complete, is Collinsville, founded by the Collins Company, in the town of Canton. From its establishment in 1826 until it closed in 1966, the company produced axes, machetes, and other edge tools for an international market. Because its site, chosen for the waterpower produced by the Farmington River, was near no existing settlement, the company built an entire town in addition to its factory. Housing and commercial and civic buildings all belonged to the Collins Company, which determined, in many cases, how they were used.

Closest to the river is the Collins factory. Its structures were arranged in lines for efficient power transmission and to follow the sequence of manufacturing: casting at the south end, forging and finishing in the center, and packing and shipping at the north. Buildings were tailored to the processes they housed; for instance, foundries and forges have monitor roofs with long raised sections along the ridge to provide light and to vent fumes.

The company's public face was its office, with roof cresting in the form of the Collins trademark, a hand rising from a crown and wielding a hammer. The office is constructed of Foster block, an early form of concrete block that varied greatly in durability (see Noroton Presbyterian Church, place 10). The blocks used here have held up well; they are still crisp-edged and haven't been painted, so they retain their original soft gray color.

On Main Street is a small business district. The Valley House, a large, mansard-roofed hotel, faces the Collinsville Green, balancing the Doric portico of the Collinsville Congregational Church at the other end. Originally, the green was a grassy rectangle, lined with trees and comfortable houses, anchored by the hotel and church at either end, and crossed by two paths that formed an X. With the advent of automobiles and road paving, the paths were widened, reducing the grassy space to two triangular traffic islands at the ends of what is now a wide street. But whether planted or paved, the green remains a focal point of the village, set apart by its openness and formal design.

The bulk of the community consists of Collins Company housing. Double cottages, constructed in 1831 and 1832, are the most distinctive type. The one-and-a-half-story

structures are larger than they seem, thanks to rear ells. Tenants were required to take in boarders, both to house more workers and as a form of social control, ensuring that unmarried men lived in a stable family environment. Two cottages, at 6–8 and 10–12 Market Street, are typical. Moved from Main Street to make way for the Valley House, they also illustrate the company's thrifty practice of moving rather than demolishing buildings as it grew. Similar cottages are also found on North and Main Streets and across the river on Church and Bridge Streets.

Like many mill villages in Connecticut and other New England states, Collinsville was built because the waterpower the factory required wasn't near an existing community. In order to attract and retain workers, the company had to give them a place to live and provide community amenities, from churches to schools to stores. As local author David Leff observes, in addition to providing dwellings for the workforce, the aim was to organize that workforce for maximum production. Leff writes, "The village, no less than the production lines ... was an engine of industry, without which business would have been impossible."

THE PLACE
COLLINSVILLE
1826 and later
Main Street and nearby streets, Collinsville

FURTHER READING
Leff, David K. *The Last Undiscovered Place*. Charlottesville: University of Virginia Press, 2004.
Paine, Carole Anstress. "Collinsville Historic District." National Register of Historic Places, reference number 76001994, listed June 23, 1976.

Western view of Collinsville, in Canton.

(*top*) FIGURE 108. Main Street, Collinsville. Patrick L. Pinnell
(*bottom*) FIGURE 109. *Western View of Collinsville, in Canton*, from John Warner Barber, *Connecticut Historical Collections*, 1836

32

IRON MAKING

BECKLEY FURNACE,
NORTH CANAAN

Although it is now primarily rural, Litchfield County in northwestern Connecticut was once a manufacturing center. The regional specialty was iron, smelted in a string of furnaces stretching from Kent to North Canaan. During the Revolution and the Civil War, Connecticut iron makers provided much-needed cannon. In the later nineteenth century they were known for railroad wheels, which required iron of particular hardness.

John Adam Beckley, a fourth-generation iron maker, built Beckley Furnace on the Blackberry River in 1847. In 1857 ownership passed to the Barnum Richardson Company, based in the Lime Rock section of Salisbury, which was consolidating the region's iron production. The furnace is a square tower of local white marble, thirty feet across at the base and forty feet high (increased from thirty-two feet in 1896). Essentially a giant fireplace and chimney, it has big pointed-arch openings on all four sides. A fire was built inside the furnace; to make it burn hotter, hot air was blasted in through nozzles called tuyeres (hence the name "blast furnace"). Workers fed ore, charcoal, and limestone in from the top (called "charging the furnace"), and molten iron dripped through to the crucible in the bottom. Periodically, the iron was released and flowed out into molds, while molten waste, called slag, was drawn off separately and discarded.

When it was in operation, the furnace was almost completely encased by buildings, including sheds for storing raw materials, an enclosed bridge leading to the top of the furnace, and the casting shed. The original wooden buildings burned in 1896 and were replaced with brick structures, but these were demolished after the furnace closed. Surviving retaining walls, next to the furnace and across the road, formed foundations for some of these structures. Slightly upstream are the dam and remains of the water system that powered some of the machinery.

When the furnace was built, everything it needed was close at hand: ore from mines in Salisbury, limestone flux (used to remove impurities) from a quarry just a mile away, and charcoal from trees cut on the surrounding hillsides. By the 1890s, this advantage had disappeared. Salisbury miners had to dig deeper, raising the cost of ore, while the hillsides had been stripped bare of trees, forcing the company to bring in charcoal from elsewhere.

The biggest problem was the antiquated Beckley furnace itself, and the other Litchfield County furnaces like it. Having decided not to invest in the new Bessemer process, Barnum Richardson was producing what amounted to artisanal iron. The firm couldn't compete with the massive, automated steel mills of Pittsburgh. When Barnum Richardson ceased operations in 1923, it was the last of Connecticut's ironworks; the firm had closed the Beckley furnace four years before.

Iron making had a drastic impact on the countryside. Mines were open pits, charcoal makers stripped the forests for fuel, rivers were dammed for waterpower, and villages clustered around the furnaces and foundries. Today, few traces of the industry remain. The forests have grown back, most of the factories and foundries have been demolished, and the workers' housing is no longer identifiable as such. Only the remains of the furnace are visible, with the Blackberry River flowing past it through a now-pastoral valley that once was filled with smoke, steam, and the clang of machinery.

THE PLACE
BECKLEY IRON FURNACE
http://beckleyfurnace.org
1847, 1896. 1998–1999, restored.
130 Lower Road, North Canaan. Open to the public.

FURTHER READING
Clouette, Bruce. "Beckley Furnace." National Register of Historic Places, reference number 78002847, listed February 14, 1978.
Gordon, Robert B., and Michael Raber. *Industrial Heritage in Northwest Connecticut: A Guide to History and Archaeology.* New Haven: Connecticut Academy of Arts and Sciences, 2000.

FIGURE 110. Beckley Furnace, Canaan. Library of Congress, Prints & Photographs Division, LC-DIG-highsm-20224, photograph by Carol H. Highsmith

33

INDUSTRIAL STRUCTURE AND AESTHETICS

HOCKANUM MILL, ROCKVILLE

Technological innovation in nineteenth-century Connecticut affected not only manufacturing methods and machinery, but also the buildings that housed them. One site that displays several stages in the development of industrial architecture is the Hockanum Mill in Rockville, an industrial city in the town of Vernon. The mill was founded in 1838 and initially produced satinet, a sturdy fabric with a cotton warp and a woolen weft (the action of early looms was too rough for wool alone). With improvements to machinery, the company later switched to all-woolen fabrics.

The mill's oldest surviving section, built of wood, is structurally similar to contemporary barns or meetinghouses. Its timber framework was massive enough to support the weight of the machinery and extensively braced to withstand vibrations. Later sections, added in the 1880s, were constructed of brick for its greater strength and resistance to fire. Their interior framing, however, was still of wood, of a type called "slow-burning" construction. In a fire the heavy timbers would char on the outside but not burn through, whereas cast iron weakened and collapsed in high temperatures. The windows are bigger than in the wooden mill; the walls between them thicken into piers for structural stability. The shallow roof pitch represents improvements in roofing materials as well as the influence of insurers, who required eliminating cluttered attics to reduce the risk of fire.

The final section of the mill was built about 1910. An early example of reinforced concrete construction, it shows how design could lag behind technology as aesthetic expectations adjusted to new conditions. Concrete construction allowed broad, smooth piers and wide windows significantly different from the textured brick or clapboards and the tall, narrow windows that people were accustomed to. So the builder scored the piers to look like blocks of stone and added a nonstructural pier to subdivide each bay into two narrow windows. Within a few years, though, smoother piers and wide openings became the norm.

Through all these phases, the basic form of the buildings remains constant. Long, tall, narrow, and lit by regular rows of big windows, they are known as "lofts."

Their multistory construction saved expensive foundations, and narrow footprints allowed natural light to penetrate throughout the building, reducing the need for gas or oil lighting, which could increase the risk of fire. The interiors offered flexible open space, adaptable to a variety of processes and types of machinery. Some operations required specialized structures such as powerhouses or weave sheds, but most manufacturing took place in these general-purpose lofts.

Although often seen as utilitarian, these buildings are not completely unadorned. The wood mill has Greek Revival frieze windows and cornice returns, and its tower

FIGURE 112. Hockanum Mill, Rockville.
Connecticut Trust for Historic Preservation

once boasted an elaborate belfry. Corbelling ornaments the brick mills, and the concrete section has scored decoration and a cornice. Nineteenth-century eyes also admired the mills' massive construction and tidy layout, which were often depicted in advertisements as evidence of a

company's prosperity and, by extension, the quality of its products.

Charles T. Main, a prolific mill engineer of the late nineteenth and early twentieth centuries, explained the industrial aesthetic in 1886 (see further reading). "Architectural beauty," Main wrote, "may be obtained at no increase of expense, if we consider beauty in architecture as it really is—the adaptation of each part to symmetrically form the whole structure, and the adaptation of the whole structure to the purposes required."

THE PLACE
HOCKANUM MILL

1854, wooden mill (tower, ca. 1870). 1880, office. 1881, 1885, brick mills. ca. 1910, concrete mill.
200 West Main Street, Rockville

FURTHER READING

Abbott, S. Ardis, and Robert Hurd. "Rockville Historic District." National Register of Historic Places, reference number 84001173, listed September 13, 1984.
Bradley, Betsy Hunter. *The Works: The Industrial Architecture of the United States*. New York: Oxford University Press, 1999.
Main, Charles T. "Notes on Mill Construction." New England Cotton Manufacturers' Association *Proceedings*, no. 41 (1886): 60–130.

34

THE POWER OF WATER

OUSATONIC DAM, DERBY AND SHELTON

Water has the power to move objects, wash away obstacles, and power machinery. Since the seventeenth century, the people of Connecticut have put water to work. The first dams built for waterpower were small, located on subsidiary streams. But by the 1860s construction technology had advanced to the point where it was possible to dam a river as big as the Housatonic, and manufacturing technology had advanced to the point where it could fully exploit the power generated by such a massive installation. The result was the Ousatonic Dam, built between the towns of Derby and Shelton. Constructed of stone with granite caps, the dam is 870 feet long, curving gently to form an arch that can better withstand the force of the water pressing against it. The face slopes, too, so that the water flowing over it will land gently and not erode the riverbed.

In addition to the dam itself, the Ousatonic Water Power Company and its industrial tenants constructed canals, sluice gates, gatehouses, grilles (to catch debris and keep it out of the machinery), wheel pits, and turbines. From the dam, water travels through canals, one on each riverbank, to mill sites. Gatehouses shelter sluice gates that control the water flow. Each mill has its own gate, too, leading to a wheel pit into which the water falls, turning turbines connected to gears that operate machinery, or to generators that produce electricity. Then, its work done, the water returns to the river.

This waterpower system altered the surrounding landscape. To ensure an adequate supply when the river is low, the dam holds back water in reserve. Upstream, land is flooded, requiring the company to negotiate with landowners for permission to flood their acres, and to compensate them for the loss of value. Under pressure from the industrial lobby, Connecticut changed its laws in 1864. After that, landowners still were entitled to compensation, but it became almost impossible for them to refuse permission to those seeking to build dams. It was probably no coincidence that the Ousatonic company was chartered just two years later. In the twentieth century this flooded upstream landscape became a popular location for vacation cottages and restaurants along Roosevelt Drive in Derby. The downstream landscape was affected, too. In dry periods, water flow was reduced, cutting off supplies to other users and hampering navigation. On the other hand, the danger of flooding also was reduced.

The biggest change was urban growth, as the increased waterpower made possible the construction of new factories. In Derby, a new industrial section spread northward from the existing downtown. Across the river, in what then was the town of Huntington, a whole new city sprang up. By 1882, Shelton (named for the president of the Ousatonic company) boasted twelve companies employing more than one thousand persons; in later years the city claimed "a mile of factories." Today, some have been demolished, some have been converted to other uses, and a few still house industrial operations.

The Ousatonic Water Power Company's office still stands on Main Street in Derby. It is small in size but big in scale (that is, *apparent* size). Ornamental brickwork, oversize brackets and windows, plus a pair of massive pilasters that push a little pediment up above the main roof, make it the very embodiment of the power of water.

THE PLACES
OUSATONIC DAM
1867–1870, William E. Worthen and Henry T. Potter. 1891, rebuilt.
Housatonic River between Shelton and Derby; visible from Roosevelt Drive (Connecticut Route 34) in Derby, and Riverview Park in Shelton

FACTORIES
ca. 1870 and later
Canal Street, Shelton, and Roosevelt Drive, Derby

OUSATONIC WATER COMPANY OFFICE
ca. 1880
127 Main Street, Derby

FURTHER READING
Roth, Matthew. *Connecticut: An Inventory of Historic Engineering and Industrial Sites.* Washington, D.C.: Society for Industrial Archeology, 1981.

(*top*) FIGURE 113. Ousatonic Dam, Derby and Shelton.
James A. Robertson, www.flickr.com/photos/jimrob
(*bottom*) FIGURE 114. Ousatonic Company Office, Derby.
Connecticut Trust for Historic Preservation

35

INDUSTRIAL SPECIALIZATION

CLARK BROTHERS FACTORY, SOUTHINGTON

The textile industry introduced general-purpose loft buildings like those of the Hockanum Mill. By the end of the nineteenth century the growing size and particular needs of metal-producing concerns fueled the development of more specialized industrial building forms.

In Southington, located between New Haven and Hartford, nineteenth-century manufacturers developed an expertise in forging. Forging, essentially the mechanization of a blacksmith's work, involves shaping iron or steel by hammering, rather than casting or cutting. Connecticut companies developed huge drop forges, which used water or steam power to hoist a ram to a height of ten or twenty feet, then release it to fall and strike a piece of iron or steel, using a die to guide it to the desired shape.

To accommodate the massive machinery, metals manufacturers constructed tall, one-story forging buildings, with roofs raised in the center to provide a clerestory, or monitor, for light and ventilation. The open, single-level spaces also made it easier to move heavy bulk materials. At the same time, sawtooth roofs, with repeated parallel skylights, allowed the construction of broad, evenly lit manufacturing floors to house other operations needed to finish forged items. Both these roof types were made possible by improvements in steel framing and by advances in roof flashing to prevent leaks.

Founded in 1854, the Clark Brothers Bolt Company originally made bolts for New Haven carriage makers in a water-powered plant located on the Quinnipiac River. Around 1900 the company erected an office and shipping building on this site beside the Canal Line Railroad (constructed along the path of the failed Farmington Canal) in Southington. In 1911 the company moved all its operations here. By the time of World War I it was producing a wide assortment of nuts, bolts, rivets, and other fasteners.

Stretching out along the railroad tracks, the Clark Brothers factory offers examples of the new building forms developed for metal manufacturing processes. Starting at the northern end of the complex, the first building is the forge, with a tall roof to accommodate the drop forges, and a monitor, parallel to the road, to vent off heat and fumes. Next is a manufacturing shed with sawtooth roof, its glazed portions facing north for glare-free light and to avoid heat from the sun. Next is a heat-treatment building, where nuts, bolts, and rivets were hardened or tempered, with another, somewhat smaller, monitor, this time turned perpendicular to the street. Then, another sawtooth manufacturing shed, which is the biggest part of the plant, with a footprint measuring 133 by 238 feet—far wider than any loft building. At the southern end are two office buildings, one two stories high with a pitched roof and a bit of decorative brickwork, the other one story with a flat roof and a parapet.

Marching in a line up the street, the different roof forms reflect the increasing specialization of industrial processes. It is easy to understand how this lively procession of shapes appealed to Modernist architects, who appreciated their industrial associations and functional design and found inspiration in their varied and interesting geometry.

But that aesthetic appeal is rooted in functional needs and the care engineers took to meet them.

THE PLACE
CLARK BROTHERS BOLT COMPANY

1911–1918 and later
409 Canal Street, Southington

FURTHER READING

Clouette, Bruce, and Matthew Roth. "Clark Brothers Bolt Company, Factory No. 2." Historic Industrial Complexes of Southington Thematic Resource. National Register of Historic Places, reference number 88002680, listed December 8, 1988.

McVarish, Douglas C. *American Industrial Archaeology: A Field Guide*. Walnut Creek, Calif.: Left Coast, 2008.

Roth, Emery, II. *Brass Valley: The Fall of an American Industry*. Atglen, Pa.: Schiffer, 2015.

FIGURE 115. Clark Brothers factory, Southington. Robert Egleston

36

INDUSTRIAL CAMPANILE

REMINGTON SHOT TOWER, BRIDGEPORT

One of Connecticut's principal industrial products has long been arms and armaments. In the early twentieth century, as European powers edged toward world war, the state's manufacturing cities exploded with industrial activity. A leader in the industry was the Remington Union Metallic Cartridge Company, in Bridgeport. At the center of its main plant stands an unusual building that played an important part in the munitions boom: the ten-story brick shot tower completed in 1909.

In 1908, the cost of the shot that Remington bought for use in its cartridges increased sharply. The plant manager suggested to the company owner, Marcellus Hartley Dodge, that it build a tower and produce its own shot. The process was described in a report written for the Historic American Engineering Record in 1981, while ammunition still was being produced at the Bridgeport site. "On the top floor," the report explains, "are two kettles to melt the lead alloy, which is then piped into two steel pans with pin-holed bottoms. The shot, formed as the molten alloy passes through the holes, falls 133' to water tanks below, from which it is conducted back up to the ninth floor by a bucket conveyor. From there it travels down, fed by gravity, through a series of operations: sorting for roundness and size, cleaning, polishing and applying graphite." Shot production at Bridgeport ceased in the mid-1980s. Since then the tower has served only as storage and a base for bristling cell-phone antennas. These uses at least keep it standing, unlike many of the nearby factory buildings, which are increasingly vulnerable to decay, fire, or demolition.

When Dodge agreed to build the shot tower, he decided to finance it himself, rather than risk the company's resources on what might be an unsuccessful venture. This gave him personal control over the design, which he insisted be not only functional but attractive, referring to it as a "campanile" for Bridgeport. While most shot towers are square or circular, looking like chimneys or plain towers, the Remington tower is more monumental, a full-fledged *building*. It starts with a six-story base measuring about seventy-six by ninety feet. From the base's hipped roof rises a four-story tower. Broad windows provide ample light for the interior, while decorative brickwork and cast-stone trim that culminates in a rooftop balustrade fulfill Dodge's desire to make the tower a civic asset.

The Remington shot tower is not only monumental— it is extremely rare. Only a handful of shot towers are left in the United States, and probably fewer than two dozen in the whole world. It is not open to the public, but anyone can admire it from the street, from the train, from hundreds of spots in Bridgeport, and even from Long Island Sound.

THE PLACE
REMINGTON UNION METALLIC CARTRIDGE COMPANY SHOT TOWER
1908–1909
Helen and Arctic Streets, Bridgeport

FURTHER READING
Roth, Matthew. *Connecticut: An Inventory of Historic Engineering and Industrial Sites.* Washington, D.C.: Society for Industrial Archaeology, 1981.

FIGURE 116. Remington Shot Tower, Bridgeport. Patrick L. Pinnell

MEANS OF PRODUCTION

37

INDUSTRY IN THE SUBURBS
MEDWAY BUSINESS PARK,
MERIDEN AND WALLINGFORD

As more and more Connecticut residents moved to the suburbs after World War II, businesses and manufacturers followed them. Meriden had prospered in the nineteenth century with factories that produced silverware, hardware, and textiles. By the 1950s many of those companies had gone out of business or moved away, and the city sought to diversify its economic base.

In 1959, the Chamber of Commerce formed the Meriden Industrial Development Commission (MIDC) to develop an office park focused on research and development, taking advantage of the construction of Interstate 91, which offered easy access to New Haven, Hartford, and beyond. The MIDC acquired a tract of land east of the interstate, away from the city center. Finding research and development clients proved difficult, however. The MIDC eventually allowed manufacturing and distribution facilities as well, but this change didn't materially affect the character of the office park. In 1977, it was taken over by Farmington-based FIP Corporation, a major developer of suburban office and light-industrial parks in central Connecticut.

The park's site plan was the corporate/industrial equivalent of the residential subdivision: a spacious landscape of individual buildings set in broad lawns sited along a curving, well-planted roadway. Buildings could cover only 20 percent of each lot, and minimum setbacks preserved the parklike atmosphere. The buildings are almost universally low and sprawling, reflecting inexpensive land, Modernist taste, and the horizontal patterns of assembly-line manufacturing.

However, the old architectural division between utilitarian processing structures and more stylish office sections still holds. See, for instance, the lower office block on the plant originally constructed for AMF Cuno, a maker of water purifiers (1968; 400 Research Parkway). At the International Silver Company Stainless Steel Center (1968; 500 Research Parkway), offices are incorporated within the mass of the building but indicated by rows of smaller windows within the walls of precast concrete.

One of the most notable occupants of the business park was a new headquarters for Meriden's preeminent corporation, the International Silver Company, rebranded in 1969 as Insilco. The low building (1969, Jeter and Cook;

FIGURE 117. Medway Business Park, former headquarters of International Silver Company (Insilco), Meriden. Robert Egleston

1000 Research Parkway) has a colonnade of brick piers and precast lintels surrounding the front office block, with Miesian-inspired steel-framed sections behind it. A curving drive passes through brick gateposts before climbing to a formal parking area planted with feathery locust trees and globe-on-post lights facing a rectilinear entry court.

A later example is the Southern New England Telephone Company Data Center (1984, Rose, Beacon and Rose Architects and Engineers; 84 Deerfield Lane), a V-shaped multistory building with ribbon windows set in vertically striated precast concrete.

Reflecting the importance of the highway transportation network, the U.S. Postal Service Distribution Center (1996; 24 Research Parkway, Wallingford), turns its back to Research Parkway, presenting its façade instead to Interstate 91, where four small square towers rise from the high-bay working section, and the office block steps down in narrow parallel strips lined with rows of small square windows.

The biggest occupant of the park is the former Bristol-Myers Squibb Richard L. Gelb Center for Pharmaceutical Research and Development (1985; 5 Research Drive, Wallingford), a massive W-shaped building with a quasi-classical Postmodernist design. The wings have long skylights that illuminate the top-floor laboratories. Set amid curving drives and naturalistic plantings and guarded by a gatehouse, the facility seems to abandon the suburban imagery for something grander: an English country estate.

THE PLACE
MEDWAY BUSINESS PARK

1966, Goodkind and O'Dea, engineers and planners
Research Parkway, Meriden and Wallingford

FURTHER READING
Mozingo, Louise A. *Pastoral Capitalism: A History of Suburban Corporate Landscapes.* Cambridge, Mass.: MIT Press, 2011.

38

CORPORATE PRIDE

UNION CARBIDE HEADQUARTERS, DANBURY

The Union Carbide building is immense—a quarter mile long, encompassing 1.3 million square feet of space—but since it is hidden by woods, the only way to see the entire structure is from the air. Perched on slender columns, clad in sandblasted aluminum and reflective glass, its fractal-shaped pods reaching into the surrounding forest, the building invites fanciful comparisons. *Architecture* magazine likened it to "a dinosaur-sized, many-legged, splay-toed lizard."

The building is one of a series of projects in which Kevin Roche, the design partner at Roche and Dinkeloo, explored ways of avoiding the barren surface parking lots that have eaten away at cities or disfigured suburban sites. The series began with the New Haven Coliseum (1969; demolished 2007), where a parking garage sat atop the arena. At the Richardson-Vicks company headquarters in Wilton (1974), the building stands on piers above the parking area, where cars sit with their noses pointing to the trees standing just beyond their bumpers. By far the largest of the three, the Union Carbide building has offices wrapped around two multilevel parking garages. Between the garages a central core houses a cafeteria, shops, a gym, and conference rooms, while numerous entries from the garages give workers easy access to their offices.

In addition to hiding parking, another aim at Union Carbide was to eliminate the competitive and disruptive jockeying for desirable offices that reflected rank within the corporate hierarchy. Every office, except those of the very top brass, is the same size, and each has a wall with a window (hence the many-fingered design). This democratic approach was balanced by providing workers with a menu of decorative schemes to personalize their spaces, and with consistently high-quality construction and materials throughout.

In building this luxurious suburban headquarters, Union Carbide was following the precedent set by the Connecticut General Life Insurance Company (later Cigna), which moved from Hartford to Bloomfield in 1957 (see figure 47). But by the end of the century, corporate culture was changing. Instead of broadcasting success with impressive architecture, companies increasingly were judged solely by stock value and dividend payments. Rather than tie up money in high-quality design and

FIGURE 118. Union Carbide Company headquarters, Danbury. Kevin Roche John Dinkeloo and Associates LLC

materials, many companies chose to rent space, making it easier to move as they merged and reorganized, and freeing up cash for acquisitions or fighting takeovers. When companies did build, as Duracell did in Bethel (1995, Herbert S. Newman and Partners), the buildings were purposely designed for easy conversion to multi-tenant use.

Union Carbide unwillingly anticipated this trend. After a massive chemical leak at its plant in Bhopal, India, in 1984, lawsuits and resulting settlements crippled the company, forcing it to sell its headquarters. Today the building houses multiple tenants, many of whom continue to use the original furnishings and décor.

THE PLACE
UNION CARBIDE HEADQUARTERS

(Now Corporate Center)
1976–1982, Kevin Roche John Dinkeloo and Associates
39 Old Ridgebury Road, Danbury

FURTHER READING
Dean, Andrea Oppenheimer. "Corporate Contrast in the Suburbs." *Architecture*, February 1985, 60–65.

Part Six

TOWNSCAPES AND CITYSCAPES

Much of Connecticut's most interesting architecture is not individual buildings, but larger groupings—towns or cities or neighborhoods. Some have been designed as a single entity and are the result of a specific vision or moment in time. If that vision is clear, the result can be a masterpiece. Other groupings have been created piece by piece, over longer periods, by a number of hands. These frequently work better, since they have been adjusted or corrected over time. They often are more satisfying, too, since successive layers of additions over the years give them greater richness and variety. Rather than monologues, they are conversations.

39

THE IDEAL VILLAGE
COLEBROOK CENTER

With its grassy green, from which the white-columned meetinghouse overlooks white-painted colonial or Federal or Greek Revival houses, Colebrook Center represents the New England hill town as it appears on countless calendars and magazine covers. Flourishing in the years between the Revolution and the advent of railroads, these towns, with their tidy buildings and pastoral landscapes, have been celebrated as the outward expression of a New England society of independent farmers united by Congregational faith and small-town democracy.

The appeal of Colebrook and other towns like it lies not so much in individual buildings, but in the framework that knits them into a larger whole. Fences and trees, set back from the roadway, define a long, irregularly shaped space extending from Thompson Road in the south to approximately Schoolhouse Road in the north. This entire space is public land.

Originally this area probably functioned as a town square: a gathering place on which stood public buildings such as the meetinghouse or a school. Utilitarian rather than ornamental, it was crisscrossed by paths or ruts, while the less-traveled portions grew up in grass or weeds. The fenced-in green and the grassy setbacks that seem to belong to the house lots are, in fact, part of this public space. Around the space, houses stand behind the fence/tree line, while public buildings like the store and tavern (now the historical society) step right up to it for easy access. The new town hall, built in 2002, follows this pattern, which, as much as its architecture, helps it fit into the existing townscape.

Three things happened to this landscape to create Colebrook as it appears today. In the early nineteenth century, people across New England began cleaning up and improving their towns. They rebuilt public buildings, graded and fenced greens, improved roads, and planted trees for shade and ornament. In Colebrook it was probably at the time the current Congregational church was built, in 1843, that the area in front of it—a small portion of the central open space—was graded and fenced to form what now is officially considered the town green. Later in the century, most of the town's industries ceased operation, driven to relocate or to close by competition with bigger enterprises in the growing cities along the railroads. This,

FIGURE 119.
Colebrook Center. Connecticut
Trust for Historic Preservation

along with agricultural decline in the twentieth century, removed sources of dirt and noise, making Colebrook more attractive to people seeking summer and weekend retreats. Finally, the roads were paved, splitting the once-unified public space into road and not-road.

Yet the original framework remains in Colebrook's DNA. Fences or trees still mostly follow property boundaries, so that what appears to be the outer portions of the house lots is still public land. By holding the buildings back from the traveled roadway, behind a border of green, this setback gives the town a spaciousness and orderliness that enhances its buildings and establishes its distinctive identity.

THE PLACE
COLEBROOK CENTER

ca. 1765 and later
Colebrook Road (Connecticut Route 183) at Rockwell
    Road (Connecticut Route 182A), Colebrook

FURTHER READING
Cunningham, Jan. "Colebrook Center Historic District." National
    Register of Historic Places, reference number 91000953, listed
    July 26, 1991.
Town Greens of Connecticut. www.towngreens.com.

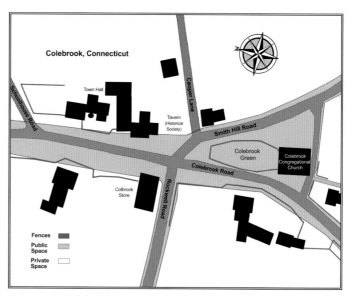

FIGURE 120. Colebrook Center, schematic map. Ann F. Peabody

40

CIVIC EMBELLISHMENT
NEW HAVEN GREEN

New Haven's founders created one of the enduring images of American city planning: a perfect square divided into nine smaller squares with the center one reserved for open space. (A trapezoidal tenth block reached toward the harbor.) No one really knows who conceived the plan. Architectural historian Elizabeth Mills Brown argued that John Brockett, who usually gets the credit, was merely the surveyor who laid out a plan created by someone else. One potential candidate is Lion Gardiner, an experienced military engineer and friend of John Davenport, New Haven's first minister.

Even more difficult than the questions of authorship are those of derivation and meaning. Writers have pointed to sources ranging from the ancient Roman architect Vitruvius to the biblical prophet Ezekiel's description of heaven, and to precedents from Puritan theology to English settlements in Ireland. What is certain is that New Haven belongs to a tradition of rational, rectilinear plans that extends from ancient Greece to the American courthouse square. In seventeenth-century Connecticut this tradition also shaped the layouts of Fairfield, Saybrook Point, and Guilford. New Haven stands out as the most ambitiously scaled, the most precisely executed, and the best-preserved of its period. Whether or not the plan is unique, it is truly a classic of American town planning.

The New Haven Green as it appears today owes much to a later generation. In the beginning, it was a utilitarian space that served many public needs, from market to drill field to burying ground. The meetinghouse stood more or less at the center, and over the years the city added or removed, as needed, other buildings and facilities: schools, statehouses, a whipping post, a town pump.

The Federal era brought a concerted program of improvements that included planting elm trees, erecting a fence, closing the burying ground and removing most of the gravestones, and razing extraneous buildings.

A major element of the improvement program was the construction of three imposing and fashionable new churches at the same time. Looking at them, one cannot help but conclude that their design was coordinated as a unified statement of New Haven's prosperity, taste, and civic virtue. Center Church, with its portico, lofty spire, and bold ornament, dominates. The other two are deferential,

E. VIEW OF THE PUBLIC SQUARE OR GREEN, IN NEW HAVEN CON.

(top) FIGURE 121. *E. View of the Public Square or Green, in New Haven Con.* [*sic*], from John Warner Barber and Lemuel S. Punderson, *History and Antiquities of New Haven, Conn.*, 1856
(bottom) FIGURE 122. New Haven Green, aerial view.
Michael Marsland / Yale University

but each distinguished in its own way: United Church by its more delicate elegance, and Trinity Episcopal by its groundbreaking Gothic Revival design and the rich color of its traprock walls. As with the town plan, the records frustratingly refuse to identify the minds behind this coordination.

Since then, the green's overall character has remained remarkably constant, and it has attained iconic status. With a simple palette of grass, trees, fence, and paths, it accommodates a wide variety of activities while continuing to serve its most important function, as a visible symbol of New Haven, the physical and emotional heart of the city.

THE PLACES
NEW HAVEN GREEN
ca. 1638 and later
Bounded by Elm, Church, Chapel, and College Streets, New Haven
CENTER CHURCH ON THE GREEN
(First Congregational Church, United Church of Christ)
1812–1815, Asher Benjamin; Ithiel Town, builder
250 Temple Street
UNITED CHURCH ON THE GREEN
(United Church of Christ)
1812–1815, Ebenezer Johnson Jr.; David Hoadley, builder
270 Temple Street
TRINITY CHURCH ON THE GREEN
(Episcopal)
1814–1816, Ithiel Town
230 Temple Street

FURTHER READING
Brown, Elizabeth Mills. *New Haven: A Guide to Architecture and Urban Design*. New Haven, Conn.: Yale University Press, 1976.
National Park Service Staff. "New Haven Green." National Historic Landmark. National Register of Historic Places, reference number 70000838, designated December 30, 1970.
Town Greens of Connecticut. www.towngreens.com.

GREATER THAN ITS PARTS

DOWNTOWN NORWICH

From a distance, downtown Norwich appears as a series of tiers rising above the river—a view visitors have admired for more than two hundred years. But seen up close, it is a tangle of narrow streets clinging to the steep hillside. The area got its start when eighteenth-century Norwich merchants built wharves and warehouses at the point where the Shetucket and Yantic Rivers join to form the Thames. By the nineteenth century it had become Norwich's commercial and civic center. Like the old drawing of a vase that morphs into two silhouetted faces, downtown Norwich can be looked at in terms either of its buildings or of the spaces between them.

Many of the buildings are what the nineteenth century called "blocks"—three- or four-story structures, mostly of brick, with shop fronts at ground level and rows of windows lighting offices or living spaces above. To maximize usable space, they fill the entire width of their lots. This form emerged in the 1830s to accommodate the demands of expanding commercial activity, and it remained constant over the next hundred years or so, as architectural styles came and went. Examples include the Greek Doric entablature of the Strand Building (1831; 203–215 Main Street), the polychrome masonry of the Richards Building (1868, W. T. Hallett; 87–93 Main Street), and the skeletal iron front of the Shannon Building (ca. 1898; 82 Water Street). Ornament balances the desire to proclaim the occupants' importance with the business owner's reluctance to waste funds on nonessentials.

So dominant was this form that some older Norwich buildings were remodeled to fit the pattern. In the 1860s the Timothy Ayers House (ca. 1753; 88–90 Main Street) and the Elihu Marvin House (1784; 94–100 Main Street) were raised up onto new ground floors and given Italianate cornices. Despite these changes, the eighteenth-century two-one-two window spacing remains visible on their façades.

Shifting focus from buildings to spaces, the streets are enclosed by the continuous wall of buildings, forming corridors that rise and fall and bend to follow the land, offering both ever-changing vistas and a sense of containment. Occasionally the corridors open out into rooms, like Franklin Square or the plaza in front of the Superior Courthouse (1982, Richard Sharpe; Main and

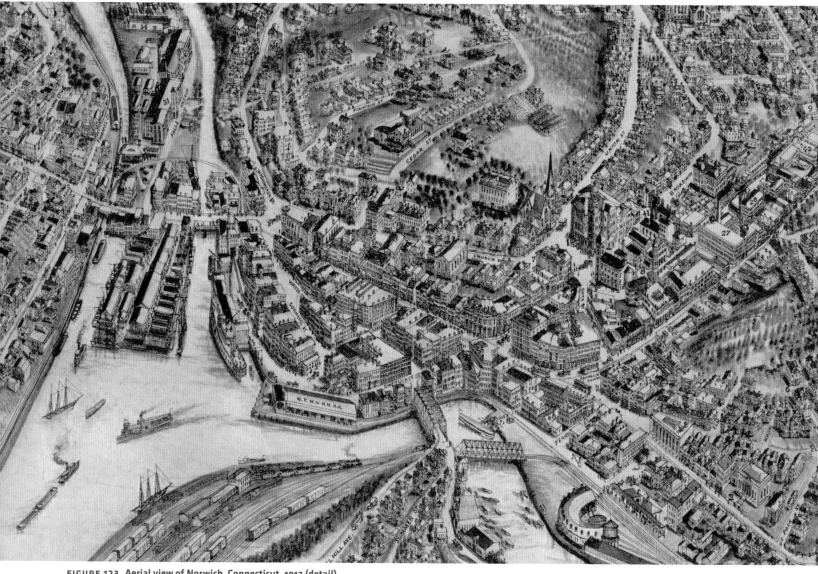

FIGURE 123. Aerial view of Norwich, Connecticut, 1912 (detail).
The Connecticut Historical Society

Shetucket Streets). Defining public space is an important part of the buildings' function. Some, like the Norwich Savings Society (1893–1895; 162–164 Main Street), curve to follow bends in the streets, while others, like the Rockwell Building (1861, 1895; 97–105 Main Street), come to points at sharp intersections. It feels as though the streets and squares have been carved from the solid mass of buildings—a reminder that the city itself is an entity, a whole that is greater than the sum of its parts.

In contrast there is Water Street, where twentieth-century urban renewal projects cleared away the old warehouses, and new buildings stand as separate objects each surrounded by an insulating layer of open space. Here, the public realm has no particular shape; it is the background for the buildings, rather than the other way round. Fortunately, modern construction on Main Street has mostly hewed to the old way of building. Except for the pointless park behind the courthouse and vacant lots at the western end of the street, the wall of buildings has been maintained, and the street keeps its traditional shape.

THE PLACE
DOWNTOWN NORWICH
Main Street between Church Street and Railroad Place

FURTHER READING
Harby, Stephen W. *Norwich, Connecticut: A Guide to Its Architecture.* New Haven, Conn.: Circa Series, 1976.
Plummer, Dale S. "Downtown Norwich Historic District." National Register of Historic Places, reference number 85000707, listed April 4, 1985.

FIGURE 124. Main Street, Norwich.
Connecticut Trust for Historic Preservation

UNDER THE MILL TOWERS
NORTH GROSVENORDALE

Nineteenth-century industrialists knew that the adage "a place for everything and everything in its place" applied not only to housekeeping but also to factory villages. The Grosvenor-Dale Company demonstrated this when it built the village of North Grosvenordale around its massive cotton factories in the town of Thompson.

Begun in 1870 on the site of an older textile mill, the North Grosvenordale mill was one of the biggest of its kind in New England; by 1900 it employed 1,750 people to produce high-quality fabrics. However, the mill can be understood only in relation to the village around it. North Grosvenordale was built not only to provide housing for employees and their families, but also to reinforce the hierarchy that governed the company and the various ethnic groups that made up the workforce. Unlike comparable mill towns, such as Taftville or Baltic, that were laid out on uniform grids, North Grosvenordale is divided into smaller clusters, constructed on level plots between the river, the railroad, and existing roads. Some of the company housing has been demolished, but four principal clusters remain.

In three of these clusters the buildings are all of frame construction, composed of basic two-family units (one down, one up) combined into multifamily structures. Differences between the clusters lie in the length of the buildings and how much space they are given, with regard both to one another and to the street. South of the mill is Three Rows, on Central and Marshall Streets, built at the same time as the mill. Three rows of four-family buildings line two parallel streets. From the beginning, their occupants were unskilled or semiskilled workers from Quebec, for whom this cluster was sometimes called Little Canada. West of Three Rows is Swede Village, a separate cluster constructed in the 1880s when the company was recruiting Swedish immigrants. Reflecting their higher skill levels, the buildings, while similar to Three Rows, are more generously spaced. A third cluster, on Market Street, contains four longer buildings that initially housed twelve families each, also French Canadians. After about 1900, as immigration patterns changed, these buildings were occupied by unmarried men from Southern and Eastern Europe, including Turkey, Albania, and Romania. In a bit of Yankee ethnocentrism, they were lumped together

FIGURES 125 AND 126. North Grosvenordale, Greek Village (*top*) and Grosvenor-Dale Company Mill (*bottom*). Robert Egleston (Greek Village); Connecticut Trust for Historic Preservation (mill)

under a single term, giving this cluster the name Greek Village.

Houses for supervisors, located north of the mill on Riverside Avenue, were different in character. Constructed of brick and accommodating only two families each, they provided a degree of privacy and solidity that distinguished their occupants from ordinary workers. Near them stands a large brick building that served as the company store and offices.

Although North Grosvenordale lacks the unifying gridiron plan of many mill communities, it still was readily identifiable as a company town, thanks to its uniform architecture and regular planning (as far as the topography allowed). Emphasizing that uniformity is contrasting private development along Main Street, where ambitious employees and outside investors erected stores, saloons (alcohol was prohibited on company property), housing, and social and religious institutions free from company control. The result is an irregular streetscape with a variety of styles and materials. However, even this free-market town remained in sight of the mill's towers. In addition to stairs and toilets and water tanks, the towers housed the bells that regulated life in the village, from the opening of the factory at 6 a.m. to noontime dinner to the 9 p.m. curfew. Rising above everything else, they stood as symbols of the company's ultimate control of the village and its inhabitants.

THE PLACE
NORTH GROSVENORDALE

1870–ca. 1900
Main Street and Riverside Avenue (Connecticut Route 12),
    North Grosvenordale

FURTHER READING
Clouette, Bruce, and Maura Cronin. "North Grosvenordale
    Mill Historic District." National Register of Historic Places,
    reference number 93000288, listed April 16, 1993.

43

CONSUMER CULTURE
THE ARCADE, BRIDGEPORT

The door to 1001 Main Street would appear to be the entry to a typical mid-nineteenth-century commercial block. Instead, it opens onto a long, dim passage, with a bend that blocks the view to the end. There is light, though, and perhaps the sound of activity to draw the visitor along. The passage ends with an arch, beyond which the space opens up to a sunlight-flooded iron-and-glass atrium ringed with shop fronts on two levels. Lacy railings line the balcony, echoed by filigree trusses supporting the glass roof. The roof trusses and floor are white, making them seem to melt away in the dazzling light, highlighting the wares on display in the shop windows. The message is unmistakable: buy something.

When the Arcade was built, in the 1880s, growing demand for downtown space was driving up the cost of land. Main Street was already lined with multistory commercial buildings like the Sterling Block, built in two stages, in 1841 and about 1850. In the late 1880s, the building's owners, brothers William D. and A. H. Bishop, wanted to put the vacant interior of their deep lot to work. Without street frontage, commercial development seemed unlikely to succeed.

Fortunately for the Bishops, a new post office was being built at the intersection of Broad and Cannon Streets, at the far corner of the block. The Bishops realized that they could create a public shortcut from Main Street to the post office, which would attract enough foot traffic to support shops. The final touch, roofing the shortcut, turned a mere passage into a *place*. It would encourage pedestrians to linger and window-shop rather than huddle into their coats against New England's all-too-frequent rain or snow.

Geared to Bridgeport's upper crust, the Arcade attracted elite businesses, and every space was leased before opening day in 1889. The first tenants included carpet, jewelry, shoe, and drug stores, a confectioner, a tailor, a photographer, a hairdresser, two artists, a broker, a dressmaker, and the Women's Exchange, a charitable organization that helped needy women discreetly earn a living by making and selling fancy work.

The structure displayed the latest in modern engineering, employing industrial materials that promised to revolutionize architecture: iron with its lightness, strength, and malleability, and glass with its transparency.

Combined, they suggested other building types associated with interesting activities—conservatories filled with exotic tropical plants, railroad sheds promising the excitement of travel, and exhibition halls offering the visual and intellectual stimulation of fairs.

The Bridgeport Arcade wasn't an original idea; a much bigger one opened the same year in Cleveland. Nearby Providence had an older arcade, built in 1828. Some European cities had arcades dating to the eighteenth century. But this type of structure fulfilled the demands created by Connecticut's booming late nineteenth-century economy. Factories were producing increasing numbers of new goods, at more affordable prices. Well-paid manufacturing jobs were increasing the public's disposable income. This still-uncommon building type was perfectly suited to the nascent consumer culture; the Bishops had built Connecticut's first shopping mall.

THE PLACE
THE ARCADE
(Originally Sterling Block and Post Office Arcade)
Sterling Block: 1841, ca. 1850. Arcade: 1889, Longstaff and
    Hurd; 2011, restored, Cutsogeorge Tooman & Allen
    Architects.
1001 Main Street, Bridgeport. Open to the public.

FURTHER READING
Brilvitch, Charles. "Sterling Block–Bishop Arcade." National
    Register of Historic Places, reference number 78002841, listed
    December 20, 1978.

FIGURE 127. The Arcade, Bridgeport. Robert Gregson

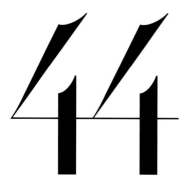

UNNECESSARY EXCELLENCE
SEASIDE VILLAGE, BRIDGEPORT

A pocket of tranquility where Colonial-style brick houses line winding, tree-shaded streets, Seaside Village is the largest of the projects constructed in Connecticut by the U.S. Housing Corporation (USHC) to accommodate munitions workers during World War I. Even before the United States entered the war, Bridgeport's armaments factories were hiring thousands of new workers to supply the European belligerents. The city's population grew by 50 percent between 1914 and 1916. In response to the resulting housing crisis, the Chamber of Commerce formed the Bridgeport Housing Company (BHC) in 1916, which was superseded in 1918 by the United States Housing Corporation. Between them, the BHC and USHC built seven complexes in Bridgeport, as well as one each in Fairfield and Stratford, creating the largest concentration of government-subsidized wartime worker housing in Connecticut and, at the time, one of the largest in the country.

Led by a team of nationally known architects, landscape architects, and planners, the BHC and USHC were driven by an ambitious, long-range goal: to provide models for postwar construction that would transform the way American cities were built. Drawing on the Garden City movement and on privately constructed model industrial housing (such as Connecticut Gables, in Danielson, figure 32), they created complexes that were sturdily built, carefully detailed, and attractively laid out and landscaped. After the war, this level of quality drew charges of "unnecessary excellence" in congressional hearings. But on the eve of World War II, national architectural journals were still citing USHC projects, including Seaside Village, as models of good housing design.

A major challenge was to make the developments of small, relatively uniform structures varied and attractive. Frederick Law Olmsted Jr., manager of the USHC's Town Planning Division, outlined principles to address this concern in the *Monthly Labor Review* in 1919. These included comparatively short streets with curves to block long views; avoiding rigid symmetry and balance, which would create an institutional appearance; and also avoiding too much variety or picturesqueness, which could look like a stage set rather than a real neighborhood. In keeping with Olmsted's principles, landscape architect

Arthur Shurtleff (who later changed his name to Shurcliff; see place 6) arranged the houses along gently winding streets or clustered them around grassy courts. Some of the bends in the streets were planned to save existing trees. Houses on the edges of the complex turn inward to create a sense of enclosure and privacy from the surrounding city, while a landscaped square provides a focal point for the enclave.

The houses themselves, designed by architects R. Clipston Sturgis and Andrew Hepburn, are broken down into small units on an intimate scale. Flemish-bond brickwork and Georgian-inspired trim suggest Virginia buildings. Interestingly, Hepburn's firm served as the restoration architects for Colonial Williamsburg beginning in the 1920s. Seaside Village shows that he was aware of Virginia architecture a decade before that project.

After the war, the USHC sold Seaside Village to a cooperative association, in which residents own a share in the total development, rather than a specific unit. This gave them a stake in the property's future and helped ensure its continued maintenance. Thanks to resident ownership and the quality of its design and construction, Seaside Village shows that affordable housing can be humane and attractive and retain its value long after other "model housing" has deteriorated into slums.

THE PLACE
SEASIDE VILLAGE

1917–1919, R. Clipston Sturgis and A. H. Hepburn, architects; Arthur A. Shurtleff, planner
Sims, Cole, and Burnham Streets, off Iranistan Avenue, Bridgeport

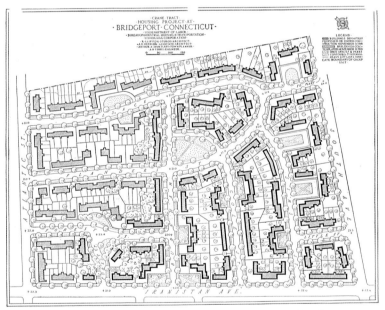

(*top*) FIGURE 128. Seaside Village, Bridgeport. Patrick L. Pinnell
(*bottom*) FIGURE 129. Seaside Village, site plan from United States Department of Labor, *Report of the United States Housing Corporation*, 1919

FURTHER READING
Bedford, Steven, and Nora Lucas. "Seaside Village Historic District" Wartime Emergency Housing in Bridgeport, 1916–1920, Multiple Property Resource. National Register of Historic Places, reference number 90001424, listed September 26, 1990.
Wright, Gwendolyn. *Building the Dream: A Social History of Housing in America*. Cambridge, Mass.: MIT Press, 1981.

45

FANTASY PALACE
WARNER THEATRE, TORRINGTON

At the turn of the twentieth century, moving pictures emerged as a new, largely American art form, and they fostered the emergence of a new building type: the movie theater. While similar to earlier dramatic theaters, movie theaters needed no backstage, and their acoustics were more stable, since sound came from speakers rather than unpredictable actors. As early as the 1910s, competitive operators were making their buildings more and more lavish, turning movie *theaters* into movie *palaces*. If the movies were a form of escape that allowed their viewers to immerse themselves in projected images flickering in a darkened room, then the movie palace brought the spectacle down off the screen and completely enveloped the audience in a fantasy world.

By the 1920s, two closely related architectural styles proved a perfect medium for such theaters. Known as Art Deco and Art Moderne, or simply Deco and Moderne, they utilized decoration based on hard-edged, stylized motifs such as chevrons, streamlined flowers and animals, zigzag sunrays, and waterfalls. Aside from the ornament, both styles favored smooth, glossy surfaces and, when possible, luxurious or exotic materials. The result could be as sharp and smart as the movie heroine who balanced a cigarette and a martini while trading machine-gun-rapid banter with the hero. It was as different from the history-laden buildings of the previous century as the heroine was from her Victorian foremothers.

At the Warner Theatre, Connecticut's best-preserved movie palace, rich materials, abundant ornament, and subtle color effects made going to the movies an unforgettable event. The exterior is boldly sculptural, with a ziggurat tower forming a backdrop for the brightly lit marquee to entice customers. In the lobby, a processional stair climbs up one wall between murals depicting idealized scenes from Torrington's history. A curtain, pulled to one side, screens the landing at the top. The lobby ceiling is scalloped to suggest more draperies, as if the entire space were a giant tent.

In the auditorium, blood-orange velour and gold brocade draperies cover the walls, highlighted with wood-grained pilasters and sconces of frosted glass, while a jazzy, multicolored carpet covers the floors. The decoration

reaches a climax in the ceiling, where gold-stenciled peacocks and floral filigrees surround a giant eight-pointed, trompe-l'oeil star. From the center of the star hangs a glass-tiered lamp. Here and in the lobbies, colored lightbulbs were used to create different moods, a dazzling use of new lighting technology.

Historian Maggie Valentine argues that such theaters could play important roles in small cities like Torrington. They drew all classes together, enhancing community identity. They brought bustle and activity to downtown commercial districts after business hours. With their architectural imagery of sophistication, they were "microcosms of allure and excitement of the big city theater district."

The building was as much an attraction as the shows it presented. For a generation that had survived world war only to fall into depression, it offered a few hours of escape in surroundings whose glamour matched the spectacle on-screen. Structure and technology were important only as they fed the fantasy. The show was the thing.

THE PLACE
WARNER THEATRE

www.warnertheatre.org

1930–1931, Thomas W. Lamb. 2002, Sevigny Architects,
EverGreene Architectural Arts.

68 Main Street, Torrington. Open to the public.

FURTHER READING

Roraback, Louisa, and William Devlin. "Warner Theater." National
Register of Historic Places, reference number 84001098, listed
February 16, 1984.

Valentine, Maggie. *The Show Starts at the Sidewalk: An
Architectural History of the Movie Theatre*. New Haven, Conn.:
Yale University Press: 1994.

FIGURE 131. Warner Theatre, Torrington. William Hosley

RENEWING THE CITY
CONSTITUTION PLAZA AND THE PHOENIX BUILDING, HARTFORD

Throughout the Depression and a construction moratorium imposed during World War II, America's cities suffered years of neglect. After the war, Congress passed Title I of the Housing Act of 1949, under which the federal government subsidized two-thirds of the cost of redeveloping blighted areas. Strongly shaped by Modernist doctrine, the program favored demolishing buildings and even entire neighborhoods considered substandard and replacing them with new construction.

Hartford focused on the area between Main Street and the Connecticut River, a deteriorated eleven-acre neighborhood historically related to the city's river port. The city cleared the whole area for new highways and an office and shopping district, called Constitution Plaza, intended to supplement the downtown. The master plan created by local architect Charles DuBose, with Sasaki, Walker and Associates, was unusual among urban renewal efforts for the prominent role of landscape design in its genesis. The plan called for office and apartment towers, plus a hotel and stores, arranged around open plazas and sheltered garden rooms, all sitting atop parking garages. Tying the disparate buildings together, the landscape elements gave Constitution Plaza a greater degree of coordination than many similar projects.

The buildings were designed by various firms within guidelines established by DuBose. Most have glass curtain walls over steel frames; an exception is the Hotel America, clad in panels of precast concrete and bridging Kinsley Street on immense steel trusses. Connected to Constitution Plaza by a bridge, but not technically a part of the project, the Phoenix Life Insurance Company building is Hartford's best-known Modernist structure. Thanks to its location next to Interstate 91 and its eye-catching shape—a long, pointed oval that gives the structure its nickname of the "Boat Building"—it was an advertisement both for the company and for Hartford as a whole.

Constitution Plaza illustrates a basic problem of twentieth-century Modernism that plagued many urban renewal projects: it doesn't play well with others. Conceived as a self-sufficient entity, the plaza sits with its back to the city, raised above the surrounding streets on a pedestal. (Connecting walkways to Main Street were planned but never built.) This isolation eventually doomed the plaza's shops and restaurants to failure.

Constitution Plaza also illustrates the central flaw of urban renewal: tearing everything down and starting from scratch rarely works. Cities are like ecosystems, in which actions in one place have consequences in others, often in unpredictable ways. Traditional cities grow gradually, evolving to meet changing needs and to correct problems as they arise. After fifty years, that process is beginning at Constitution Plaza. The conversion of the Hotel America to apartments, completed in 2015, promises to bring it some round-the-clock activity at a time when people are returning from the suburbs and want to live downtown. Perhaps other changes could be made to improve the plaza's connections to the rest of the city.

THE PLACES
CONSTITUTION PLAZA
1959–1964, Charles DuBose, coordinating architect;
    Sasaki, Walker and Associates, landscape architects
State, Market, Talbot Streets and Columbus Boulevard,
    Hartford

HOTEL AMERICA
(Now Spectra Boutique Apartments)
1961–1964, Curtis & Davis; 2013–2015, Crosskey Architects
5 Constitution Plaza, Hartford

PHOENIX LIFE INSURANCE COMPANY BUILDING
1961–1963, Harrison and Abramovitz
1 American Row, Hartford

FIGURE 132. Constitution Plaza, Hartford. Library of Congress, Prints & Photographs Division, LC-DIG-highsm-19393, photograph by Carol H. Highsmith

FURTHER READING
Andrews, Gregory E., and David F. Ransom. *Structures and Styles: Guided Tours of Hartford Architecture*. Hartford: Connecticut Historical Society and Connecticut Architecture Foundation, 1988.
Cunningham, Jan. "Phoenix Life Insurance Company Building." National Register of Historic Places, reference number 04001462, listed January 21, 2005.
Garvin, Alexander. *The American City: What Works, What Doesn't*. 2nd ed. New York: McGraw-Hill, 2002.
Karmazinas, Lucas. "Hotel America." National Register of Historic Places, reference number 12000359, listed September 7, 2012.

47

NEW URBANISM

BLUE BACK SQUARE, WEST HARTFORD

By the 1980s it was becoming clear that urban renewal had largely failed to revitalize America's cities. The practice of demolishing vast swaths of a city, then building Modernist plazas surrounded by free-standing high-rises like Constitution Plaza in Hartford (place 46), or suburban-style shopping centers like Dixwell Plaza in New Haven (place 99), almost never produced successful downtowns or neighborhoods. Inspired in part by Yale's charismatic architectural historian, Vincent Scully, one group of architects and planners sought to emulate the design of traditional cities. This New Urbanism movement is usually identified with the University of Miami, with which its leading proponents, Andrés Duany and Elizabeth Plater-Zyberk, are affiliated. However, it is in some ways a Connecticut product, influenced by their graduate-student exposure to New Haven's neighborhoods.

Eventually, developers got into the act, and Blue Back Square is one result. A cross between a suburban shopping mall and a traditional downtown, it has elements of each. As with a mall, a single owner controls the entire environment. Everything was built at once to a single plan, and the retail tenants are predominantly national chains. But as in a downtown, the buildings face streets rather than a private, enclosed space. They employ a variety of styles and shapes, and they contain a mix of uses, with offices and housing in addition to shops. Even the existing town library was incorporated into the plan, gaining a new entry onto one of the new streets.

While Blue Back Square's streets fit smoothly into the existing road network, the buildings are less convincing. Their varied façades, designed to look like a series of separate structures, are patently a veneer over larger bodies, particularly on the big, boxlike apartment blocks. One critic called them "smarmy postmodern fakery."

Commercially, Blue Back Square has been a resounding success. The development has benefited from its connection to West Hartford's existing commercial district, which lies just across the street. Although the downtown had suffered a setback after Westfarms Mall opened in 1974 on the West Hartford / Farmington line, it bounced back by attracting upscale shops and restaurants and building on its small-town atmosphere. Instead of starting from scratch, Blue Back has been able to draw on

FIGURE 133.
Blue Back Square,
West Hartford.
Deb Cohen

customers already in the area. Without this foundation to build on, it's a question whether it would have become the attraction it is.

Blue Back Square raises the larger issue of what makes a city. Are varied architecture and streets with parking enough? Much of the appeal of traditional city neighborhoods is the sense of organic variety that results from development over time by many different hands. This, Blue Back Square obviously lacks. Like urban renewal projects or suburban developments, it is the product of a single hand and a single moment. As a result, it feels artificial, more stage set than downtown.

But—it is still new. Perhaps after a few decades, Blue Back Square may settle into the surrounding town, its buildings (if they hold up) may develop a bit of patina, or some of them may be remodeled so that the sense of development over time becomes a fact rather than an illusion. Time will tell. In the meantime, the scale of Blue Back Square, the efforts made to encourage foot traffic, and even the Postmodern architecture have succeeded in creating a more humane environment than urban renewal plazas or enclosed auto-destination malls, and that is an important development.

THE PLACE
BLUE BACK SQUARE

2003–2008, Street-Works
South Main Street, Memorial and Isham Roads, West
    Hartford. Open to the public.

FURTHER READING

Kunstler, James Howard. *Home from Nowhere: Remaking Our Everyday World for the 21st Century.* New York: Simon & Schuster, 1996.
Scully, Vincent. *American Architecture and Urbanism.* New York: Praeger, 1969, 1976.

48

SUBURBAN CHINATOWN
MONTVILLE

Immigrants to the United States have long followed a pattern of settling first in cities, which offered job opportunities, inexpensive housing, and the chance to congregate with fellow immigrants for support. Subsequent generations, after establishing themselves economically and socially, might then join the migration to the suburbs. In the last third of the twentieth century, that pattern increasingly broke down as more and more employers also left the cities, and new immigrants followed them.

Since it opened in 1996, the Mohegan Sun casino, located in the Uncasville section of the town of Montville, has employed large numbers of immigrants, many of them from China. In part, these numbers reflect the casino's many Chinese customers, thanks to cultural traditions that favor gambling. And in part they reflect rising levels of immigration from China and the many entry-level jobs offered by the casino. From 2000 to 2010, Montville's Chinese-born population grew from 110 to 949, an increase of 763 percent during a period when the town's total population grew by only 5.5 percent. The influx of Chinese immigrants is changing the face of Montville. Most visible are growing numbers of Chinese restaurants, markets, and other businesses along area roads.

The influx also affects residential areas. Mostly employed in low-paying positions, immigrants tend to share houses—ordinary split-levels or raised ranches intended for American nuclear families. As architect Stephen Fan documents, the immigrants use and modify these houses to accommodate groups of unrelated persons and to fit Chinese cultural patterns. Within the houses occupants have their own bedrooms while sharing kitchens, bathrooms, and other common spaces. Some spaces intended to be common, such as living rooms, may be subdivided into additional bedrooms. Garages, with their doors left open, may serve as porches where occupants sit to watch the world and chat with passing neighbors. Changes extend to the surrounding landscape as well. Vegetables grow in front yards, spreading out under trees or climbing on homemade trellises built from branches collected in nearby woods. Laundry and even fish hang out to dry. Since many of the immigrants do not own cars, they walk to work and elsewhere, wearing paths along roads that have no sidewalks, while traffic whizzes by.

These choices are largely a matter of economics. Most

immigrants cannot afford to live by themselves or buy cars; and growing their own food also saves money. But, according to Fan, there are other factors to consider. Shared housing provides companionship and mutual assistance that in China would be supplied by extended families. Walking rather than driving provides healthful exercise and fresh air for workers in the windowless casino. And vegetable gardens can supply foods not available in local stores while giving the gardeners a sense of fulfillment.

Sometimes, these different ways of living create friction with earlier residents. Legally, the immigrants may run up against building and zoning codes, which limit the number of unrelated people who may share a single-family dwelling or regulate how spaces are divided. Socially, they run up against suburban customs, such as those that relegate socializing and functional uses to back yards, leaving front yards for display. These regulations or customs are typically justified as needed to protect public health and safety or property values. However, they may also reflect cultural biases. Why, for instance, would ten unrelated people necessarily be more crowded or noisy than ten related people?

In a sense, perhaps the most serious violation is the revelation of diversity among Montville's residents. Reviewing the exhibit *Sub-Urbanisms*, Matthew Lasner of Hunter College wrote, "For all our ethnic pride and diversity, we Americans tend to hide our differences behind closed doors. As Dianne Harris and others have argued, a central purpose of suburbia—and perhaps much of the U.S. built environment—is to obscure difference. In peeling back some of architecture's superficial uniformity, *SubUrbanisms* ... made America easier to see."

THE PLACE
MONTVILLE

Holly Hill Drive, Crestview Drive, Cedar Lane, Fort Shantok Road, and others

FURTHER READING

Fan, Stephen, ed. *Sub-Urbanisms: Casino Urbanization, Chinatowns, and the Contested American Landscape.* New London, Conn.: Lyman Allyn Museum, 2014.

Harris, Dianne. *Little White Houses: How the Postwar Home Constructed Race in America.* Minneapolis: University of Minnesota Press, 2013.

CURRENTLY INHABITED
Upper Level Plan

Exterior porch
-> Kitchen

Exterior siding
-> Sink backsplash

A bedroom has been inserted into an existing bedroom

Kitchen
-> Bedroom

Additional bedrooms block two former windows, but the large living room window provides adequate lighting

Interior vestibule adds an additional public and private threshold

Living Room
-> "Courtyard" flanked by bedrooms

Lower Level Plan

New bathroom inserted under existing bathroom maximizes use of existing plumbing

Garage
-> Semi-permeable social front porch that stays cool in the summer.

(top) FIGURE 134. House and garden, Montville. Stephen Fan
(bottom) FIGURE 135. Plan of modified house, Montville. Drawing by Stephen Fan

Part Seven

FROM PLACE TO PLACE

The need to move people and goods has contributed to shaping Connecticut, and advancing transportation technology has produced works that are significant parts of the state's landscape. Roads, canals, and bridges are conceived primarily for their functional qualities, but like buildings such as railroad stations and roadside businesses, they have expressive, symbolic, and social qualities, too. They can enhance the traveler's experience or celebrate the connections that tie a people together. Additionally, transportation networks can enable the transmission of architectural ideas from one place to another.

49

LIGHTS ALONG THE SHORE
HARBOR AND LEDGE LIGHTHOUSES, NEW LONDON

In the century separating the Harbor and Ledge lighthouses at New London, lighthouse construction changed significantly. From the time of the first European settlement, maritime transportation was crucial to the development of commerce, defense, and communications. But sailing could be dangerous. Shoals and ledges were hazards, and important harbors and rivers needed to be identified. As an aid to navigation, Connecticut built just the fourth lighthouse in the Americas at New London in 1760, marking the entrance to Connecticut's deepest harbor. By 1800 that structure had developed serious cracks, and the United States Treasury Department, which had assumed responsibility for lighthouses in 1789, commissioned a replacement.

The new Harbor lighthouse was an octagonal stone tower, eighty-nine feet tall. Not much different from medieval or even ancient lighthouses, it had thick walls and a tapering form to give it stability against winds and waves. The original light was an oil lamp with a reflector housed in an iron-and-glass lantern atop the tower. The lantern was replaced in 1833, and new lights were installed as technology improved, with oil giving way to acetylene and then electricity and more powerful lenses being devised. The tower itself remains essentially unchanged. Next to it is the keeper's house, rebuilt in 1863. Other buildings, no longer extant, included a barn and an oil-storage shed.

Throughout the first half of the nineteenth century, American lighthouses lagged behind European ones technologically, owing to neglect by Treasury Department officials. In 1852, Congress created a separate Lighthouse Board, which pursued improvements more aggressively. The board introduced new equipment and new types of lighthouses.

By the 1870s, the most common lighthouse form was a houselike structure with the light on its roof. This was more stable in exposed locations than a tower, and it provided sheltered access to the light from the keeper's quarters. From the 1880s to the 1920s, a third type, a truncated cone formed of prefabricated cast-iron plates, dominated lighthouse building. Prefabrication simplified construction, particularly in offshore locations, and standardized designs saved money.

The board returned to the house form, though, when a new lighthouse was built at New London in 1909 to mark an underwater ledge at the mouth of the harbor. At the same time, it experimented with an innovative type of construction. Instead of cast iron, the new lighthouse used cinder concrete and steel I-beams in its structure. Known as reinforced concrete, this was just emerging as a building material; the first lighthouse employing it had gone up only the year before, on the Pacific Coast, and industrial designers were beginning to use it for factories such as Hockanum Mill (place 33).

New London's lighthouses look quite different from each other—one a traditional stone tower, the other resembling a house with an oversize cupola somehow stranded in the middle of the harbor. Unexpectedly, this difference has little to do with their primary function, which is to cast a bright light for a long distance, or with advances in lighting technology. Instead, it derives more from changes in construction practices, which saw a shift from stone to iron to concrete, and in planning, allowing keepers direct access from their quarters to the light, even in bad weather.

THE PLACES
NEW LONDON HARBOR LIGHTHOUSE
1801, Abishai Woodward. 1833, Charles H. Smith. 1863, keeper's house.
810 Pequot Avenue, New London
NEW LONDON LEDGE LIGHTHOUSE
1909, Hamilton R. Douglas Company, builder
Visible from Pequot Avenue, New London

FURTHER READING
Templeton, Dorothy B. "New London Harbor Lighthouse." National Register of Historic Places, reference number 89001470, listed May 29, 1990.
———. "New London Ledge Lighthouse." National Register of Historic Places, reference number 89001471, listed May 29, 1990.
———. "Operating Lighthouses in the State of Connecticut Multiple Property Submission." National Register of Historic Places, reference number 64500080, listed October 5, 1989.

FIGURES 136 AND 137. New London Harbor Lighthouse (*top*) and New London Ledge Lighthouse (*bottom*). New London Maritime Society

50

ARCHITECTURE TRAVELS NEW ROADS

TWO HOUSES, THOMPSON HILL

Settled soon after 1700, Thompson Hill, the central settlement in the northeast Connecticut town of Thompson, remained a sleepy farming village gathered around a meetinghouse until the early nineteenth century, when new two turnpikes crossed here: the Hartford-Boston Turnpike (1797) and the Providence-Springfield Turnpike (1803). The roads, privately operated under state charters, brought new business to Thompson Hill. The community soon sprouted an inn, shops, a bank, and the beginnings of industry. This flush of prosperity expressed itself in fashionable new buildings.

The new turnpikes brought not only people and goods to previously isolated rural communities, but new architectural ideas as well. Since Thompson borders on both Rhode Island and Massachusetts, outside influences are particularly visible here.

At the southeastern corner of the town's common (note the use of "common," a Massachusetts / Rhode Island term, instead of the Connecticut "green") stands the Joseph Gay house, better known as the home of the nineteenth-century historian Ellen Larned. Built about 1814, it is a restrained Federal house with the delicate door surround and Palladian window typical of the period. But the brick end walls of this otherwise wood-framed and clapboarded building are distinctly different; sometimes found in Rhode Island and more often in Massachusetts, they appear almost nowhere else in Connecticut. Wide corner boards outline the edges of the house and cover the junction of brick and wood. (On some brick-enders, wooden quoins perform this function, their more elaborate design actually accentuating the difference in materials.)

A more eye-catching example of outside influence is the Daniel Wickham House, built facing the common about 1820. Its low hipped roof has a monitor that provides light, ventilation, and headroom for the attic. In Rhode Island, monitors like the one on the Wickham House were a trademark of John Holden Greene (1777–1850) a builder-architect of the Federal era. Several houses Greene built in Providence have roofs like this, some still with balustrades lining the eaves on both levels, to hide the roofs and give the house a decorative edging. It is likely that the Wickham House once had similar balustrades. The doorway offers another suggestion of Greene's work. The exaggeratedly

FIGURE 138. Joseph Gay (Ellen Larned) House, Thompson Hill.
Connecticut Trust for Historic Preservation

FIGURE 139. Daniel Wickham House, Thompson Hill.
Connecticut Trust for Historic Preservation

slender columns flanking the door and sidelights have flared capitals and rings around their middles, an unusual Gothic touch that Greene frequently used on otherwise Neoclassical houses.

Did John Holden Greene design the Wickham House? Or was someone copying his work? It is impossible to tell, but his influence is clear. It provides a visible sign of Thompson's growing connections with the outside world, thanks to the turnpikes. These connections weren't just mercantile and industrial; they were cultural as well.

THE PLACES
JOSEPH GAY HOUSE
(Ellen Larned House)

ca. 1814

327 Thompson Road, Thompson Hill. Private residence.

DANIEL WICKHAM HOUSE

ca. 1820

343 Thompson Road, Thompson Hill. Private residence.

FURTHER READING

Ransom, David, and Gregory Andrews. "Thompson Hill Historic District." National Register of Historic Places, reference number 87002186, listed December 31, 1987.

51

CANAL ENGINEERING

ENFIELD FALLS CANAL,
WINDSOR LOCKS AND SUFFIELD

Since the New Haven Colony was absorbed into the Connecticut Colony under the Charter of 1662, Hartford and New Haven have vied for the title of Connecticut's leading city. In trade, New Haven dominated the coast, and Hartford the hinterlands, thanks to its location on the Connecticut River, which provided direct access through Massachusetts into New Hampshire and Vermont. There was, however, one significant obstacle on this watery highway: the rapids at Enfield. Goods had to be unloaded from vessels, carried around the rapids, and reloaded before continuing upstream or down.

In the 1820s, New Haven merchants began work on a scheme to bypass Hartford and gain direct water access to the interior of New England via a canal from New Haven to Northampton, Massachusetts. Construction on what was known popularly as the Farmington Canal began in 1825; the first section opened in 1828, and the full route to Northampton was completed in 1835.

Around the same time, Hartford interests formed the Connecticut River Company to build a canal bypassing the Enfield rapids. Construction of what was known as the Enfield Falls Canal began in 1827 and was completed in 1829. Both were part of a national canal-building movement that produced the Erie Canal between Albany and Buffalo, New York, and the Chesapeake and Ohio Canal, from Washington, D.C., to Cumberland, Maryland, among others.

For design and construction oversight, the Connecticut River Company turned to Canvass White (1790–1834), who had practical experience from working on the Erie Canal, which he augmented by a study trip to England. Construction was done by hand, requiring hundreds of laborers, many of them Irish immigrants, a new and foreign presence in Connecticut's population. The canal is five and a half miles long and averages eighty feet wide and about four and a half feet deep. It has four locks, plus a 104-foot aqueduct over Stony Brook.

On its face, the Farmington Canal was a more impressive engineering achievement. At eighty miles it was much longer than the Enfield Falls Canal, and it traveled difficult terrain that required complex engineering, including construction of twenty-eight locks and a 280-foot aqueduct over the Farmington River. To save money, the canal walls were built mostly of earth, and were plagued by leaks. The Farmington Canal never turned a profit; it was abandoned in 1846, and its towpath was used to build a railroad.

The Enfield Falls Canal was more forward looking. Canvass White specified more expensive, but more durable, masonry walls. The masonry leaked less and was able to withstand the turbulence produced by the paddle wheels of steamboats, as earthen walls never could have done. In another bit of foresight, the Connecticut River Company also laid out sites for mills that could use water from the canal to power their machinery. After railroads took over the canal's transportation function, this industrial use kept it economically relevant and ensured its preservation.

Though Connecticut's canal era was short, it marked the beginning of the revolution in transportation that fostered commercial and industrial growth in the nineteenth century and changed the shape of the state. New communities grew up around transportation nodes and factories like those along the Enfield Falls Canal, which formed the heart of the new town of Windsor Locks, incorporated in 1854. Some of those industrial sites are still in use, and the towpath is currently maintained as a state park.

THE PLACE
ENFIELD FALLS CANAL
(Windsor Locks Canal State Park)

1827–1829, Canvass White, engineer

Access at Bridge Street (Connecticut Route 140), Windsor Locks, and Canal Road, Suffield. Open to the public.

FURTHER READING

Clouette, Bruce. "Enfield Canal." National Register of Historic Places, reference number 76001998, listed April 22, 1976.

FIGURE 140. Enfield Falls Canal, Windsor Locks. William Hosley

RIVER TRAFFIC

STEAMBOAT DOCK, ESSEX

For three hundred years after Europeans arrived in Connecticut, the Connecticut River was a working highway, the easiest path for moving people and goods. The shores of Connecticut waterfront towns and cities teemed with activity and were crowded with piers, warehouses, shipyards, and other structures to accommodate it.

Essex was one of those towns. Since the 1660s there has been a landing at the foot of Main Street at which farmers sent livestock and crops to coastal cities and the West Indies, and merchants imported goods for their stores. Thriving shipyards constructed sailing vessels until the mid-nineteenth century. Even after the building of the railroads, steamboats continued to stop at Essex for passengers and freight, ceasing service only in 1931.

Today the landing is known as Steamboat Dock, and the dockhouse, a barnlike wooden building with a gawky cupola, is the most visible survivor of Essex's maritime history. The dockhouse was built in 1878 for Phoebe Hayden, the granddaughter, niece, daughter, and widow of shipyard proprietors who was also an important landowner. Her grandson, William H. Parmelee, operated a store in the building, but its main function was as a warehouse and depot serving steamboat traffic.

Although balloon framing was rapidly taking over residential construction in Connecticut in the 1870s, the dockhouse has a timber frame like a barn or factory—the better to accommodate heavy loads. Modern technology is apparent, though, in the use of iron structural posts in the upper story, and in a hoist, still usable and accessed through trapdoors in the floors. The building originally stood on piles, overhanging the river; in 1951 it was moved back onto dry land. Like a railroad station, Steamboat Dock served as a gateway to Essex, the first thing arriving passengers would see. Its cupola and balcony also provided lookouts from which to watch for approaching ships.

Near the dockhouse, three other buildings from earlier, more promising days illustrate the intertwined family relationships that dominated Essex's maritime economy. Overlooking the water, the Uriah Hayden House was home to a prominent shipbuilder, Phoebe's grandfather. Its high basement, a common feature of waterfront houses of the eighteenth century, provided storage with easy access to boats anchored in front of the house. Next to it is a

FIGURE 141. Steamboat Dock (Connecticut River Museum), Essex. Connecticut River Museum, photograph by Jody Dole

brick store built by Phoebe's father and two of his cousins (who also were his brothers-in-law), its durable material suggesting the value of the goods they dealt in. The Hayden Chandlery, built by Richard Hayden (a cousin of both Phoebe's mother and her father-in-law), sold supplies and equipment for seamen and ships. Its elegant Federal-style façade speaks to the glory days of river shipping, when merchants and shipbuilders could make fortunes. The chandlery originally stood next to Richard's brick house, at 40 Main Street—the finest in town.

In the twentieth century Essex successfully reinvented itself as a chic shopping and dining destination. Unlike many structures of the working waterfront, the dockhouse has survived. After serving as a marina, a store, apartments, and a restaurant, it is now a museum dedicated to the Connecticut River.

THE PLACES

STEAMBOAT DOCK

(Now Connecticut River Museum,
    www.ctrivermuseum.org)

1878. 1951, moved. 1981, 1988, Glen Arbonies of
    Centerbrook Architects.

67 Main Street, Essex. Open to the public.

HAYDEN CHANDLERY

1813. 1948, moved.

67 Main Street, Essex

HAYDEN-STARKEY STORE

1809

48 Main Street, Essex. Private.

URIAH HAYDEN HOUSE

1765–1766, with older rear ell

66 Main Street, Essex. Private.

FURTHER READING

Delaney, Edmund. *The Connecticut River: New England's Historic Waterway.* Chester, Conn.: Globe Pequot, 1983.

Ransom, David F. "Steamboat Dock Site." National Register of Historic Places, reference number 82003768, listed April 1, 1982.

53

GATEWAY TO THE CITY
UNION STATION, NEW LONDON

Built in the late nineteenth century when railroads were the principal means of long-distance transportation, Union Station was New London's front door, the first thing travelers to the city would see. Even ship or ferry passengers disembarking at the city's piers had to pass by it. The station dominates the Parade, the central square where several major streets converge: State Street coming down the hill, Bank Street curving in from the south, and Eugene O'Neill Drive (originally Main Street) from the north. Other civic landmarks like City Hall or big churches make do with subsidiary sites; the station's only rival for location is the venerable New London County Courthouse (place 9) at the head of State Street. But the courthouse sits at the edge of downtown; Union Station is at its heart.

Fortunately, the station lives up to its setting. It was the last and, in the eyes of many critics, the best of the railroad stations designed by H. H. Richardson (1838–1886). Like Robert Adam before him or Frank Lloyd Wright after him, Richardson gave his name to an architectural style: Richardsonian. He is known for his personal reinterpretation of medieval Romanesque architecture, characterized by massive and picturesque forms, rugged stonework often in contrasting colors, and big round arches. All of this Richardson married to the clear planning taught at the École des Beaux-Arts, in Paris, where he was trained. The Cheney Block, in Hartford (1875), shows Richardson himself working in his eponymous style. Examples of his influence on others include the New London Public Library (1890), by Shepley, Rutan and Coolidge, the former employees who succeeded to Richardson's office, and his style, after his death.

But Richardson himself was not always Richardsonian. At Union Station, as at Sever Hall at Harvard (1878) and Emmanuel Episcopal Church in Pittsburgh (1883), he abandoned his trademark rugged, two-toned stonework in favor of smooth walls of monochrome brick, and simplified the overall shape of the building. From a distance, the station appears as a massive, simple form capped by an unbroken hipped roof. A front gable, dormers, and chimneys animate the shape but barely break the silhouette. At closer view, details not visible from farther away become apparent. A shallow overhang at the second-story level casts a narrow shadow. Carved stone blocks (red, like the brick) anchor the corners of the front gable; strips of dentils line the cornice and overhang; and recessed panels undergird the second-story windows. Still closer, basketweave patterning highlights the gable, and wide arches cap windows and doors while remaining in the wall plane, perfectly flat.

This was a trend in Richardson's career that most of his imitators didn't grasp: his turn toward simplicity. But it was simplicity on nineteenth-century terms. Not the machinelike bareness of twentieth-century Modernism, it employed coherent form, straightforward planning, restrained color, and ornament that plays a distinctly secondary role to overall effect. Instead of out-shouting the many voices of downtown New London, Union Station asserts its primacy by standing massive and serene while the busy traffic swirls around it.

THE PLACE
UNION STATION

1885–1887, H. H. Richardson. 1974–1976, Anderson Notter Associates. 2004, Barun Basu Associates.

Water Street, New London

FURTHER READING

Luyster, Constance. "New London Railroad Station." National Register of Historic Places, reference number 71000913, listed June 28, 1971.

Ochsner, Jeffrey Karl. *H. H. Richardson: Complete Architectural Works*. Cambridge, Mass.: MIT Press, 1982.

O'Gorman, James F. *Three American Architects: Richardson, Sullivan, and Wright, 1865–1915*. Chicago: University of Chicago Press, 1991.

FIGURE 142. Union Station, New London. Connecticut Trust for Historic Preservation

54

TO ENJOY AS WE GO
THE MERRITT PARKWAY

At the groundbreaking for the Merritt Parkway in 1934, the road's namesake, Congressman Schuyler Merritt, summarized the road's purpose. "It is not being built primarily to get [from] one place to another as rapidly as possible," he said, "but is being built to enjoy as you go."

The Merritt grew out of efforts to bypass congestion on the Boston Post Road through Fairfield County. But instead of a wider, faster version of the Post Road, the Connecticut Highway Department built a *parkway*—a road in a landscaped park, designed for pleasurable driving. This idea was inspired by the City Beautiful movement of the late nineteenth and early twentieth centuries, which produced grand public works based on the conviction that beauty was a valuable public asset.

The Merritt's bridges are well known because they are unusual. Typical parkway bridges of rustic stone were too expensive for Depression-wracked Connecticut. So the highway department's architect, George Dunkelberger (1891–1960), molded ordinary concrete into works of art or whimsy. But the bridges are just a garnish, intended to enhance the real star of the show, the landscape.

For Thayer Chase (1908–2003), the landscape architect, the task was to heal the scars of construction and blend the parkway seamlessly into the surrounding countryside. To accomplish this, Chase used indigenous plants, grouped informally and matched to what was growing nearby—willows and red maples in swampy areas, cedars and birches on abandoned farmland, and black birches on the rock ledges. In some cases, he imitated natural succession, planting quick-growing "weed trees" to shelter laurels until slower-growing oaks could mature. "It was a great satisfaction to me," Chase said, "when people would ask, 'But what did you *do*?'"

Although Chase wanted the landscape to look natural, it was carefully designed. He sited plantings to enhance the bridges or to lead the eye to views beyond the right-of-way. At curves and exits, shrubs shielded drivers' eyes from oncoming headlights. And Chase specified more flowering plants than would occur naturally, including tens of thousands of mountain laurels, Connecticut's state flower.

The landscape matured as intended through the 1940s. But as maintenance budgets were cut and development increased, new growth obscured Chase's vistas and enclosed the roadway in a nearly continuous green tunnel. Since the 1990s the Connecticut Department of Transportation has been removing overgrowth and restoring plantings as it gradually repairs and improves the parkway. However, as this is being written in 2016, the department is clear-cutting a wide swath along the parkway to remove trees perceived as potential hazards. Because this is considered emergency work, it is being done without waiting to complete plans or secure funding for restoring the landscape. The effect is devastating, as weeds and brush take over the barren cleared areas with amazing speed.

Fortunately, Chase's work of the 1930s offers hope. Today's builders can design a landscape that heals the scars, just as he did. The concept is flexible—details can be quite different, as long as the concept of a road in a natural-looking park remains constant. What is important is the *experience* of the parkway. With care, the Merritt can continue to be a road to enjoy as we go.

THE PLACE
MERRITT PARKWAY

1934–1940, Connecticut Highway Department: Warren
    Creamer and Leslie G. Sumner, engineers; George
    Dunkelberger, architect; Weld Thayer Chase, landscape
    architect
Connecticut Route 15, Greenwich to Stratford

FURTHER READING
Heiss, Laurie, and Jill Smyth. *The Merritt Parkway: The Road That Shaped a Region.* Charleston, S.C.: History Press, 2014.
Larned, Larry. *Traveling the Merritt Parkway.* Charleston, S.C.: Arcadia, 1998.
Lynn, Catherine, and Christopher Wigren. "Merritt Parkway." National Register of Historic Places, reference number 91000410, listed April 17, 1991.

FIGURES 143 AND 144. Merritt Parkway, roadway in summer (*top*), and James Farm Road Bridge, Stratford (*bottom*). Merritt Parkway Conservancy

55

HIGHWAY CULTURE

THE BERLIN TURNPIKE, BERLIN AND NEWINGTON

After completing the Merritt Parkway, the Connecticut Highway Department intended to continue it past the Housatonic River, to New Haven, Hartford, and Massachusetts. The section from Trumbull to Meriden was built as a parkway named in honor of former governor Wilbur Cross. From Meriden to Hartford the Department chose another model for what is variously called the Wilbur Cross Highway or the Berlin Turnpike. Completed in 1942, this road followed the path of the old Hartford and New Haven Turnpike, chartered in 1798 by James Hillhouse, Eli Whitney, and other New Haven investors.

Unlike the parkways, the new highway allowed direct access to roadside property. As a segment of the inland route from New York to Boston, it attracted businesses catering to travelers—restaurants, motels, and the service stations that gave the road the nickname "Gasoline Alley." After Interstate 91 opened in 1965, through traffic bypassed the turnpike, leaving its businesses to close or adapt to serve a local clientele. Nonetheless, through Berlin and Newington the road remains one of the best places in Connecticut to spot post–World War II roadside architecture.

To capture the attention of fast-moving travelers, businesses resorted to eye-catching designs. Signs are big, brightly colored, and, at night, brightly lit. Free-standing or mounted on roofs, they had to communicate their message in time for the driver to make a decision, slow down, and turn off the road. On many signs, easy-to-read block letters identify the service being offered (Diner, Motel), while the name of the specific business (Olympia, Grantmoor) appears in more decorative, if somewhat less legible, cursive letters. Sometimes the building itself becomes a sign, by virtue of unusual shape or material or decoration. Before chains took over with standardized designs for easy recognition, the roadside was a cacophony of voices, each trying to out-shout the others.

One of the biggest car-oriented businesses remaining along the Berlin Turnpike is the Grantmoor Motor Lodge, an epitome of the flashy commercial strain of Modernist design known as "Googie." Its zigzag roof reads well from a fast-moving car, while the pleated canopies, slim proportions, and bright panels in primary colors on the balcony railings (since removed) promised modernity and fun. By the late 1950s, ambitious motel operators were adding amusements in the ever-escalating war to attract customers. The Grantmoor offered a swimming pool, golf course, driving range, and restaurant. The restaurant (now a Shriners' temple) continues the Googie theme with its swooping roof and busy combination of stone, brick, stucco, and glass. This variety probably was derived from orthodox Modernists' use of different materials to indicate different structural functions, but here it is purely decorative. The idea is to create a jazzy setting for vacation pleasure-seeking—aesthetics in the service of function.

Though some decried the visual (and literal) noise of the Berlin Turnpike, others found it vital and exciting. In the 1950s it spoke of prosperity and relaxation to a people emerging from years of economic depression and war. Today, it conjures up a vision of a past when even the strip was localized, before corporate standardization made every place look the same. And yet, in its businesses' use of similar tactics to attract customers, it carried the seeds of that very standardization.

THE PLACES
BERLIN TURNPIKE / WILBUR CROSS HIGHWAY
1942
Connecticut Route 15 through Meriden, Berlin, Newington, and Wethersfield
GRANTMOOR MOTOR LODGE
1959–1960
3000 Berlin Turnpike, Newington

FURTHER READING
Donohue, Mary. "A Hip Road Trip." *Connecticut Explored* 8, no. 1 (Winter 2009–2010): 24–29.
Larned, Larry. *Route 15: The Road to Hartford*. Charleston, S.C.: Arcadia, 2002.

FIGURE 145. Grantmoor Motor Lodge, Newington. Robert Gregson

Part Eight

BODY, MIND, AND SOUL

Apart from the basic needs of shelter and a site to pursue a livelihood, architecture in Connecticut has created places that serve people's intellectual, health, and spiritual needs. Starting with the meetinghouses of the original Puritans' God-centered settlements, churches, synagogues, and other houses of worship have pointed beyond the visible world. Education quickly became one of the state's principal industries, serving Connecticut's own residents and attracting students and teachers from elsewhere. Public and private institutions alike have provided innovative physical and mental health care. In all these cases, architecture has been part of the program: to accommodate and further the specific activities, and also to embody the values behind them.

56

PURITAN FINERY

FIRST CHURCH OF CHRIST, WETHERSFIELD

What kind of building was best in which to worship God? In England, the Puritans had used existing church buildings. But in New England, they had to start afresh. They tried various solutions, always hewing to the principle that the buildings had to accommodate a variety of uses, not just worship. While this goal was partly due to practicality under circumstances where erecting a structure was a major undertaking, it also reflected the Puritan conviction that the "church" was not a building, but the congregation of God's people. The resulting "meetinghouse" was a place for public gatherings of all kinds.

None of the first generation of meetinghouses survives in Connecticut. Although evidence is unclear, it seems likely that most were poorly constructed and plain. There is a popular notion that this plainness was a deliberate choice, but in towns that could afford it, the records refer to such finery as bell turrets, ornamental spindle rails along the tops of pews, and general "comeliness." Plainness seems to have been more the consequence of scarce resources amid the difficulty of establishing a stable society.

What eventually emerged in the eighteenth century as a nearly standard meetinghouse type was a rectangular structure with a pitched roof. The main entrance was on the broad front, opening onto an aisle that led to the pulpit on the opposite wall. On more ambitious buildings, a tower was attached to one end, but the main door remained on the long side. Modern viewers often describe these buildings as "side-openers," not realizing that when they were constructed the long wall with the door was considered the *front*.

Inside these meetinghouses everything focused on the pulpit. Lifted almost to gallery height, topped by a sounding board, and lit by the building's only arched window—in the eighteenth century an indicator of high status—it clearly is the building's hub, the physical embodiment of the power of the word of God.

In 1761 the wealthy town of Wethersfield began the most luxurious of Connecticut's surviving colonial meetinghouses. It is constructed of brick—only the seventh such in New England—laid in a Dutch cross bond usually associated with builders from the Hudson

FIGURE 146.
First Church of Christ,
Wethersfield. Deb Cohen

CONNECTICUT ARCHITECTURE

Valley, and ornamented with glazed-header diapering. In a demonstration of sophisticated planning, the building committee specified that the gallery stairs be located in the porch and tower at the ends, "so that the congregation may not be interrupted by such as go into the galleries … and that there may be more room in the house." Another bit of finery is the original pulpit, bedecked with paneled pilasters, rosettes (a common Connecticut Valley motif), and beautifully carved festoons of fruit and flowers. Putting the lie to notions of meetinghouse austerity, its richness matches that of contemporary merchants' mansions such as Ebenezer Grant's house in East Windsor (place 87).

Wethersfield's was also one of the first Congregational meetinghouses to have a tower on which multiple stages ornamented with pinnacles and urns were layered to create a steeple. This was an Anglican type, copied from Trinity Church in Newport, Rhode Island (1726, Richard Munday; steeple 1741), itself copied from Christ Church (Old North Church), in Boston (1722, William Price; steeple ca. 1735). Historian Peter Benes interprets this as an early stage in the gradual change taking place in Congregational practice, which after the Revolution would inspire the shift from meetinghouses to buildings that looked like, and eventually were called, churches.

THE PLACE
FIRST CHURCH OF CHRIST

1761–1764. 1971–1973 restored, Jeter, Cook and Jepson. 250 Main Street, Wethersfield. Open to the public.

FURTHER READING
Benes, Peter. *Meetinghouses of Early New England*. Amherst: University of Massachusetts Press, 2012.
Luyster, Constance. "Old Wethersfield Historic District." National Register of Historic Places, reference number 70000719, listed December 29, 1970.

FIGURE 147. First Church of Christ, Wethersfield. Connecticut Trust for Historic Preservation

57

SCHOOLS FOR ALL
LITTLE RED SCHOOL, WINCHESTER

From its founding, Connecticut has valued public education. The Puritans taught that all believers should be able to read the Bible, and so made ecclesiastical societies responsible for local schools. Later, towns formed school districts to raise money for buildings and teachers' salaries through taxes and school fees. In 1795 Connecticut set aside proceeds from the sale of its Western Reserve lands in Ohio as a School Fund to supplement local funds.

In practice, however, support for schools was uneven. When Winchester's Eighth District School burned in the 1790s, a replacement wasn't built until sometime between 1812 and 1815. In the meantime, the students met wherever they could, including in a barn. Like most rural schools, the new building was utilitarian, with a post-and-beam frame, uneven clapboards, and unadorned door and window openings. Given the school's nickname, it must have been painted red at some point, but very possibly not at first. Apart from a narrow vestibule, it contains a single classroom, lit by windows on three sides and heated by a stove, which replaced the original fireplace. Plain board wainscoting lines the lower part of the classroom walls, with plaster above.

The school does have one touch of architectural distinction: a barrel-vaulted plaster ceiling. In fact, a surprising number of country schools from the Federal era have (or had) ceilings like this, including two others in Winchester. The reason for them is not clear. Perhaps the vaults were thought to improve acoustics. Perhaps the additional height made packed classrooms seem less crowded. Perhaps the arched shape, which required greater skill and labor to execute, was a reminder that, despite its spartan appearance, this building fulfilled an important civic function and was worthy of respect.

What was it like to attend the Little Red School? The writing shelf that runs partway around the room offers a hint. Such shelves were typical of early nineteenth-century schools, but few survive. Having students sit with their backs to the teacher may seem inconvenient, but the children attending rural schools varied widely in age and level of learning. Teachers would assign quiet work to some students while they gave lessons to or heard recitations from others. Facing the wall might have helped those working on their own to concentrate.

Although nineteenth-century Connecticut schools had a good reputation, they apparently had many shortcomings. A report to the General Assembly in 1837 found that most of the state's rural schools suffered from insufficient funding, low parent interest, poorly qualified teachers, and ill-constructed buildings. Of 103 schools examined, only 31 were considered in good repair. Ironically, the School Fund was partly to blame for this sad state of affairs. Although it was envisioned as a supplement for local funding, some districts took its availability as an excuse to eliminate school taxes, with the result that spending for education actually declined in some communities. The 1837 report sparked efforts to improve and modernize Connecticut's schools, a process that eventually led to the closing of the Little Red School in 1908.

Neglect and reform both contributed to the preservation of the Little Red School. The district never significantly updated the building, leaving it almost entirely unchanged. After it closed, the school was bought by Clifford Bristol as a memorial to his father, Charles, a longtime member of the Winchester school board and a proponent of educational improvement. It is now operated as a museum by a private association.

THE PLACE
DISTRICT 8 SCHOOL
(Little Red School)
ca. 1812–1815
Intersection of Platt Hill and Taylor Brook Roads,
    Winchester

FURTHER READING
Carley, Rachel D. "Little Red School House, Structural Analysis."
    Little Red School House Association of Winchester, 2013.

FIGURE 148. Little Red School, Winchester, ca. 1900.
DeMars Images Collection

58

THE BIG HOUSE

MIDDLETOWN ALMS HOUSE, MIDDLETOWN

Most colonial Connecticut towns assigned their poor to individual households where they could live and work in an intimate but closely supervised setting. By the early nineteenth century this system was falling apart, particularly in larger communities, and towns began to build dedicated facilities to care for the poor. Middletown's alms house is the earliest surviving structure built specifically for housing the poor in Connecticut and one of the oldest in the country. It provides a glimpse into the process of developing a new type of building, one its builders had never before erected and may never have even seen examples of elsewhere.

One model that proved suitable to many situations was a building with a pedimented center block and wings with rooms on both sides of the corridors. In outline, it looked like a simpler version of Georgian country houses like Mount Vernon or the White House, themselves adapted from English models. Even before the Revolution, builders used this big-house model for college buildings; perhaps the oldest surviving example is the Wren Building at the College of William and Mary in Williamsburg (1695; rebuilt 1705; restored 1928).

In the Federal era, as social institutions proliferated, this building form proved useful for many new purposes. The wings could be made longer or shorter to accommodate needed functions, while the center pavilion provided a visual focus. Degrees of importance could be indicated by architectural features such as (in roughly rising order of status) pedimented center pavilions, arched windows, cupolas, or porticos. In Connecticut, examples include the Old State House (place 88); academic buildings such as North College at Wesleyan University in Middletown (1825; burned 1906); health-care institutions such as the American Asylum for the Deaf and Dumb (1820; demolished); and even ambitious factories like Samuel Colt's Patent Fire Arms Manufacturing Company armory in Hartford (1855; burned 1864; rebuilt 1867).

The Middletown Alms House has a shallow central pavilion; the pediment that originally crowned it has been removed. Also gone is the cupola, which announced the building's civic function. According to early descriptions, the interior contained a workroom, kitchen, dungeon, steward's rooms, "victualling rooms," thirteen lodging rooms (four with fireplaces), and, in the attic, twenty more rooms, which must have been scarcely bigger than closets. Illustrating the type's flexibility, the alms house was converted to a factory in the 1850s; it now contains apartments, a gym, and a beauty salon.

In the twentieth century, Colonial Revival builders rediscovered the big-house model, employing it for institutional or civic buildings such as Stratford's town hall (1936), the Housatonic Valley High School, in Falls Village (1939), and the American School for the Deaf, in West Hartford (1921), the successor to the Hartford Asylum. For this new generation, the type offered not only flexibility and dignity, but also a link to a period of confidence and accomplishment, when Connecticut and the nation were building a new republic.

THE PLACE
MIDDLETOWN ALMS HOUSE

1813–1814
53 Warwick Street, Middletown

FURTHER READING

Loether, J. Paul, and Janice Cunningham. "Middletown Alms House." National Register of Historic Places, reference number 82003772, listed April 29, 1982.

FIGURE 149. Middletown Alms House, Middletown. Patrick L. Pinnell

59

MEETINGHOUSE TO CHURCH
WARREN CONGREGATIONAL CHURCH, WARREN

Sitting high and proud on its hilltop, the Warren church was one of the flood of new Congregational houses of worship built in the Federal era, when rising prosperity and new fashions spread from the cities to the countryside. At the same time, the disestablishment of the Congregational Church under Connecticut's new state constitution of 1818 forced religious denominations to compete for members, and architecture became one means of doing this.

In fact, the new constitution only made official changes that had been coming for some time. By 1818, Congregationalists were moving away from the Puritan insistence that the word "church" meant only the body of believers, and not a structure. They began referring to their meetinghouses as "churches" or "temples," and in some cases took votes forbidding use of the buildings for nonreligious purposes. With this came a shift to houses of worship that looked more like traditional churches: long and narrow rather than wide and short, with elaborate steeples centered on their façades. Romantic sensibilities, which saw a beautiful setting as conducive to meaningful worship, inspired adoption of the new Federal style with its emphasis on lightness and grace.

Begun in the constitutional year of 1818, the Warren church shows the effects of these changes. More complex in outline than the old boxy meetinghouses, it has a large rectangular block with a pitched roof for the main body; a smaller, shallow block for the vestibule; and a narrow tower rising above their junction. The boxes are subtly outlined with corner boards and molded cornices. On the vestibule, shallow pilasters and a pediment suggest a classical temple. A Georgian architect might have used the same motif, but here the pilasters are more slender, the moldings more complex, and flush-board siding makes them stand out more clearly.

Crowning the building, the steeple stretches upward, its movement emphasized by the pointed spire and the little railings running around each change in level. Everywhere there is a proliferation of the curved forms favored during the Federal period: fanlights on the doors, elliptical false windows in the tower, arches on the belfry, and curlicues at the top level of the steeple. The white paint is important,

FIGURE 150. Warren Congregational Church, Warren. Daniel Sterner

too, contrasting with the shadows to highlight even the smallest details.

Inside, windows on three sides flood the audience room with light. Galleries on the sides, supported by slender Ionic columns, and an arched central ceiling accentuate the length of the room (which actually is nearly square). Most remarkable is the high pulpit. Made of butternut stained to look like mahogany, it is notable for its lightness of proportion and complex geometry. As the room's principal focus, this architectural finery emphasizes the continued centrality of the sermon in Congregational worship.

The Warren church bears a strong family resemblance to others in western Connecticut, including ones built about the same time in East Canaan, North Cornwall, and Norfolk. Warren's is said to have been modeled on Norfolk's, and in turn it was specified as the model for Derby's, built in 1820. With their contemporaries in other places, these churches reflected changes in religious practice and in the role of organized religion in Connecticut society.

THE PLACE
WARREN CONGREGATIONAL CHURCH

1818–1820, James Jennings, builder. 1939, restored,
   J. Frederick Kelly. 1997, parish house, Bob Fox.
4 Sackett Hill Road, Warren. Open to the public.

FURTHER READING

Buggeln, Gretchen. *Temples of Grace: The Material Transformation of Connecticut's Churches, 1790–1840.* Hanover, N.H.: University Press of New England, 2003.

Clouette, Bruce, and Matthew Roth. "Warren Congregational Church." National Register of Historic Places, reference number 91001743, listed November 29, 1991.

Kelly, J. Frederick. *Early Connecticut Meetinghouses.* 2 vols. New York: Columbia University Press, 1948.

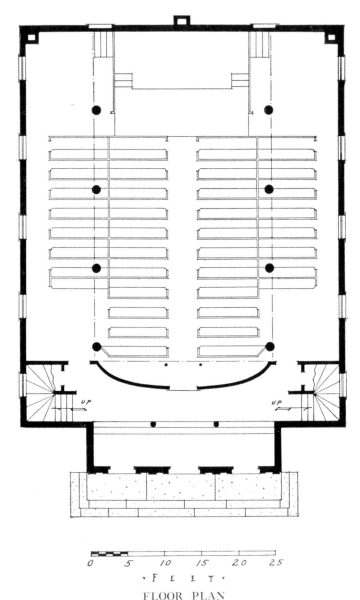

FLOOR PLAN

FIGURE 151. Warren Congregational Church, plan. From J. Frederick Kelly, *Early Connecticut Meetinghouses*, 1948. Reprinted with permission from Columbia University Press

60

One of the most notorious episodes of the Revolutionary War was the battle of Groton Heights, in 1781, at which a British invasion force killed more than eighty American defenders, most after they had surrendered. This event, termed a massacre by the Americans, inspired one of the first large-scale patriotic monuments in the United States. In the earliest years of the Republic, such monuments had been considered antidemocratic, even monarchical. But by the 1820s, as the Revolutionary generation died off, the desire to commemorate the war began to overcome those objections. Then the question became, how to design a monument?

In 1826, the Groton Monument Association was founded to erect a memorial to the victims of the Groton Heights massacre. Just a year earlier, a similar organization had begun work on the Bunker Hill Monument in Charlestown, Massachusetts, which was designed as a stone obelisk, 221 feet tall (it wasn't completed until 1843, well after the Groton monument). Originating in ancient Egypt, obelisks were considered appropriate for their association with death; since the eighteenth century they often were used as grave monuments. But Egyptian obelisks were single stones—objects. The Bunker Hill monument was much bigger—an obelisk-shaped *building*.

For Groton, Ithiel Town designed another obelisk/building, 127 feet tall. He didn't follow the ancient form precisely, though. Instead, he truncated the top to create a viewing platform and set the shaft atop a square pedestal, increasing its resemblance to a gigantic grave marker. For the one-hundredth anniversary of the battle, in 1881, the Monument Association enclosed the platform and added a pyramidal cap. This raised the monument's height to 135 feet and gave it a more classical appearance.

Town's design employed a set of characteristics for monuments long established in Europe. First of all, the monument captures attention. Towering over the surrounding landscape from its hilltop location, the Groton obelisk can be seen from miles away (even farther in the 1830s, when much of the countryside had been cleared for farming). With its tall, narrow proportions, the obelisk clearly marks a particular spot. "This is the place!" it says.

Up close, inscriptions indicate the monument's function. One, over the door, describes the massacre. Just inside the door, a marble plaque lists the names of the dead, while opposite it, another plaque bears an inscription from the biblical book of Judges: "Zebulon and Naphtali were a people that jeoparded [*sic*] their lives unto the death, in the high places of the field."

Even without the inscriptions, visitors would have understood much of the monument's meaning. Then as now, Egyptian civilization was identified with death rituals. Perhaps Town's decision to give the monument a pedestal, making it look like a grave marker, was intended to make the funerary connection more explicit. The use of a motif from antiquity, coupled with the rough-faced stone blocks, also made the monument seem like something ancient and primitive, battered by the passage of time. To nineteenth-century minds, this would have inspired feelings of awe and reverence, emotions deemed appropriate to those contemplating the heroic sacrifice of the Revolutionary soldiers.

After the Civil War, the trauma of which touched every community in the state, a memorial to war dead came to be seen as almost a necessary feature of any town center or green. The characteristics of the Groton monument— size and visibility, commemorative inscriptions, and an appeal to the emotions—continued to influence these monuments.

THE PLACE
GROTON BATTLE MONUMENT

1826–1830, Ithiel Town, with A. J. Davis
Monument Street, Groton. Open to the public.

FURTHER READING
Luyster, Constance. "Fort Griswold." National Register of Historic
  Places, reference number 70000694, listed October 6, 1970.

FIGURE 152. Groton Battle Monument, Groton. Daniel Sterner

61

CHURCH IN SOCIETY

SAINT MARY OF THE IMMACULATE CONCEPTION CATHOLIC CHURCH COMPLEX, BALTIC

Baltic, located in the town of Sprague, was a mill town, but since the massive granite mill burned in 1999, the village's dominant architectural presence has been a row of big brick buildings affiliated with the Roman Catholic Church. Such complexes appear in almost every Connecticut mill town. Built by the workers themselves (not the Protestant mill owners), they offered the only rivals in scale and solidity to the mill buildings and stand as reminders of the immigrants who provided labor for Connecticut's industries and changed the face of its population.

It took decades for the first Catholic immigrants, Irish laborers arriving in the 1820s, to overcome long-standing hostility to Catholicism. By 1872, though, Connecticut became an independent diocese with its own bishop. In the years that followed, as Catholic immigrants began arriving in great numbers from Italy and Eastern Europe, the Diocese of Hartford intentionally worked to accommodate these new arrivals.

Between the antebellum Irish and Germans and the later Italians and Eastern Europeans came the French Canadians, who began arriving in numbers in the 1860s. One of the places they first settled was Baltic, where the Sprague family, industrialists from Rhode Island, erected a huge cotton mill in 1857 (for greater control, they engineered the incorporation of the town of Sprague in 1860). By 1864, approximately half the mill's fourteen hundred employees were from Canada, and a Catholic mission church had been built on a hill outside town. The church received a resident pastor in 1866, and in 1874 he recruited Dutch nuns from the Sisters of Charity to open a parochial school, Saint Joseph's, and the Academy of the Holy Family.

Fire destroyed the mill in 1887, workers left, and Baltic remained a virtual ghost town until 1899, when Pawcatuck industrialist Frederick Sayles opened the Baltic Manufacturing Company in the reconstructed mill. With the mill going again, Saint Mary's built a big new church in 1911—on West Main Street rather than outside the town. Over the years, the Academy and Saint Joseph's erected new buildings, too. Although enrollment dwindled after the mill closed in 1967, the schools rebounded in the '70s as the Diocese of Norwich (separated from Hartford in

FIGURE 153. Saint Mary of the Immaculate Conception Catholic Church complex, Baltic. Connecticut Trust for Historic Preservation

1953) adopted policies to reinvigorate Catholic education. The Sisters of Charity, granted independence from their European order in 1970, made Saint Mary's convent their motherhouse. Thus, unlike many churches and church-related institutions, the buildings on West Main Street remain active.

The creation of complexes like this is characteristic of Catholicism. To be sure, Protestants established educational and charitable institutions as well, but they rarely brought them together in one place. Appearing in Congregationalist Connecticut, these Catholic complexes strongly asserted the immigrants' presence in a society

FIGURE 154. Saint Mary of the Immaculate Conception Catholic Church complex, Baltic. Connecticut Trust for Historic Preservation

activities that take place here. And finally they spoke of the faith and work and contributions—often sacrifices—of the faithful who made it all possible.

that did not always welcome them. More than that, the complexes also proclaimed a distinctively Catholic notion of religion and its place in society. They spoke of the unmarried clergy and religious who lived in community and dedicated their lives to service. They spoke of the importance of education that incorporates religious instruction. They spoke of the church itself as a center of daily worship and of faith as the foundation for the

THE PLACES
SAINT MARY OF THE IMMACULATE CONCEPTION CATHOLIC CHURCH
1911. 1930, rectory.
70 West Main Street, Baltic
SAINT MARY CONVENT, SISTERS OF CHARITY MOTHERHOUSE
1888
54 West Main Street, Baltic
ACADEMY OF THE HOLY FAMILY
1914 and later
54 West Main Street, Baltic
SAINT JOSEPH SCHOOL
1950, Alfred Reinhardt
10 School Hill Road, Baltic

FURTHER READING
Roth, Matthew, et al. "Baltic Historic District." National Register of Historic Places, reference number 87001247, listed August 3, 1987.
Williams, Peter W. *Houses of God: Region, Religion, and Architecture in America.* New York: Pilgrim, 1995.

62

THERAPEUTIC LANDSCAPE
THE INSTITUTE OF LIVING,
HARTFORD

Nineteenth-century Romantic thought believed strongly in the restorative qualities of nature. As Frederick Law Olmsted (1822–1903), the Hartford-born pioneer of American landscape architecture, wrote: "The enjoyment of scenery employs the mind without fatigue and yet exercises it, tranquilizes it and yet enlivens it; and thus gives the effect of refreshing rest and reinvigoration of the whole system." This belief lay behind the development of urban parks in that period. New York's Central Park, by Olmsted and Calvert Vaux, is the best-known example, although Hartford's Bushnell Park actually came slightly before it.

Hartford also boasts a more direct example of landscape design for healing. In 1824 one of the country's first mental hospitals, the Connecticut Retreat for the Insane (later renamed the Hartford Retreat), opened here. Located on the city's southern outskirts, the Retreat was housed in a pedimented building with side wings, very like the Middletown Alms House (place 58). By 1860, the Retreat's superintendent, John S. Butler, wanted to improve the hospital's grounds, which he considered rough and wet and "of little use." He envisioned a setting that would contribute to the treatment of patients—a "therapeutic Arcadia."

Butler commissioned a design from Olmsted and Vaux. However, with the outbreak of the Civil War, Olmsted left to run the United States Sanitary Commission. Jacob Weidenmann (1829–1893), a Swiss immigrant, was engaged to finalize and execute the plan. Trained in architecture, engineering, and horticulture, he was overseeing the design and construction of Bushnell Park at the same time.

Though smaller, the Retreat landscape resembled Central and Bushnell Parks. Around the edges of the property, dense plantings created a buffer against the growing city. Inside this were rolling lawns dotted with trees, either specimens or in clumps. Grading and drainage improvements solved the wetness problem, forming a base for winding paths and roads. A flower garden and a small activities building, called the Museum, provided opportunities for patient therapy. In 1868 Vaux, with his partner Frederick Clark Withers, expanded the Retreat building, adding verandas and turrets and decorative gable trusses that give the structure a picturesque outline in harmony with the landscape.

Over the years the Retreat—now called the Institute of Living and affiliated with Hartford Hospital—continued to grow. New buildings and parking lots have replaced much of the planted outer buffer. The central area remains largely unchanged, with its lawns, curving paths, and naturalistic clumps of shrubs and trees. Some of the specimen trees survive from Weidenmann's day.

In Butler's vision, this landscape served a broader audience than just the Retreat's patients. From the first, he opened the grounds to the public, to demonstrate "that the externals of a lunatic asylum need not be repulsive, and … that its inner life is not without its cheerful, home-like aspects." He signaled this intention by calling the grounds "Retreat Park." The Institute of Living still continues this tradition, offering this peaceful, verdant setting to patients and public alike for "refreshing rest and reinvigoration of the whole system."

THE PLACE
THE INSTITUTE OF LIVING

(Originally Connecticut Retreat for the Insane)
Buildings, 1822 and later. Landscape, 1861–1863, Olmsted and Vaux; modified and executed by Jacob Weidenmann.
200 Retreat Avenue, Hartford. Open to the public.

FURTHER READING

Favretti, Rudy J. *Jacob Weidenmann: Pioneer Landscape Architect.* Hartford, Conn.: Cedar Hill Cemetery Foundation, in cooperation with Wesleyan University Press, 2007.
Weidenmann, Jacob. *Beautifying Country Homes: A Handbook of Landscape Gardening.* New York: Orange Judd, 1870. Facsimile, American Life Foundation, 1978.

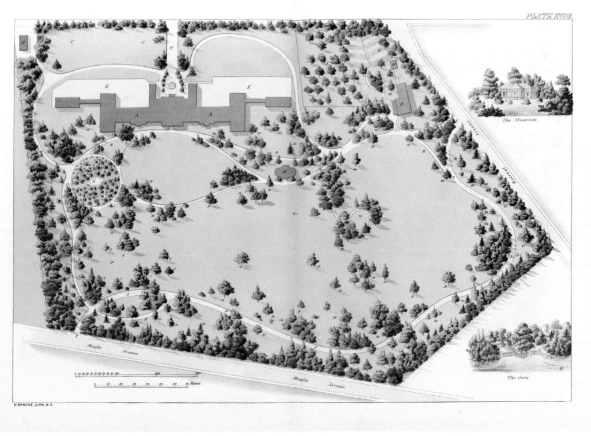

FIGURE 155. Retreat for the Insane (Institute of Living), Hartford, plan. From Jacob Weidenmann, *Beautifying Country Homes*, 1870, plate XVIII. Collection of the New-York Historical Society

63

HOLY RETREAT

PLAINVILLE CAMPGROUND, PLAINVILLE

Although suburban houses crowd around it, the Plainville Campground still feels like a peaceful retreat from the busy world. It has been that since its founding in 1865 by the New Haven District of the Methodist Episcopal Church as a place to find tranquility and reconnect with God.

The campground traces its lineage to frontier revival meetings held at the close of the eighteenth century. Intended as religious events, camp meetings from the first also provided an escape from daily routines. For city dwellers, they offered access to nature; for isolated rural folk, a chance to socialize. In other words, they were forerunners to vacations.

Beginning in the 1830s, many of these temporary gatherings became institutionalized as multiday annual events held at permanent campgrounds with distinct arrangements and architecture. The model, for Plainville and many others, was the campground at Oak Bluffs, on Martha's Vineyard. At the center of the Plainville Campground is the Auditorium, built in 1902, an open pavilion for worship services and other gatherings. Congregations and other church groups built cottages in a big circle around the Auditorium, and smaller cottages line "avenues" (scarcely wider than footpaths, really) radiating from the circle.

The gingerbread cottages follow the model developed on Martha's Vineyard: toylike frame buildings with their narrow end to the street and wide double doors opening onto a front porch or platform. The tightly packed cottages with their big porches and wide-open doors fostered social interaction; above all, camp meetings were and are communal events.

This cottage form evolved from the tents used at earlier camp meetings, which were erected on platforms and opened up during the daytime, and which often bore decorative trim. Characterized by their small size, light construction, and plentiful but fragile ornament, the cottages follow not only the plan and decoration of the tents, but also their insubstantiality, which means many haven't survived to the present. The form was soon copied for secular vacation cottages as well. Examples can be seen in many of Connecticut's nineteenth-century lakeside and seaside resorts, built by vacationers from New York

FIGURE 156. The Circle, Plainville Campground, Plainville.
Connecticut Trust for Historic Preservation

or from the state's own cities intent on rediscovering the countryside.

Most of the Plainville cottages were built between about 1880 and 1910, with a few as late as 1925. Notable ones include "Much Room" at 16 Meriden Avenue, also known as the Mushroom Cottage for its unusual cutout porch. The building's sinuous curves have an Art Nouveau flavor rarely found in Connecticut. Round-arched door and windows distinguish 16 Hartford Avenue. More typical is 11 Meriden Avenue, which has a two-story porch under the low roof, a common configuration. The wooded setting is important as well; camp meeting planners typically chose groves for their cooling shade and a sense of enclosure and intimacy.

Like most of its peers, the Plainville Campground

gradually became secularized. By 1901 it also offered Chautauquas—educational and cultural programs that didn't necessarily have religious connections. In 1957, the Methodist Church sold the campground to a nondenominational association that holds the land and leases lots to cottage owners. While the association continues to offer religious events, the campground's focus remains the distinctive combination of nature and society that has defined it since 1865.

THE PLACE
PLAINVILLE CAMPGROUND
(New Haven District Campground)
1865 and later
320 Camp Street, Plainville

FURTHER READING
Pope, Arthur K. *The Heart Strangely Warmed: The Chautauqua and Methodist Campgrounds at Plainville, Connecticut.* Victoria, B.C.: Trafford, 2006.
Weiss, Ellen. *City in the Woods: The Life and Design of an American Camp Meeting on Martha's Vineyard.* Boston: Northeastern University Press, 1998.
Zimmerman, Sarah. "New Haven District Campground." National Register of Historic Places, reference number 80004065, listed May 19, 1980.

FIGURE 157. 11 Meriden Avenue, Plainville Campground, Plainville. Connecticut Trust for Historic Preservation

6 4

MODEL SCHOOL

LOCUST AVENUE SCHOOL, DANBURY

As Connecticut's industrial cities prospered after the Civil War, they struggled to provide schools for their rapidly growing populations. At the same time, new theories of instruction and architecture were reshaping education and school design.

Warren R. Briggs (1850–1933), the architect of the Locust Avenue School, had an extensive practice in Bridgeport. He also produced commercial and institutional buildings across the state, including county courthouses in Bridgeport, Danbury, and Willimantic. Briggs considered himself an expert in school construction. In 1899 he published *Modern American School Buildings*, which contained up-to-date information on classroom size and fixtures, as well as lighting, heating, and ventilation.

In his book, Briggs included views and plans of the Locust Avenue School to illustrate his ideas about scientific school architecture. The classrooms, designed to accommodate between fifty and sixty students each, are laid out with banks of windows to provide unobstructed light from the pupils' left sides (the assumption being they all would write with their right hands). The actual glass surface, according to Briggs, should equal at least one-sixth of the room's floor space. The windows should be grouped in a continuous bank to minimize shadows cast by piers or mullions. Other facilities include cloakrooms for students and basement playrooms for exercise in bad weather.

Safety features in the school include masonry construction and slow-burning timber framing on the interior for fire resistance. Staircases are separated from the inner structure and enclosed to slow the spread of fire and prevent students from falling over railings.

Heating and particularly ventilation were a common concern of nineteenth-century builders as buildings grew bigger, accommodating larger numbers of people, and as germ theory advanced understanding of the spread of diseases. Briggs had been experimenting with ventilation systems since the 1870s, with financial support and technical suggestions from Nathaniel Wheeler, a Bridgeport industrialist. The result, patented in 1883, was called the Wheeler system, and Briggs specified it for all his school. In his words, "A device by which the heat-generating surface of each room could be concentrated and controlled, and the centralization of the entire heating-surface of the building at or near its centre, were its principal features." Careful proportion of incoming and outgoing flues and the relative position and amount of heating surface for each room were key to its successful application. Briggs highlighted this system by treating its chimneys and turret-like intake ventilators as decorative features.

Originally an elementary school, the Locust Avenue building was taken over in 1905 by the Danbury State Normal School (which eventually became Western Connecticut State University) and used as a model school for teacher training until 1965. Since 1976 it has housed the city's Alternative High School, continuing the tradition of progressive education embodied in Briggs's design.

THE PLACE
LOCUST AVENUE SCHOOL

(Now Alternative Center for Education)
1896, Warren R. Briggs
26 Locust Avenue, Danbury

FURTHER READING

Briggs, Warren Richard. *Modern American School Buildings, Being a Treatise upon, and Designs for, the Construction of School Buildings.* New York: John Wiley & Sons, 1899.

Devlin, William E. "Locust Avenue School." National Register of Historic Places, reference number 85001162, listed May 30, 1985.

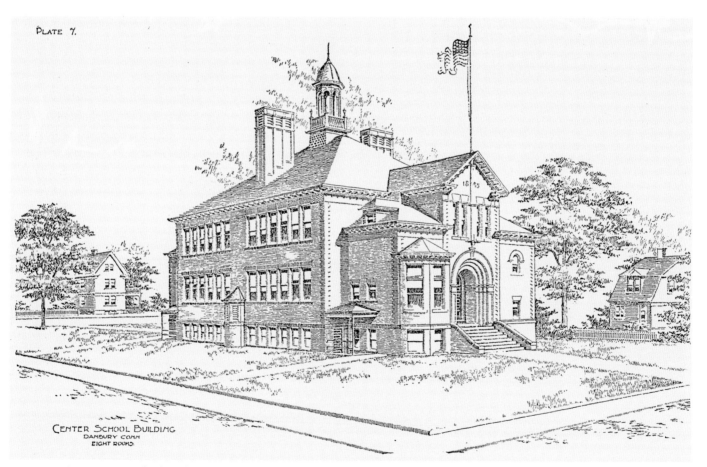

FIGURE 158. Locust Avenue School, Danbury. From Warren R. Briggs, *Modern American School Buildings*, 1899

65

BUILT FOR HEALING
THE SEASIDE, WATERFORD

Can a building heal disease? Not literally, but one might be designed to foster successful treatment. And a special kind of treatment might require a very special building. That is what led the State of Connecticut to build the Seaside sanatorium.

Before the twentieth century, there was no cure for tuberculosis. But by the turn of the century, European researchers found that prolonged exposure to sunshine and ocean air could be effective treatment for the bone and glandular forms of tuberculosis commonly found in children. The Connecticut State Tuberculosis Commission introduced this treatment, known as heliotherapy, to the United States in 1918, establishing a children's sanatorium in a converted hotel at Niantic. In 1930, the commission began planning a permanent facility, the first in the United States specifically designed for heliotherapy for children. Aware that they were breaking new ground, the commissioners deliberately chose to use the most up-to-date construction and equipment, and just as deliberately selected a nationally known architect, Cass Gilbert (1859–1934).

Gilbert's design shows how a traditionalist might approach new architectural needs: by searching out possible models from the past and adapting them to different purposes. This was based on the belief that there is no such thing as starting from scratch, and that the past could suggest designs for new functions. Writing in *Pencil Points* after his father's death, Cass Gilbert Jr. identified the style of the hospital as "Norman farmhouse." But, he added, the functional requirements "made it impossible to follow any style so that the architect had to evolve something of his own to meet the requirements."

The hospital building is a large, U-shaped structure facing the water. Each room opened onto stepped, south-facing terraces where swimsuit-clad children soaked up the rays, even in winter. The tiered massing certainly has no precedent in Norman architecture; it is more reminiscent of something like a pueblo. But it is executed in a believable Norman vocabulary of brick and stone, with big arches, steep-pitched roof and dormers, and a slender, French-looking flèche atop the ventilation cupola. The rough textures and earthy colors lend the complex an air of informality in keeping with the aim of creating

FIGURE 159.
The Seaside, Waterford,
ca. 1940. Seaside
Sanitarium, PG 170,
State Archives,
Connecticut State
Library

a noninstitutional atmosphere. This extended to the interior, where descriptions mention paint colors chosen to harmonize with the autumn foliage outside.

Subsidiary buildings, including a nurses' dormitory and houses for the superintendent and medical staff, resemble the hospital in style, although architecturally they are more orthodox. Drawings and contemporary references firmly identify Gilbert, who died before the complex was dedicated, as the designer only of the main building, but the dormitory is attributed to him on the basis of indirect evidence. The smaller houses are attributed to Fred S. Langdon, a New London architect.

Antibiotic treatment for tuberculosis, introduced in the 1940s, rapidly reduced the need for residential institutions like Seaside. The sanatorium closed in the 1950s. In 1961 the building was transferred to the Department of Mental Retardation; it closed for good in 1997. After years of neglect and an interrupted redevelopment attempt, the state decided to turn the waterfront site into a park. It is not certain that the buildings will survive, but their picturesque design, more like a seaside estate or hotel than a hospital, could easily be at home in a park.

THE PLACE
THE SEASIDE

1931–1934, Cass Gilbert, some buildings by Fred S.
    Langdon
36 Shore Road, Waterford

FURTHER READING

Cunningham, Jan. "The Seaside." National Register of Historic
    Places, reference number 95001007, listed August 15, 1995.
Harrison, Ann, and Mark H. Jones. "Sun and Sea Harnessed to
    Fight Tuberculosis." *Hog River Journal* 5, no. 2 (Spring 2007):
    14–19.

66

AGING REVOLUTIONARY

ANSONIA HIGH SCHOOL

In 1937, Ansonia was on the cutting edge of American architecture. Its new high school, designed by the Swiss-born architect William Lescaze (1896–1969), was attracting worldwide attention as a model of the latest in modern architecture. Closer to home, many could appreciate the school's up-to-date facilities, but were baffled—outraged, even—by its appearance.

Time has caught up with this revolutionary building, rendering its trend-setting features commonplace. Now it looks like thousands of other schools across the country, and people wonder what the fuss was all about, if they even know there was a fuss. But Ansonia High School was among the first of its kind, the work of an architect who played a pioneering role in introducing European Modernism to the United States. It was just the second significant public building of the Modernist movement in Connecticut (following the Wadsworth Atheneum's Avery Wing, which was Modernist only on its interior).

Then as now, ribbon windows, a flat roof, and the absence of applied ornament caught the viewer's attention first. But the plan was innovative, too. Most schools of the time were built in a T shape, with a long block of classrooms fronting on the street and an auditorium projecting from the center of the rear. (Hamden High School, built in 1935, follows this traditional pattern.) Lescaze wrapped the Ansonia High School around the edges of its lot in a C shape that left space at the center for playing fields. In keeping with Modernist ideas of functionality, he made the various parts of the building clearly identifiable: the auditorium by its splayed walls following the seating plan, the gymnasium by its high windows, the classrooms by their long window strips, and the offices by their stone cladding.

Additions and alterations have obscured the original design somewhat. The porch between the offices and auditorium was enclosed in 1961, when another classroom wing was built in the rear, encroaching on the fields. A more complete overhaul in 2000 gave the building a new brick skin. It also reduced the size of the windows, though they still combine with stucco panels to suggest continuous strips.

Ansonia High School was produced in a moment of social and architectural optimism: the Depression was easing, and a new way of building promised to harness the latest scientific and technological developments for the benefit of ordinary people. Since then, World War II, the Cold War, Vietnam, terrorist attacks, and growing social and economic inequality have eroded that optimism, while many of the school's experimental features have proved less than successful. The inexpensive industrial materials have not always worn well, and spaces designed for specific functions have not always adjusted easily to changing needs.

But however altered, Ansonia High School is still a reminder of that 1930s dream, and of some of the positive lessons of Modernism. These include the determination to examine functional needs and meet them in imaginative ways unconstrained by traditional solutions, and the resolve to consider carefully a building's basic form and materials, and not simply rely on applied decoration to make it attractive.

THE PLACE
ANSONIA HIGH SCHOOL

(Now Ansonia Middle School)

1935–1937, William Lescaze; Vernon F. Sears, associate. 1961, additions. 2000, remodeled, Kaestle Boos Associates.

115 Howard Avenue, Ansonia

FURTHER READING

"Ansonia High School, Ansonia, Conn." *Architectural Forum*, December 1937, 487–491.

Benassi, Martin. "Ansonia High School's Historic 'International Style.'" *AIA/CT News*, March/April 1998.

FIGURE 160. Ansonia High School (now Ansonia Middle School), Ansonia. Martin A. Benassi, AIA

67

COMFORT FOR THE DYING

CONNECTICUT HOSPICE, BRANFORD

One of the great forward steps in humane health care in the twentieth century was the introduction of the hospice movement in the 1970s, to provide palliative physical and emotional care to dying patients. First developed in England, the concept was brought to the United States by Florence Wald, then dean of the Yale School of Nursing, in 1971. She helped found the Connecticut Hospice, the country's first, which constructed the first American building specifically designed for a hospice. Paul Goldberger, then architecture critic for the *New York Times*, called this "a significant event in the annals of social architecture."

The architect, Lo-Yi Chan (b. 1932), was chosen precisely because he had no experience in health care facilities, and therefore no preconceptions to overcome. He embarked on a period of study, epitomizing the Modernist principle of careful research to develop an architectural solution suited to particular needs. Chan's goal was to create "an environment that would be both serene and familiar to its occupants." He did this by making wards bright and cheery, connected via greenhouse-like outer corridors to outdoor terraces. Each ward held four beds, to provide social contact. Anterooms, vestibules, private counseling or visiting rooms, and a long entry driveway allowed patients, visitors, or staff members to withdraw and confront their emotions. Warm materials and ample lighting fostered a welcoming atmosphere, while not attempting to deny the inescapable institutional nature of the facility.

The building's fate was to be successful and to be outgrown. After much debate, the hospice moved, in 2001. The original facility has been converted to a convent and altered. The public is welcome at daily Mass, but otherwise the building is private.

The present Connecticut Hospice (pictured) is a former corporate headquarters overlooking Long Island Sound. There were fears that its size and character would be incompatible with the hospice's values, but the architects who renovated it followed many of the design principles established by Chan, aiming for a similar sense of openness and providing similar transitional spaces. The scenic waterfront location offers a beach, paths, and terraces with views of the Sound, all in keeping with Chan's finding—echoing Frederick Law Olmsted—that "beauty is healing."

The Connecticut Hospice was part of a broader movement in health care to provide personalized, humane care for patients in homelike environments. Another expression of this movement is Griffin Hospital, in Derby, which beginning in the 1990s has remodeled its facility to be focused on the patients' experience rather than the staff's convenience. Griffin became a leading member of the Planetree Alliance, a nonprofit organization dedicated to humanizing health care, with design as one of its areas of interest.

As Paul Goldberger wrote of the original hospice, health care facilities "remind us that architecture does not exist as pure form, that it is, inevitably, tied to certain social experiences and to certain social goals." Attention to the whole person in health-care design can contribute to healing.

THE PLACES
CONNECTICUT HOSPICE
(Now Monastery of the Glorious Cross)
1973–1980, Lo-Yi Chan of Prentice & Chan, Olhausen. Altered.
61 Burban Drive, Branford
CONNECTICUT HOSPICE
http://hospice.com
1982. 2000, Perkins/Eastman; landscape, Jack Curtis & Associates.
100 Double Beach Road, Branford

FURTHER READING
Chan, Lo-Yi. "Hospice: A New Building Type to Comfort the Dying." *AIA Journal* 65, no. 12 (December 1976): 42–45.
Verderber, Stephen, and Ben J. Refuerzo. *Innovations in Hospice Architecture*. London: Taylor & Francis, 2006.

FIGURE 161. Connecticut Hospice, Branford. Robert Egleston

Part Nine

DESIGNERS, BUILDERS, AND CLIENTS

Building is a communal activity; it requires designers, builders, and clients. In the modern world, financiers and developers must be added to the list. All of them contribute to the final product, bringing their own needs and ideas and services and skills to bear on the task at hand, in proportions that vary by project. One other factor to consider is the process of design— what motivates the search for architectural ideas, where do they come from, and how are they incorporated into new works? Sometimes roles may be shared, but for anything much bigger than a toolshed, it is impossible for one person to fill all the parts. That is for the best, since the finest results very often arise from the interactions among the players.

68

MASTER BUILDER

EPAPHRODITUS CHAMPION HOUSE, EAST HADDAM

After the American Revolution, a burst of construction was sparked by the financial successes of Connecticut merchants and mariners who expanded trade once they were released from restrictions placed on them under British rule. Epaphroditus Champion was one of these merchants, a member of a prominent family with connections from Colchester to Litchfield. In 1794, when he built a new house overlooking East Haddam's Upper Landing on the Connecticut River, Champion turned to William Sprats (ca. 1757–1810), a Litchfield joiner who had already built houses for Champion's brother Henry in Colchester and for his cousin and brother-in-law, Julius Deming, in Litchfield.

The square house sits on a steep hillside with terraces stepping down to a gambrel-roofed countinghouse near the landing site. The property projects an air of restrained classicism, seen in ornamental features that reach a climax in the front porch, a miniature classical temple with Ionic columns, a full entablature, and a pediment. All the decoration follows rules of composition and proportion laid down by Renaissance architects based on their study of Roman ruins. These rules were communicated through architectural pattern books rather than taught by master builder to apprentice.

This classicism is not just a matter of details, but also how they are put together. Unlike earlier houses such as Ebenezer Grant's (place 87), where a Baroque doorway is pasted onto a plain base, the Champion House is an entire composition where all the parts work together to form a unified whole. Quoins and moldings outline the edges of the house. The other architectural elements relate to one another in size and type, like the similar but not quite identical porches at the front and side doors, the repetition of the bulging frieze on the porches and the window hoods, and the repeated rhythm of small blocks (called modillions) on the cornices.

Not much is known of William Sprats's life. A British soldier taken prisoner during the Revolution, he remained in Connecticut after the war and worked as a joiner in Litchfield roughly from 1782 to 1797 before moving to Vermont. In addition to the Deming and Champion commissions, Sprats built the Litchfield Courthouse (1795; burned 1886) and the Zenas Cowles house in Farmington

(1790). A number of other buildings are attributed to him, some plausibly, some less so.

Sprats clearly had some background in building, and his works show a level of sophistication that had been uncommon in inland Connecticut before the war. Surprisingly, they don't look particularly English. The boxy outlines, timber construction, and clapboard siding belong to the prewar New England vernacular. This is a reminder that building is a social process. Designers can't get too far ahead of their clients' taste. Sprats's Connecticut buildings represent a compromise between the classical detailing and careful proportions of the era's stylish modern design and what his clients found an acceptable level of innovation. For Champion and his neighbors, the coordinated design and classical components of his house would have been signs of his, and the new nation's, growing refinement.

THE PLACE
EPAPHRODITUS CHAMPION HOUSE

1794, William Sprats
5 Landing Hill Road, East Haddam. Private residence.

FURTHER READING

Keiner, Hal. "East Haddam Historic District." National Register of Historic Places, reference number 83001273, listed April 29, 1983.

Warren, William L. "William Sprats and His Civil and Ecclesiastical Architecture in New England." *Old-Time New England* 44, no. 3 (Winter 1954): 65–78, and 44, no. 4 (Spring 1954): 103–114.

———. "William Sprats, Master Joiner: Connecticut's Federalist Architect." *Connecticut Antiquarian* 9, no. 2 (December 1957): 11–21.

FIGURE 162. Epaphroditus Champion House, East Haddam. Patrick L. Pinnell

69

FROM THE INSIDE OUT
PHELPS-HATHEWAY HOUSE, SUFFIELD

Throughout the seventeenth and eighteenth centuries, the Connecticut River Valley, stretching from Middletown to Hartford to Springfield and beyond, had been something of a place apart, marked by its distinct social and artistic culture. But in the years following the American Revolution, that began to change. This house illustrates the architectural side of that shift, from the provincial Baroque of the River Gods to international Neoclassicism. This change was fueled by the experiences of clients and builders who saw fashionable new buildings in coastal cities and who also had access to architectural pattern books.

Shem Burbank built the original house, a typical Connecticut Valley merchant's dwelling of the mid-eighteenth century, two stories high, with a central chimney and extensive paneling. Oliver Phelps, who bought the property in 1788, was one of the richest men in the country, a land speculator who owned millions of acres in New York State and the Ohio Country. He remodeled the exterior, adding a heavy gambrel roof and Georgian details such as quoins, window caps, and a columned entry porch.

Just a few years later, Phelps added the north wing. On the outside, the addition echoes the remodeled main house, with the same gambrel roof, quoins, and columned entry. The interiors are another matter. Here, provincial paneling gives way to the latest Neoclassical design. Each space is framed in correctly proportioned pilasters and cornices, with paneled dados and eared door and window surrounds. All are highlighted with delicately carved moldings, festoons, and urns. Covering the walls are imported French papers in intricate arabesque designs inspired by Pompeiian wall paintings. Complementing each other, the woodwork and papers create a stunningly opulent environment that would not have been out of place in Boston or Newport.

This shift in fashion was paralleled by the introduction of a new generation of builders, and the beginning of the emergence of professional architects. The Phelps House north wing is the first documented work of Asher Benjamin (1773–1845), who crafted Ionic column capitals and other woodwork. Benjamin later became an architect and published the first American builder's guide, *The*

Country Builder's Assistant, in 1797, followed in later years by six other widely influential handbooks for architects and builders.

Oliver Phelps's luxurious interior decoration represents a common pattern in architectural development, the introduction of new styles through interior decoration or garden design. A building is a big investment; if an owner takes a chance and it doesn't work out, the results will be painfully obvious for a long time. It's safer to experiment in something less visible, less permanent than an entire building: wallpaper, perhaps, or a gazebo. If that works, *then* remodel the whole house. At the same time, interiors and gardens are also more subject to later alteration as other new styles begin to emerge. The survival of Oliver Phelps's Neoclassical woodwork and wallpapers is little short of miraculous.

THE PLACE
PHELPS-HATHEWAY HOUSE
(Burbank-Phelps House / Hatheway House)

www.ctlandmarks.org

1761. 1788–1789, Eliphalet King. 1794–1795, Thomas Hayden, Ashbel King, John Lewis, Asher Benjamin.

55 South Main Street, Suffield. Open to the public.

FURTHER READING

Brockmeyer, Christine B. "Hatheway House." National Register of Historic Places, reference number 75001934, listed August 6, 1975, amended by Bruce Clouette, September 5, 2008.

Ward, Gerald W. R., and William N. Hosley Jr., eds. *The Great River: Art and Society of the Connecticut Valley, 1635–1820*. Meriden, Conn.: Stinehour Press for the Wadsworth Atheneum, Hartford, 1985.

FIGURE 163. Phelps-Hatheway House, Suffield, chamber. William Hosley

70

ARCHITECTURE FROM BOOKS

WILLIS BRISTOL HOUSE, NEW HAVEN

To judge from their houses, the inhabitants of Wooster Square, one of New Haven's most fashionable antebellum neighborhoods, were a cosmopolitan group, acquainted with ancient Greece, Renaissance France, rural Italy, even far-off India. Yet few of these people had been abroad. Nor had their architects; it's unlikely that Henry Austin (1804–1891) traveled farther than New Jersey. Yet the house Austin created for factory owner and banker Willis Bristol is a fantasia of cusped arches, windows with sinuous muntins and glints of stained glass, and columns balanced uneasily on narrow turned bases, all derived from the buildings of India. How did he do it?

It all came from books. In the early nineteenth century, with limited opportunities for travel and no formal architectural education, architects looked to books as among their most important tools. Earlier ones, such as Asher Benjamin's *The Country Builder's Assistant* of 1797, provided guidance to builders in the correct use of classical columns and moldings, or in structural intricacies like curving stairs. Later writers, such as Andrew Jackson Downing, addressed clients looking for designs that would fit harmoniously into the natural landscape.

In New Haven, Ithiel Town amassed the biggest architectural library in the country. Town generously shared his collection with local designers such as Austin, who is believed to have been a carpenter before launching his architectural practice. Austin himself collected architecture books and probably bought a number when Town's library was sold after his death in 1844.

The Bristol House's exotic ornament can be traced to travel books about India, such as illustrations in Thomas and William Daniell's *Oriental Scenery*, published in the early nineteenth century, or English landscape designer Humphry Repton's proposal for remodeling the Royal Pavilion at Brighton, England. Although Repton's design wasn't built, he published it in 1808, along with a manifesto promoting Indian architecture as less expensive and more flexible than classical or Gothic styles. On the Bristol House, the main-floor and basement windows are copied directly from Repton.

One consequence of this way of building is a certain disconnect between the book-based ornament and the underlying building. Apart from its Indian embellishment,

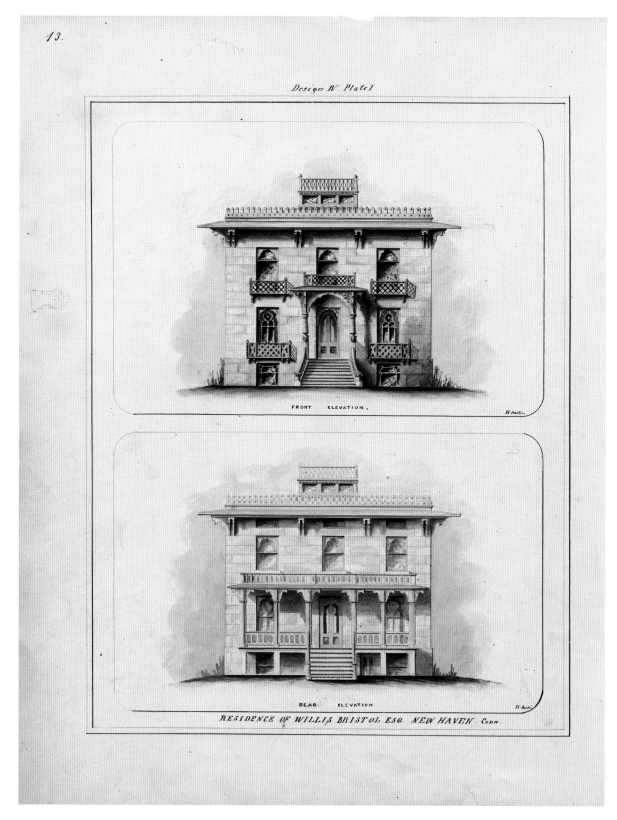

FIGURE 164.
Willis Bristol
House, New
Haven, elevation
drawings by
Henry Austin.
Henry Austin
Papers, 1851–
1865 (inclusive).
Manuscripts and
Archives, Yale
University

FIGURE 165. Willis Bristol House, doorway. Patrick L. Pinnell

the Bristol house is a typical cubical house of its time. This common form provided a plain background that could be dressed up in any way that appealed to the client's taste or the architect's inventiveness. There is a Grecian version a couple of doors away from the Bristol House (600 Chapel Street), built just a year earlier.

Henry Austin was a designer and builder, not a writer. He left behind two volumes of drawings, now at Yale, but no text to explain or promote his designs. Austin must have done his marketing in person, and done it well; his biographer, James F. O'Gorman, marvels that he managed to persuade no-nonsense businessmen like Willis Bristol to construct such flamboyant buildings.

Popular history remembers Austin chiefly for exotic designs like the Bristol House, which certainly show him at his most inventive. But they represent only a brief phase in a career that lasted some fifty years. Tastes changed, and after a brief moment in the sun, Austin seems to have retreated into the background, a skillful and locally influential designer, but never again a standout one.

THE PLACE
WILLIS BRISTOL HOUSE

1845, Henry Austin. 1993, restored, Douglas McIntosh. 584 Chapel Street, New Haven. Private.

FURTHER READING

Brown, Elizabeth Mills. *New Haven: A Guide to Architecture and Urban Design*. New Haven, Conn.: Yale University Press, 1976.
Luyster, Constance. "Wooster Square Historic District." National Register of Historic Places, reference number 71000914, listed August 5, 1971.
O'Gorman, James F. *Henry Austin: In Every Variety of Architectural Style*. Middletown, Conn.: Wesleyan University Press, 2008.

71

WALTER BUNCE HOUSE, MANCHESTER

Although African Americans lived in Connecticut from the seventeenth century, finding architectural evidence of their presence can be difficult. Only in the nineteenth century do the names of black builders begin to appear. Nonetheless, it is possible to find some traces of their role in building Connecticut.

Alpheus Quicy (d. 1875) was a free African American stonemason credited with several projects in and around Manchester in the antebellum era, including a house for Sidney Olcott, a local abolitionist, and a building and dam for the Union Manufacturing Company. Unfortunately, further information about Quicy is scarce and inconsistent.

The only standing building attributed to Quicy, the Bunce House is notable for its stonework, with alternating wide (twenty-four-inch) and narrow (four-inch) courses of granite slabs. It is formed by laying two slabs of stone vertically, filling the space between them with rubble, and then laying slabs horizontally to tie the vertical layers together. This technique is called "slab-and-binder" or the fancier "pseudo-isodomic." Relatively rare in central Connecticut, it is more common in Windham County, where, according to some sources, Quicy was born and, presumably, learned his trade. It can be cut and laid with varying degrees of precision, ranging from examples so crude that the pattern is barely recognizable, to meticulously smooth surfaces subtly animated by the alternating wide and narrow courses. The Bunce house lies somewhere between these extremes: individual stones are somewhat irregular, but the corners are sharp and the walls plumb, a testament to Quicy's skill.

There were other African Americans who contributed to Connecticut's built landscape in the early nineteenth century. In Colchester, Gideon Quash and his son James were both stonemasons at the beginning of the century. In New Haven, William Lanson built an extension to the Long Wharf in 1810 and a basin for the Farmington Canal in 1825—two difficult and exacting jobs. Less visible in the records are African Americans who worked as laborers, building under either white or black employers.

As historian Peter Hinks has written, the fortunes of African Americans in Connecticut began to decline beginning in the 1820s. As increases in European immigration reduced the demand for black labor, prominent African American businessmen like William Lanson lost business and increasingly suffered harassment from white neighbors. This same period saw the emergence of the colonization movement, which sought to solve America's racial conflict by "returning" free blacks to a colony in Africa called Liberia. Alpheus Quicy's client Walter Bunce is recorded as making a donation to the American Colonization Society in 1849. Did he regret hiring a black stonemason to build his house? Whether or not he did, the house survives, a monument to its builder.

ca. 1830, Alpheus Quicy
34 Bidwell Street, Manchester. Private.

FURTHER READING

Brilvitch, Charles. "Freeman Houses." National Register of Historic Places, reference number 99000110, listed February 22, 1999.
Connecticut Freedom Trail. www.ctfreedomtrail.org.
Hinks, Peter P. "The Successes and Struggles of New Haven Entrepreneur William Lanson." ConnecticutHistory.org, February 10, 2015.

FIGURE 166. Walter Bunce House, Manchester. Connecticut Trust for Historic Preservation

72

HOMES FOR THE PEOPLE

BARNUM-SHERWOOD
DEVELOPMENT, BRIDGEPORT

Bridgeport's most famous nineteenth-century citizen, P. T. Barnum, was not only a showman, businessman, and politician, but also a developer who left his mark on nearly every part of the city. In 1873, he and a partner, David W. Sherwood, redeveloped an old burying ground on the edge of the rapidly growing industrial city as a residential neighborhood. (The bodies were moved to Mountain Grove Cemetery, another Barnum project.) Although they mostly sold lots, Barnum and Sherwood did erect a few model houses, designed by local architect George Palliser (1846–1903), to attract buyers.

Palliser refined two distinctive house types that appear over and over in Bridgeport: modest Victorian Gothic cottages and more imposing double houses. The latter combined two units in a single structure to approximate the scale of a costly single-family dwelling. Money thus saved on construction could be used for additional ornament. Despite modern siding and lost trim, it is still possible to identify several Palliser houses in the neighborhood. The modest "cottage house" at 190 Cottage Street was one of the first model houses. At 114 Cottage Street is what Palliser called a "Model Gothic Cottage." It originally had a tower, which, alas, has been lost. The double house at 198–200 Lewis Street is also a Palliser building.

Palliser's real significance lies in his ability to extend his reach beyond Bridgeport through canny salesmanship (not for nothing was Barnum his client). Based on his experience with the Barnum-Sherwood development, Palliser realized there was a big untapped market for modest houses of good design, not only in cities like Bridgeport, but also in rural communities too small to support an architect. To capture that market, Palliser started what he claimed was the first-ever mail-order architectural practice. In 1876 he published *Palliser's Model Homes for the People: A Complete Guide to the Proper and Economical Erection of Buildings.* Inexpensively printed and populist in tone, it was a catalogue of Palliser's work, containing a list of designs with sample plans and elevations.

Unlike many of the mail-order architects who followed him, Palliser insisted that these designs were intended only as starting points. Clients were to choose one they liked and provide the company with information that would be used to modify the design to suit their needs. The result was more personal than the typical mail-order plan, but less expensive than a custom design.

In 1877 Palliser's brother, Charles (1853–ca. 1912), joined the firm, and other books followed, more than twenty in all. In addition to working-class housing, their output included larger houses, plus schools, churches, and commercial and institutional buildings, many first built in or near Bridgeport. All three of the houses mentioned above appear in *Palliser's Model Homes*: 190 Cottage Street (the model) is Design 1; 114 Cottage Street (the Model Cottage) is Design 7; and 198–200 Lewis Street (the double house) resembles Design 43.

Connecticut served as the Pallisers' architectural laboratory, but their designs had a nationwide market. In this way they contributed to the development of a national, not just a regional, architecture.

THE PLACE
BARNUM-SHERWOOD DEVELOPMENT
1873 and later
Cottage, Lewis, and Hanover Streets between Park and
    Iranistan Avenues, Bridgeport

FURTHER READING
Brilvitch, Charles. "Division Street Historic District." National
    Register of Historic Places, reference number 82004385, listed
    June 3, 1982.
Palliser, George. *Palliser's Model Homes for the People: A Complete
    Guide to the Proper and Economical Erection of Buildings.*
    Bridgeport, Conn., 1876. Reprint, Watkins Glen, N.Y.: American
    Life Foundation, 1978.
Palliser, Palliser & Co. *American Cottage Homes.* Bridgeport, Conn.,
    1878. Reprinted as *American Victorian Cottage Homes.* New
    York: Dover, 1990.

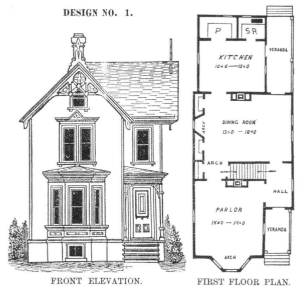

DESIGN NO. 1.

FRONT ELEVATION.   FIRST FLOOR PLAN.

Cottage house 21x48; 1st floor, parlor, dining room, kitchen, pantry, sink room and 3 closets; 2d floor, 3 chambers and 4 closets. Four of these cottages built by Hon. P. T. Barnum and D. W. Sherwood, Esq., this city, and one by J. Bird, Esq., at Woodside, N. J., cost $2,400.

Plans and specifications, $15.

(*top*) FIGURE 167. Design 1, from George Palliser, *Model Homes for the People*, 1876. Bridgeport History Center, Bridgeport Public Library
(*bottom*) FIGURE 168. 190 Cottage Street, Bridgeport.
Connecticut Trust for Historic Preservation

73

HANDMADE

AVON OLD FARMS SCHOOL, AVON

Before the advent of Modernism, American private schools tended to build Gothic or Georgian-style buildings, in a move to cultivate the image of centuries-old English institutions. None did so with the single-mindedness of Avon Old Farms, founded by Theodate Pope Riddle (1867–1946), one of the first women to practice architecture in Connecticut.

Independent and determined, Effie Pope, the daughter of a Cleveland industrialist, adopted her grandmother's name, Theodate, and set about becoming an architect. Since women could not enroll in architecture schools, she studied on her own and hired tutors. She then engaged the prominent New York firm of McKim, Mead & White to assist her in designing a home for her parents in Farmington, now the Hill-Stead Museum. In her practice Pope (who used her maiden name professionally) designed country estates, workers' houses, and three schools.

For Avon Old Farms, a memorial to her father, Pope assembled the land, planned the curriculum, and designed the buildings. The campus marries Old English forms with an Arts and Crafts emphasis on handicraft, using red sandstone and timber from the property and ironwork made on the site. Resembling a Cotswold village that grew organically over the centuries, the school's buildings sit at odd angles and surprise the viewer with unexpected changes in material and style. Walls are thick, and windows small. Eaves hug the ground, ridges sag, and roofs soar sharply up, sprouting odd dormers and strange carved beasts (notably a winged beaver, the school mascot).

This ultra-picturesque setting was the product of Pope's ideas about curriculum and architectural process. Influenced by the educator John Dewey and by her own belief that most prep schools neglected character development, Pope conceived Avon Old Farms as a self-sufficient community where students would learn by doing. In addition to academics, this "doing" included self-government and manual labor such as carpentry or farmwork.

To house the community, Pope planned the campus as a village. Dormitories and faculty cottages enclose a sheltered quadrangle. The refectory and headmaster's and dean's houses define a village green. A twisting street leads to club rooms, a post office, and the school shop. Farm

FIGURE 169. Avon Old Farms School, Avon. Connecticut Trust for Historic Preservation

buildings, plus the smithy and carpentry shop, form a separate cluster.

For Pope, how the school's buildings were constructed was as important as their design. She believed it wasn't possible to create traditional forms without employing the materials and methods that originally produced them. In short, the only way to produce buildings with the warmth and texture of hand craftsmanship was to build them by hand. To achieve this, she imported English builders to train local workers in traditional methods, and banned levels and plumb rules from the site. She explained: "a natural variation in line and surface was far more desirable in this work than accuracy."

For Theodate Pope, human appeal was crucial to architecture; buildings must be emotionally, as well as intellectually, attractive. She put this belief to work at Avon

Old Farms. To children of the machine age, let alone the digital age, the conspicuously handmade nature of the school's buildings provided unmistakable and inescapable evidence of human handiwork, permanent reminders of the humanistic purpose of education.

THE PLACE
AVON OLD FARMS SCHOOL
www.avonoldfarms.com
1921–1929, Theodate Pope
500 Old Farms Road, Avon

FURTHER READING
O'Gorman, James F. "The Modernism of Theodate Pope." *Connecticut Explored* 8, no. 1 (Winter 2009–2010): 30–35.
Paine, Judith. "Avon Old Farms School: The Architecture of Theodate Pope Riddle." *Perspecta: The Yale Architecture Journal* 18 (1982): 43–49.

FIGURE 170. Avon Old Farms School, Avon. Deb Cohen

74

WHEN IS A COPY MORE THAN A COPY?

YALE DIVINITY SCHOOL, NEW HAVEN

Historically, architects often copied from other works: sometimes a detail, sometimes a general outline, sometimes an entire building. Successful structures of the past were seen to offer useful models for later builders. This changed with the advent of Modernism, which taught that technological and social changes had severed modern life irrevocably from the past. Every project had to start from scratch with an analysis of the client's needs and then develop a unique solution to fit those specific requirements.

Embodying the pre-Modernist attitude toward architectural copying, the Yale Divinity School was based on Thomas Jefferson's University of Virginia (1817–1826). Jefferson conceived his university as a village. Professors lived and taught in two-story pavilions, arranged in two rows facing a lawn and linked by one-story ranges of student rooms. Colonnaded walkways provided sheltered access between buildings, and at the head of the lawn a half-size copy of the Roman Pantheon housed the library. In a surprising departure from symmetry, Jefferson made each pavilion different, creating a life-size display of classical architecture.

For architects Delano and Aldrich, and the Divinity School's leadership, Jefferson's plan held great appeal, both as a model for organizing a residential professional school and as a symbol of a community for learning. The architects followed the basic scheme quite closely: the two rows of pavilions and connectors, the colonnaded walkways, the dominant principal building at the head of the lawn, even Jefferson's red-brick, white-trim classicism.

But the differences are equally important. Stylistically, Delano and Aldrich swapped Jeffersonian Palladianism for New England Federal. The focal building is a chapel rather than a library, and it is modeled on a Congregational meetinghouse, not a Roman temple. Professors' houses were not required, so the pavilions contained only student rooms. Classrooms and common spaces were fitted into bigger wings flanking and behind the chapel.

The rear wings represent Delano and Aldrich's most important modification of their model. Jefferson's composition built up from the foot of the lawn to its climax in the Rotunda, but then stopped abruptly, leaving the rear of the Rotunda unfinished (Stanford White later gave it a proper façade, as Delano and Aldrich, former employees of McKim, Mead & White, doubtless knew). The Divinity School similarly builds up to the chapel, but then it tapers off again with the rear wings and the intimate courtyard between them, giving the composition a more satisfying conclusion.

At its completion, the Divinity School was widely admired as a skillful adaptation of a famous prototype. But in the 1990s, when the school began planning renovations, Modernist disdain for copying intruded on the process. The architect, Robert Kliment, opened a presentation of his plans by saying that the Divinity School wasn't very good architecture, since it was "only a copy." This attitude comes through in some of the new elements added. Clearly created to avoid any suggestion of copying, their clunky Postmodernist design clashes with Delano and Aldrich's delicate Adamesque interiors. Sometimes fitting in is more important than originality.

THE PLACE
YALE DIVINITY SCHOOL
(Sterling Divinity Quadrangle)
1931–1932, Delano and Aldrich. 2003, Robert Kliment and
    Frances Halsband Architects.
409 Prospect Street, New Haven

FURTHER READING
Cook, John W. *The Sterling Divinity Quadrangle: Building Divinity at Yale Divinity School.* New Haven, Conn.: Yale Institute of Sacred Music, 1994.
Pinnell, Patrick L. *The Campus Guide: Yale University.* New York: Princeton Architectural Press, 1999.
Ryan, Susan. "Prospect Hill Historic District." National Register of Historic Places, reference number 79002670, listed November 2, 1979.

FIGURE 171. Yale Divinity School, New Haven. Patrick L. Pinnell

75

ONION DOME IN THE COUNTRYSIDE

SAINT PHILIP THE APOSTLE CATHOLIC CHURCH, ASHFORD

One of the great surprises of the Connecticut countryside is the sight of Saint Philip's onion-domed tower, completed in 1937, rising above the crossroads village of Warrenville, in the town of Ashford. Rarely did the immigrants who moved onto Connecticut's worn-out and abandoned farms in the late nineteenth and early twentieth centuries leave so conspicuous and distinctive a mark of their presence. In Ashford, many of these immigrants were Hungarians, Slovaks, and Bohemians, and the church owes its Eastern European Baroque character both to them and to its designer, Paul Chalfin (1874–1959), who had a summer cottage in Ashford and donated the plans to the fledgling mission congregation.

Chalfin was not an architect, but rather a painter and curator—and one of those people of exquisite taste who devote themselves to helping the very rich spend their money tastefully. He is best known for Vizcaya, the palatial Florida estate where he bullied, wheedled, cajoled, and charmed his client, International Harvester heir James Deering, into ever more lavish outlays.

As at Vizcaya, in Ashford Chalfin drew on Baroque models overlaid with a delicate sensibility for texture and color. The fieldstone walls were whitewashed, then allowed to peel, creating a sense of age that accentuated their rough construction (more recently the stone has been painted with non-peeling white). The entry façade, on the other hand, is built of brick, with crisply rusticated pilasters, a stylized effect that contrasts with the genuine rusticity of the stone. Inside, angled pews and the plan's intersecting curves create a sense of movement in the lofty space, made exuberant by the inflected woodwork and a few surviving traces of the original decorative painting with its swirling, brushy motifs.

Most of the construction was done by the parishioners themselves, with their pastor, the Reverend William J. Dunn, taking the lead. (The *Hartford Courant* reported, "Missionary Padre Sheds Ecclesiastical Garb and Tackles Hard Labor with a Will.") Men with jobs donated one day's labor every week; when fund-raising allowed, out-of-work laborers were paid. Fifty years later, one worker recalled: "I was just out of school at the time—during the Depression. There wasn't much work available. When the church was under construction, we worked. There wasn't

FIGURE 172. Saint Philip the Apostle Catholic Church, Ashford. Robert Egleston

much loafing around. We worked six days and got paid for five days. One day was for the church." Women and children helped gather stones from their fields, and roof slates came from mills being demolished in Willimantic.

Did Chalfin push the farmers of Ashford as he had Deering, stretching their resources to, or even beyond, the limits of their means? If so, history records no trace of it. Instead, one finds nothing but the parishioners' pride in their ability to construct such an ambitious and handsome structure.

THE PLACE

SAINT PHILIP THE APOSTLE CATHOLIC CHURCH

saintphilipsaintjude.org

1933–1937, Paul Chalfin

64 Pompey Hollow Road (U.S. Route 44), Ashford

FURTHER READING

Saint Philip Church. *Golden Jubilee, 1937–1987*. Norwich, Conn.: Thames Printing, 1987.

YOUR TAXES AT WORK

PEOPLE'S STATE FOREST MUSEUM, BARKHAMSTED

Built of local boulders, the People's State Forest Museum seems almost a natural formation rather than a human-made structure. Its battered corners and recessed, nearly invisible, mortar joints make it appear that the stone walls have been piled up by a glacier or earthquake. Deep-set banks of windows seem cavelike, while the flared roof echoes the swooping branches of the surrounding pine trees. Everything about the little building is heavy and chunky, from the stones to the rough-hewn beams supporting the roof to the sturdy planked door with its oversize iron hardware. Yet it bears marks of artistry as well. The curving lintel of the office window suggests the rising sun, with radiating stones above as rays of light. Inside, hand-forged wall sconces have copper reflectors.

By the 1930s, this rustic style had come to be expected in parks, where its simple forms and rough textures harmonized with and enhanced the natural landscape. Its use here, and the exceptional quality of design and craftsmanship, identify the museum as a work of the Civilian Conservation Corps (CCC), one of the most successful job programs of the Great Depression. Thousands of men joined the CCC in Connecticut between 1933 and 1942. They built roads and trails, planted trees, and constructed recreational and support facilities in state parks, gaining useful skills in the process.

Other New Deal relief programs provided funding for public works projects such as town halls and schools, and infrastructure projects such as roads, bridges, and water-treatment plants. The Merritt Parkway, although primarily financed by Fairfield County bonds, received some money from the Public Works Administration. The Works Project Administration put artists to work embellishing public buildings with sculptures and murals.

By the early 1940s, with the easing of the Depression and the changing economic demands of World War II, relief programs shut down. Men went into the armed forces instead, and domestic construction ceased, apart from war-related projects. (In fact, the only New Deal program still operating is an architectural one: the Historic American Buildings Survey, which employed out-of-work architects to record historic buildings through drawings and photographs. Its charge has been expanded through parallel programs for engineering structures and landscapes.)

Even though the New Deal programs ended, their legacy of a heightened federal role in producing public works endures. In fact, the trend only increased through the remainder of the twentieth century. In contrast to the early nineteenth century, when custom houses and lighthouses were nearly the only federal structures in Connecticut, today it is nearly impossible to pass a day without encountering some built evidence of the national government. From the People's State Forest Museum to Interstate 95 to the homebuyer loan guarantees that encouraged the development of suburban subdivisions, federal programs continue to affect what is built in Connecticut. In its way, this little rustic building serves as a symbol of the increased presence of government in the everyday life of its citizens, and as a model of excellence of design and construction to serve the public good.

THE PLACE
PEOPLE'S STATE FOREST MUSEUM

www.psfnaturemuseum.org
1934–1935, Robert Lienhard, architect; Civilian
 Conservation Corps
Greenwoods Road, off East River Road, Barkhamsted.
 Open to the public.

FURTHER READING
McCahon, Mary. "People's Forest Museum." Connecticut State
 Park and Forest Depression-Era Federal Work Relief Programs
 Structures Thematic Resource. National Register of Historic
 Places, reference number 86001737, listed September 4, 1986.

FIGURE 173. People's State Forest Museum, Barkhamsted. Connecticut Trust for Historic Preservation

77

THE BUSINESS OF HOUSES
BROADVIEW LANE, WAREHOUSE POINT, EAST WINDSOR

In the years after World War II, suburban homebuilding became a big business. Before the war, developers typically sold lots to individual homeowners, who built their own houses. Now, the developers harnessed newly available financing and mass-production methods to build at a rate not seen before. The process was as much about selling as about designing or building, with a careful balance of economical construction with features that would attract buyers.

Broadview Lane, one of the many subdivisions carved out of the level, easy-to-build-on farmland of the Connecticut River Valley, was considered a model of this balancing act. After the fifty-three houses, costing $10,900 each, sold out in just thirty hours, *House & Home*, a magazine for the homebuilding business, proclaimed Broadview "the fastest-selling houses in Connecticut."

According to the magazine, careful attention to the details of planning and construction accounted for Broadview's success. It quoted one of the developers, James Bent, as saying, "The houses were the end product of many architect-engineer-salesmen conferences." Designed for families with two children, the 1,026-square-foot houses offered plentiful storage, "car porches" that served as both car shelters and outdoor living space, and dens that could be converted to additional bedrooms. Economies of scale included using precut lumber and assembling prefabricated wall frames that could be tipped up into place, speeding construction. Slab construction eliminated costly basements. Marketing experts suggested popular features such as kitchens that were accessible but not open to living rooms, fully tiled bathrooms, and radiant heating ("to bolster faith in slab-house warmth").

Many of these tips were gleaned from a homebuilders' roundtable sponsored by *House & Home*. Bent, however, credited the project's success to a refusal to skimp on architectural design. Unlike many builders, he was convinced that good design was integral to a successful development, not a frill to add on at the end of the process.

Bent's architect, David C. Barker, had worked for Skidmore, Owings & Merrill before establishing his own practice. In a statement that reflects the economic forces shaping suburban architecture, Barker told *House & Home*, "I've learned the importance of saving on each

53-house sellout in 30 hours near Hartford

"These houses," says their builder,
"resulted directly from the HOUSE & HOME Round Table
on the low-income family and the too-cheap house"

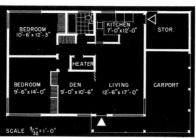

Photos: (following pages) A. J. Kiely, Jr.

No advocate of the banana split, Architect Barker used only bevel siding as facing material, says: "Nothing shows poorer taste than a jumble of materials." He persuaded builders to use 2' overhangs front and back. Previous Bent-built houses had them only in front. Trusses permitted overhangs at low cost.

Most popular model had this plan. Builders attribute sales mainly to fact that this was the furnished model. Originally kitchen had rear door, but plan was revised, as shown here, to permit access to storage room from both kitchen and garage since salesmen believed many buyers wanted it as extra room.

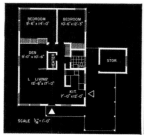

Separate storage-room plan was not as popular as house above. Access to rear yard or patio would be made from kitchen door through space between house and storage room. A rear-living-room model was discarded: builders thought added cost of split plumbing unwarranted on such a low price house.

Variety of project appearance was achieved in this plan and plan at left by facing narrow side of house to street. Carport and storage room on narrow size helped increase apparent size of house. Driveway from street to rear of carport is included with each house. All three models were offered in plans.

HOUSE & HOME

FIGURES 174 AND 175. Broadview Lane, East Windsor, from *House & Home*, August 1953. Time Inc.

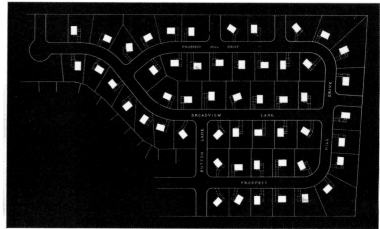

Sight seldom seen in a lower-cost house: site planning of houses to take advantage of breeze, view, avoid row-on-row development look. The 100' lot was such a buyer bonus and sales-tipping feature that all future houses will get 100' lots.

This may very well be the fastest-selling house ever offered in Connecticut. In 30 hours 53 houses sold and people still waited in line. Price on the 1,026 sq. ft. house: $10,900. FHA down payments: $1,500; no down payments for vets. The vast majority were sold VA.

Perhaps these houses could be called the Round Table development because Builder Jim Bent credits their success to the good ideas he picked up as a panel member of the Round Table on the low-income family and the too-cheap house (H&H, Oct. '52).

Before the Round Table neither Bent (who is also president of Hartford Federal Savings & Loan Assn.) nor partner Bill Stevens had ever called in an architect until plans were virtually complete. But for their Warehouse Point project, 14 miles from downtown Hartford, Bent handed Architect Dave Barker his Round Table notes, told him to design a house that would sell for under $11,000 adequate for a family with two children.

"The houses were the end product of many architect-engineer-salesmen conferences," says Bent.

LOCATION: East Windsor, Conn.
BENT & STEVENS, builders
DAVID C. BARKER, architect
LOOMIS & SULLIVAN, engineers
FRED S. DUBIN & ASSOC., consulting engineers

Architect's part. Architect Barker, on his first merchant-builder design after almost 10 years of design in Japan and Batavia (he had been with Skidmore, Owings & Merrill), was guided by these ideas from Bent's notes:

▶ Elimination of the basement with its water hazard.

▶ Provision of ample storage room to make up for the lack of basement.

▶ Use of one basic rectangular design for economy in building.

▶ Equivalent of three bedrooms.

▶ A car porch designed to double as porch and garage.

▶ Bigger lots (100' width as opposed to 30' widths in a 92-unit project in the same area last year, 60' widths the year before).

Clean-cut inside and out. Almost every square foot under roof is put to good use (see plans). Use of "landscape" colors on exteriors—bright reds of flowers, soft greens and yellows of foliage, grays and browns of rocks and earth—added more variety to project with its skillful place-

piece of lumber because the saving or loss is multiplied many times over. And I now recognize the importance of simplification and the importance of standardization."

In the development, curving roads are lined with small, evenly spaced houses similar in form but varied in orientation, color, and materials. Although all the houses followed a single plan, they are turned to present either a long or a short side to the street. Different configurations of the car porch and storage room provide further variety. Houses set at angles and one-hundred-foot-wide lots—an increase over then-standard sixty- or eighty-foot frontages—add a sense of openness to the streetscape.

The houses include such Modernist elements as

windows set at corners or in high strips, and flat-roofed carports. But the Modernism is tamed with pitched roofs, traditional brick or shingle or clapboard siding, and small scale, ensuring that the houses wouldn't be too unconventional for buyers—or lenders, at a time when many banks automatically refused loans for any design they considered "extreme."

As a successful example of the blending of architecture and product development, Broadview Lane reflects the growing influence of consumerism in mid-century American culture.

THE PLACE
BROADVIEW LANE
1953, Bent and Stevens, builders; David C. Barker, architect
Broadview Lane and Prospect Hill Drive, East Windsor. Private residences.

FURTHER READING
"53-House Sellout in 30 Hours Near Hartford." *House & Home*, August 1953, 130–133.

78

MODERNIST PATRONAGE

TORIN COMPANY BUILDINGS, TORRINGTON

Since the profession began, architects have depended on patrons—influential clients who provided commissions and referrals to other clients. This cluster of buildings is an example of patronage in the Modernist period. The story starts with Rufus (1921–2009) and Leslie Stillman (1922–2006), who after World War II moved to Litchfield (the next town south of Torrington) determined to build a house "of their own time." They chose the Bauhaus-trained architect Marcel Breuer (1902–1981), who designed a house for them in 1951. The couple built two more houses designed by Breuer in Litchfield, in 1965 and 1973, before moving back to the first one.

By themselves, the three Stillman houses document a notable ongoing relationship between architect and client. But the Stillmans' patronage led to more Modernist buildings in and around Litchfield, a remarkable collection that is usually overshadowed by the town's reputation for Colonial architecture. At the Stillmans' recommendation, friends, neighbors, and relatives commissioned houses by Breuer or other prominent Modernist architects such as John Johansen, Edward Larrabee Barnes, and Eliot Noyes. Rufus Stillman's employer, Andrew Gagarin, built two Breuer houses, in 1956 and 1973. Community involvement led to other architectural commissions: Rufus Stillman served on the town school board, which commissioned schools by Breuer and Johansen. The Connecticut Junior Republic, with Gagarin on its board, built dormitories designed by Breuer in Litchfield. Mrs. Gagarin was on the board of the Oliver Wolcott Library in Litchfield, which commissioned a building by Noyes.

Finally, there was the Torin Corporation, a manufacturer of machinery. Andrew Gagarin was its president, and Rufus Stillman its vice president and later president. Beginning in 1952, Breuer's firm designed ten buildings for Torin, including three in Torrington.

The Torin Machine Division Building, erected in 1962, is a big one-story industrial shed with an office/lab section at front. This arrangement was typical of postwar industrial architecture, but Breuer brought to it his mastery of form and materials, seen in the contrast of white enameled aluminum siding and black brick, originally highlighted with yellow mechanicals on the roof. For the Torin Administration Building, constructed in 1966, Breuer

FIGURE 176. Torin Administration Building, Torrington. Robert Gregson

chose the precast concrete panels that he favored for their strength, sculptural form, and moderate cost. (A later occupant cleared much of the building's wooded setting for parking.)

The Torin Technical Center, erected in 1971, is built of concrete block and precast concrete. Of particular note are the ribbon windows with their heavy hoods. Rufus Stillman wrote of this building, "I love the openness of the end walls contrasted with fort-like masonry and its heavy-browed windows—the primitive texture of the concrete block against the sophisticated details of the black aluminum of windows and doors. The details, the ease or simplicity reflect Breuer's sense of form."

Stillman summarized Torin's experience with Breuer: "That all this was done by a small company over a period of 20 years is, I think, an inspiring story—an object lesson in the way a corporation of this sort, concerned with quality and receptive to talent, can add some things of beauty to this world." It's also a lesson in the importance of patrons and their role in the making of architecture.

THE PLACES

TORIN MACHINE DIVISION
1962, Marcel Breuer and Robert Gatje
89 Commercial Boulevard, Torrington

TORIN ADMINISTRATION BUILDING
1966, Marcel Breuer and Herbert Beckhard
200 Kennedy Drive, Torrington

TORIN TECHNICAL CENTER
1971, Marcel Breuer and Hamilton Smith
62 Commercial Boulevard, Torrington

FURTHER READING
Litchfield Historical Society. *In Our Own Time: Modern Architecture in Litchfield, 1949–1970*. Exhibition, April 11– November 30, 2003. www.litchfieldhistoricalsociety.org.
Stillman, Rufus. "A Client and His Architect." *Architectural Forum* 136, no. 2 (March 1972): 46–51.

Part Ten

COLONIAL AND
COLONIAL REVIVAL

Connecticut is known for its heritage of colonial-era buildings. While sharing its English Puritan origins with Massachusetts, Connecticut was also influenced by multicultural New Netherland, later renamed New York. Running through the state's center and extending into Massachusetts, the Connecticut River Valley was home to a distinct provincial culture in the seventeenth and eighteenth centuries. Although architects and historians have long studied the state's colonial buildings, new research continues to help us better understand them and the unique society that created them.

After the Civil War, as Americans began to rediscover their colonial architectural heritage, Connecticut's colonial buildings helped shape the emerging national Colonial Revival movement. The state provided convenient, close-by models for New York architects. The town of Litchfield became a nationally known pioneer in restoring old buildings—and often embellishing them in the process. And Colonial Revival design dominated the state's growing suburbs, giving them a distinctive flavor and a sense of connection to the past.

79

ENGLISH BEGINNINGS
BUTTOLPH-WILLIAMS HOUSE, WETHERSFIELD

With its steep roof, unpainted clapboards, and small leaded-glass windows, the Buttolph-Williams House still seems to hunker down in a raw, unfriendly wilderness. Although built two generations after the first European settlement in Connecticut, it represents the post-medieval building traditions that the settlers brought with them from England and that persisted in the Connecticut River Valley into the eighteenth century.

The house's most distinctive feature is the wooden frame that forms its skeleton, a cage of mighty timbers hewn from old-growth trees (see figure 16). Because wood was plentiful, and iron nails scarce, the builders fitted the timbers together like puzzle pieces, using a variety of joints and wooden pegs known as "tree nails" to address particular sets of stresses and strains. Constructing a colonial house required a builder who knew which joint to use where, how to prepare the pieces—careful measuring required!—and how to assemble them with the help of a crowd of able-bodied but inexpert workers.

The colonists brought this way of building with them from England. Seen without its clapboards, the frame of the Buttolph-Williams House would look like an English half-timbered building, because that is how it is built. In the old country the spaces between the posts and beams would be filled with wattle and daub and covered with plaster. Colonial builders quickly learned that plaster did not hold up in North America's harsher climate, so they covered their buildings with clapboards, which in England were usually used only on outbuildings.

Because of the labor involved in shaping the frame's joints, a colonial house is simple in form, almost always a boxlike rectangle. But there were ways to provide variety. One used at the Buttolph-Williams House was to carve away the lower part of the posts, leaving the upper section to project a few inches. Unlike earlier framed overhangs, which were a vestige of crowded medieval European cities, this hewn version didn't create any additional space upstairs. Its purpose was purely decorative, to break up the surface, and it became particularly common in the Connecticut Valley and areas settled from the valley.

With its careful craftsmanship and finely detailed moldings the Buttolph-Williams House was clearly an expensive structure, built to impress. Inside the house,

FIGURE 177.
Buttolph-
Williams House,
Wethersfield,
chamber.
Melanie A. McCue

the framing timbers were left visible. Planed smooth, their corners chamfered and embellished with moldings and sometimes decorative painting, the framing members are dominant elements determining the character of the interior. The resulting unity of structure and ornament is visually and intellectually satisfying.

Because of the post-medieval features such as its exposed timber frame, massive center chimney, and banks of casement windows, the Buttolph-Williams House was long thought to have been built for David Buttolph in 1692. However, subsequent research determined that it actually was erected some two decades later. Tavern keeper Benjamin Belden bought the property in 1711 for £70 and sold it in 1720 for £245. The more than tripling of the property's value is evidence for construction of a new house during Belden's ownership. Nonetheless, the house retains its traditional, if incorrect, name.

In the mid-twentieth century, the Antiquarian & Landmarks Society of Connecticut (now known as

Connecticut Landmarks) acquired the Buttolph-Williams House and hired antiquarian architect Frederic C. Palmer to restore it. He uncovered the furred-out overhangs and traced the size and shape of the window openings from marks on the frame to recapture the original appearance.

THE PLACE
BUTTOLPH-WILLIAMS HOUSE

www.ctlandmarks.org
Between 1711 and 1720. Restored 1947, Frederic C. Palmer.
249 Broad Street, Wethersfield. Open to the public.

FURTHER READING

Dillon, James. "Buttolph-Williams House." National Historic Landmark. National Register of Historic Places, reference number 68000048, designated November 24, 1968.

Cummings, Abbott Lowell. *The Framed Houses of Massachusetts Bay, 1625–1725*. Cambridge, Mass.: Belknap Press of Harvard University Press, 1979.

80

THE CONNECTICUT HOUSE

DEACON ADAMS HOUSE, NEW HARTFORD

Say "Connecticut house," and something like the Deacon Adams House will pop into most minds: a colonial saltbox with a slanting rear roof, painted red with white trim, and sitting amid green fields beside a country road. Decades of magazine photographs, Hollywood happy endings, and suburban imitators have firmly fixed this image in the American psyche as a domestic ideal.

Many aspects of this image are inaccurate. The Adams House was well above the average in size and finish for its period. At the same time, it was a working house, the headquarters of a busy farm. And persistent myths about specialized "coffin doors" (multipurpose side entries) and "borning rooms" (simply downstairs bedrooms) obscure how life truly was lived here.

Still, in a sense the Adams house really *is* "the Connecticut house." By the time it was built, the colony had been established for more than one hundred years. Separated from the mother country by a wide ocean and protected by a royal charter that provided a degree of self-government rare among Britain's North American colonies, Connecticut had developed into a place with its own particular identity. Its architecture had evolved, too, adapted to suit the environment, its inhabitants' practical needs, and the social structure.

The Adams house is literally a product of its environment, constructed almost entirely of local materials: timber, stone, and possibly Litchfield County iron. Only the window glass came from far away. The house is also a product of its climate, with a center chimney economically serving many fireplaces with a single stack and radiating residual heat back into the house.

In terms of use, the house shows the common "hall-and-parlor plan" (see figure 17) with two main rooms at the front (in the colonial era, "hall" referred to a house's main everyday living space, not a passage, while "parlor" referred to the best room). Augmenting them is a separate kitchen in the rear lean-to, a development that kept the smells and bustle of cooking away from the living rooms at the front. The main door to the house opened into a vestibule containing a stair to the second floor and doors to the hall and parlor. The Adams house also has an informal side entry leading directly into the hall, a feature common in the Connecticut Valley. In the lean-to, a second staircase makes it possible to reach any part of the upper levels without passing through another room.

In terms of social conditions, the Adams house provides evidence of both stratification and relative equality. Its generous size and finely detailed doorway, window pediments, and paneling all proclaim Deacon Adams's wealth and important position in New Hartford. So too do the massive stone garden terraces, among the most imposing in the state. At the same time, the house has much in common with those of both richer and poorer Connecticut inhabitants. The range of eighteenth-century house sizes and types was considerably wider than surviving examples would suggest (see place 15), but in overall form, plan, construction, and architectural vocabulary they were quite similar. On all but the poorest levels, differences were primarily of size and decoration. This suggests, if not egalitarianism, at least a certain degree of social cohesion, especially when compared to wider extremes in the plantation societies of the South or the mercantile cities of the North.

Suited to the environmental, practical, and social needs of its time, the Adams House stands as a masterpiece of vernacular design—that is, design native to a particular location. This unity of place and architecture gives it a rightness that remains evident, however much Connecticut has changed since it was built.

THE PLACE
DEACON ADAMS HOUSE
ca. 1750–1760
146 South Road, New Hartford. Private residence.

FURTHER READING

Garvin, James L. *A Building History of Northern New England.* Hanover, N.H.: University Press of New England, 2001.

Kelly, J. Frederick. *The Early Domestic Architecture of Connecticut.* New Haven, Conn.: Yale University Press, 1924. Reprint, New York: Dover, 1963.

FIGURE 178. Deacon Adams House, New Hartford. Connecticut Trust for Historic Preservation

81

OUR OWN HISTORY

HORACE BUSHNELL CONGREGATIONAL CHURCH, HARTFORD

In 1913, Hartford's Fourth Congregational Church asked architectural firms to submit proposals for its new building on Albany Avenue. (After moving, the congregation adopted the name of the influential nineteenth-century theologian Horace Bushnell, a former member.) One firm, Davis and Brooks, suggested reusing the portico and steeple from the current building on the new church. As W. F. Brooks later wrote, this scheme "preserved the character and best features of the old church."

Brooks didn't mention, and may not have known, the back history of the features he proposed to preserve. When the old church was being planned in 1848, the building committee asked the architect, Sidney Mason Stone, to copy the portico and steeple of Center Church in New Haven, completed in 1814 (place 40). Stone did so, although he enriched the design in keeping with current taste. Instead of Center Church's Doric columns, he used the more decorative Corinthian, and he upped their number from four to six. But the steeple is very similar to its model, and the Rococo swirl of foliage in the pediment is unmistakable.

Thanks to high levels of literacy, Connecticut, like New England in general, came early to an appreciation of its own history. As early as 1797, Benjamin Trumbull published his *Complete History of Connecticut, Civil and Ecclesiastical*. By the 1830s there were glimmerings of interest in early buildings, as seen in the engravings amateur historian John Warner Barber included in his *Connecticut Historical Collections*, first published in 1836.

Barber's illustrations didn't affect contemporary architectural practice, though. Antebellum American builders and clients still looked to Europe for inspiration. So we don't know why the Fourth Church specified that its building be patterned after the New Haven church. But the idea apparently struck a chord with Stone. Over the next decade he designed several other churches resembling Federal meetinghouses, in New Haven, Waterbury, Naugatuck, and West Haven. Henry Austin, Stone's contemporary, also designed Federal-style churches in New Haven and Danbury, and there are some similar buildings by unidentified designers. One can, it is true, find colonial-inspired antebellum buildings elsewhere in the country, but nowhere is there so concentrated a cluster as these

Connecticut churches. Moreover, builders in other places looked to the much older buildings of the seventeenth or early eighteenth century. Stone's and Austin's use of relatively recent models from the early nineteenth century stands alone.

It is not certain whether these buildings represent a conservative survival of earlier modes or a foretaste of the Colonial Revival that would emerge after the Civil War. Perhaps they were a Congregationalist response to the Episcopalians' adoption of Gothic as an architectural brand, an assertion of denominational identity through imitation of buildings that had Congregational heritage and also (unlike primitive colonial meetinghouses) appealed to the current taste for architectural enrichment. The search for appropriate architectural styles for churches was a topic of great interest; just a few years later Stone would contribute drawings to a book promoting Romanesque design as a Congregationalist alternative to Gothic.

Davis and Brooks got the job, and they did indeed reuse the older portico and steeple on a new Georgian-style building that harmonizes well with Stone's 1850s-flavored classicism. By persuading the congregation to reuse parts of their building, Davis and Brooks not only set an example of historic preservation and architectural recycling, but also preserved evidence of a little-known episode in Connecticut's architectural history. As Liberty Christian Center International, the building continues to tell that story.

THE PLACE
HORACE BUSHNELL CONGREGATIONAL CHURCH
(Now Liberty Christian Center International)
1913–1914, Davis and Brooks; steeple and portico, 1848–
    1850, Sidney Mason Stone
750 Albany Avenue, Hartford

FURTHER READING
Brooks, W. F. "The Fourth Congregational Church of Hartford: Old Traditions Embodied in the New Building." *Architecture* 42, no. 2 (August 1920): 238.
Plummer, Dale S. "Fourth Congregational Church." National Register of Historic Places, reference number 82004409, listed April 12, 1982.

FIGURE 179. Horace Bushnell Congregational Church (Liberty Christian Center), Hartford. Connecticut Trust for Historic Preservation

82

INVENTING RESTORATION
HYLAND HOUSE, GUILFORD

It is often easy to forget that the colonial buildings Connecticut is known for have almost invariably been restored—altered to recapture their assumed appearance at some previous time. Like any other building alteration, restoration reflects the preconceptions and tastes of the restorers and their clients.

Clearly built by a person of means and fashionable taste, the Hyland House was notable particularly for its unusual chamfered overhangs and a high-style chamber chimneypiece. But in 1916 the house barely escaped demolition for a garage when it was bought by the Dorothy Whitfield Historic Society, a women's group named for the wife of Guilford's first minister. Unlike earlier preservation efforts, this one was motivated not by the house's association with an historic event or person, but rather by its architecture.

Over the years the Hyland house had undergone many alterations. These included an added lean-to; new doors and windows; and, inside, new mantels, trim, and partitions. To restore the house, the Dorothies (as later generations called them) hired Providence architect Norman Morrison Isham (1864–1943), an expert in early Connecticut and Rhode Island architecture and a pioneer in professional restoration. Isham's work at the Hyland House reveals patterns that would characterize later restoration projects.

Much depended on when the house was built. Relying on written records, the Dorothies had arrived at a date of 1660. From his examination of the structure, Isham dated it to about 1720 and based many of his design decisions on that conclusion. The matter wasn't settled until 2015, when dendrochronology (analysis of tree rings) determined that the trees for the frame had been cut in 1712 and 1713. Since frames typically were constructed of green wood, 1713 is now the accepted date.

Unlike romantic restorers such as the antiquarian Wallace Nutting, Isham championed a scientific approach to restoration. He recommended retaining elements of later periods rather than replacing them with modern re-creations of what might have previously been in place, particularly where clear evidence for the original was lacking. Nonetheless, at the Hyland House Isham did remove historic items from the later eighteenth and early

FIGURE 180. Hyland House, Guilford, during restoration, 1916. Guilford Keeping Society Library Collection

FIGURE 181. Hyland House after restoration, 1940. Library of Congress, Prints & Photographs Division, Historic American Buildings Survey, HABS CONN,5-GUIL,19-1, Stanley P. Mixon, photographer

nineteenth centuries and replaced them with items such as paneling and leaded sash windows representative of the early eighteenth century. Where these were conjectural, he defended them as "compatible" with the original period. One hundred years later, it can be difficult to distinguish some of Isham's now-aged additions from older materials.

Since the restorer's knowledge is never complete, any restoration will involve a certain amount of invention. The result is neither the original building nor the building-as-found, but rather a third building, in which origins and intermediate history and present day are tangled together. For this reason, modern preservationists often advocate preserving what currently exists instead of trying to recapture some period in the past.

The truly unaltered colonial house doesn't exist. It must be recognized that surviving early buildings are the products of centuries of change—including restoration—influenced by the needs and values of their own times. These changes can add layers of meaning, express the passage of time, and provide evidence of the successive generations who inhabited and used these buildings, not just the people who built them.

THE PLACE
HYLAND HOUSE

hylandhouse.org
1713. 1916–17, restored, Norman M. Isham.
84 Boston Street, Guilford. Open to the public.

FURTHER READING
Brockmeyer, Christine R. "Hyland-Wildman House." National Register of Historic Places, reference number 76001989, listed March 26, 1976.
Green, Bryan Clark, and James Sexton. "An Early Connecticut House: The Hyland House, Historic Structure Report." Guilford, Conn.: Dorothy Whitfield Historic Society, 1996.
Isham, Norman M., and Albert F. Brown. *Early Connecticut Houses: An Historical and Architectural Study*. Providence: Preston and Rounds, 1900. Facsimile reprint, New York: Dover, 1965.

83

AMERICAN STYLE
WATERBURY CITY HALL,
WATERBURY

In the mid-nineteenth century, American builders often sought an architectural style that would express the nation's ideals in government and society—a truly *American* architecture. There were many candidates; various champions advocated Greek design, to equate American democracy with that of the ancient Greeks; Italian country villas, as appropriate models of republican simplicity; and even Romanesque and Hindu styles, among others.

A more lasting solution began to emerge with the centennial celebration of the Declaration of Independence in 1876, which called attention to early American buildings, first for their ties to historic events and then for their architectural appeal. Over the following decades, architects gradually created a new style that applied colonial forms and decorative motifs to modern needs. This style, called "Colonial Revival," has developed and changed with the times but continues to exert a powerful hold on the American imagination.

In the early twentieth century, the Colonial Revival was seen not only as a celebration of the American past, but also as a tool for integrating recent immigrants into American society. Rooted in the era when the principles of freedom and democracy were first articulated, the style would constitute an element of common cultural grounding for all Americans, whatever their ethnic background, and a physical symbol of American values. A related but less benign interpretation views Colonial Revival design as a means by which the native-born elite, as descendants of Revolutionary heroes, attempted to assert their social and political dominance over the newcomers. Whether one or both of these motives was in play, it was hardly surprising that Waterbury—a city proud of its colonial past and also a thriving industrial center with a growing immigrant population—chose for its new city hall a design that *Time* magazine later called "pure Colonial."

In 1913 the term "Colonial" in architecture could refer to anything from early post-medieval buildings to mid-eighteenth-century Baroque, Georgian, and Federal structures. In a pinch, even Greek Revival could qualify. Often motifs from several historical periods were incorporated into a single building. The goal wasn't scholarly correctness but evocation of early American heroism, elegance, or democracy.

For Waterbury, architect Cass Gilbert looked primarily to the Federal era of the late eighteenth and early nineteenth centuries. He took inspiration from the rusticated ground floors and slender upper-story pilasters favored by Boston's Charles Bulfinch; from Federal houses' slim window surrounds with their elegant swags; and from the roof balustrade and tall, slim cupola of New York's City Hall. Perhaps he was also paying tribute to David Hoadley, a Waterbury native and one of Connecticut's most famous Federal-era builders.

Despite Gilbert's historical references, the City Hall is clearly a product of its own age. It is much bigger than any Federal structure, built to handle the complex needs of a modern industrial city. It is also much more richly ornamented, reflecting the wealth generated by Waterbury's factories and other businesses.

The early twentieth century took seriously the power of public buildings to convey messages about the people who create and use them. Through the quality of its design and construction, its appeal to local and national history, and its use of symbolic ornament, the Waterbury City Hall proclaimed the power of democracy, the efficacy of government, and the dignity and duties of citizenship. Thanks to sensitive restoration, it still does.

THE PLACE
WATERBURY CITY HALL

1913–1915, Cass Gilbert. 2007–2010, restored, DeCarlo and
    Doll Inc.
235 Grand Street, Waterbury. Open to the public.

FURTHER READING
Wrenn, Tony P. "Waterbury Municipal Center Complex." National
    Register of Historic Places, reference number 78002882, listed
    October 10, 1978.

FIGURE 182. Waterbury City Hall. Robert W. Grzywacz

84

TOWNWIDE MAKEOVER
LITCHFIELD

The first thing that travelers from the north or east see of Litchfield is the tall, white spire of the First Congregational Church, identifying the town as the ultimate colonial community. Like other components of that image, the church owes as much, if not more, to the Colonial Revival era as to earlier periods.

Founded in 1715, Litchfield by 1900 was a bustling county seat. The town center boasted a variety of well-built houses—new ones in current fashions and older ones updated to keep up with the times. In 1873, the First Congregational Church had replaced its Federal meetinghouse with a stylish new Gothic Revival church. And after two fires in the 1880s, the business district had been rebuilt with red-brick commercial blocks and a Richardsonian Romanesque courthouse.

Amid this up-to-date Victoriana, Litchfield was more than typically in touch with its past. Its leading citizens still included prosperous descendants of the eighteenth-century elite, either year-round or summer residents. The historical society, established in 1856, was a power to be reckoned with. An active village improvement society tended the green and, in 1882, introduced one of the country's first plaque programs to identify historic structures.

Before the turn of the twentieth century, Litchfield's interest in its own past began to take physical form as residents, inspired by the Colonial Revival movement, began restoring old houses or constructing new ones in colonial style. Building on these individual efforts, the village improvement society launched a campaign in 1913 to redesign the business district. The society oversaw the remodeling of the courthouse with a Georgian-style cupola, and commissioned sample plans for adding Colonial Revival storefronts to the commercial blocks.

The re-Colonialization effort was more about image than historical accuracy. Restored houses often were more elaborate than anything that actually existed in the eighteenth century, sometimes even employing southern models alongside New England ones. If all else failed, owners could camouflage nonconforming dwellings with white paint and black or dark-green shutters, a color scheme thought to be as integral to colonial architecture as raised paneling and narrow clapboards. The improvement society re-landscaped the town green with grass and arching elms to create a parklike setting that wasn't at all colonial but gave the town a tasteful centerpiece.

The high point of the makeover was the First Congregational Church. In 1929 the congregation demolished its Gothic Revival building and moved back to the site the Federal-style meetinghouse, which since its replacement had been reused as a warehouse, a movie theater, and a gymnasium. Richard Henry Dana Jr. (1879–1933), a leading Colonial Revival architect, oversaw its restoration. Dana's seamless re-creations of the galleries, pulpit, and spire are a tribute to his mastery of Federal models.

By the 1940s, Litchfield was known across the country as the archetypal New England colonial town. Images of its houses and church appeared on calendars and in magazines. Museum re-creations like Historic Deerfield and Old Sturbridge Village in Massachusetts looked to it for inspiration. At home, the transformation was fully institutionalized in 1959, when the town established Connecticut's first local historic district. The ordinance required that a town commission approve any new construction or alteration within the district, thus ensuring that Litchfield would remain a model of Colonial—that is, Colonial *Revival*—architecture.

THE PLACE
FIRST CONGREGATIONAL
CHURCH OF LITCHFIELD

1828–1829. 1929, Richard Henry Dana Jr.
21 Torrington Road, Litchfield

FURTHER READING
Carley, Rachel. *Litchfield: The Making of a New England Town*. Litchfield, Conn.: Litchfield Historical Society, 2011.
"Litchfield Historic District." National Historic Landmark. National Register of Historic Places reference number 68000050, designated November 24, 1968, and number 78003456, designated November 29, 1978.

FIGURE 183. First Congregational Church, Litchfield. Daniel Sterner

85

THE LAST VERNACULAR
HOUSES BY ALICE WASHBURN, HAMDEN

In the New Haven real estate market, the name Washburn is a valued brand, guaranteed to add a premium to the price of a house—and for good reason. Distinguished by gracious flowing spaces, easily recognizable signature features, and exceptional detail, Washburn houses are a cut above ordinary suburban dwellings of the 1920s.

A teacher and housewife, Alice Washburn (1870–1958) began designing and building houses just after World War I, putting together her own crew to control every aspect of construction. Eventually she erected nearly ninety houses in Hamden, Cheshire, New Haven, and Woodbridge, some commissioned by clients, but many built on speculation. Like many small builders, however, Washburn went bankrupt during the Depression, and she dropped out of the business entirely.

A dense concentration of Washburn's work is found on Harmon and Swarthmore Streets in Hamden's Spring Glen section. This suburban community grew up along Whitney Avenue in the 1910s and '20s, made possible by streetcar service and increasing automobile ownership. Three houses, all built on speculation, serve as examples:

Seventy-Nine Harmon Street (1926): The saltbox profile, readily identified with colonial houses, appears in a number of Washburn's designs. Here it faces the street for maximum visual impact. Two robust columns frame the front door, set farther apart than usual to make an imposing statement.

Ninety Harmon Street (1924): Washburn gave this modest structure an elegant doorway with Doric half-columns, a subtly detailed entablature, and a small parapet. From inside the house her characteristic wide windows feel even bigger than they appear from outside. Narrow side windows flanking the door spice up the rhythm.

Thirty-Five Swarthmore Street (1930): This building has the emphatic breadth often seen on Washburn's larger houses. The handsome doorway puts small-scale details where approaching visitors can easily see them. Above it, two arched windows light small rooms, probably bathrooms or closets, an uncommon but successful alternative to the more common practice of installing a grand Palladian window in this central spot, despite the less-than-grand spaces behind it. The garage retains its

original swinging doors, plus pilasters that relate it to the house.

Washburn had no formal training in architecture; how and where she acquired her design skills remains a mystery. The only clue is a family tradition of drives in the country to sketch old houses. Her crew's skills contributed much, but clients' reminiscences make it clear that she was firmly in charge, and the designs were indeed *hers*.

Although Washburn's houses stand out, the early twentieth-century suburbs saw a blossoming of self-taught builder-designers like her. Coming primarily from the construction industry, they produced streets full of solid, attractive dwellings for the growing middle class, particularly in the Colonial Revival manner. Consistently evolving since the 1870s, the Colonial Revival style had become such an integral part of popular culture in this period that it functioned nearly as a vernacular, a design language identified with a particular place and time and transmitted informally, outside the world of trained professionals. In a sense, it was in the air, and Alice Washburn breathed it deeply.

THE PLACES
HOUSES BY ALICE WASHBURN

1919–1930. 79, 80, 84, and 90 Harmon Street, Hamden. 35, 43, 46, 51, 56, 57, 61, 64, 70, and 75 Swarthmore Street, Hamden. Private residences.

FURTHER READING
Yellig, Martha Finder. *Alice F. Washburn, Architect.* Hamden, Conn.: Tiger Lily Press for the Eli Whitney Museum, 1990.

FIGURES 184 AND 185. 35 Swarthmore Street (*top*) and 92 Harmon Street (*bottom*), Hamden. Connecticut Trust for Historic Preservation

86

BACK TO HISTORY

SALISBURY TOWN HALL, SALISBURY

The town hall stands in the middle of Salisbury's historic town center, amid buildings spanning nearly all of the town's 270-year history. Unsurprisingly, it is a rectangular building with white clapboard siding, a cupola, and a big Doric portico. Surprisingly, it is barely thirty years old, replacing an earlier building that burned down in 1985. That building, originally constructed in 1751 as the meetinghouse, had been expanded and remodeled over the years, acquiring porches and a mansarded tower. In 1913, it was re-Colonialized, with a dignified Doric portico.

After the fire, the town debated what to do. Should they copy the beloved old building, or build something "of their own time"? Keep the same location, or find a more spacious lot with plenty of parking? The decision was made to keep the same site, on a corner shared with the Congregational church and the Romanesque Revival library. The design was to be compatible with the character of the historic district.

The new town hall is typically described as a modern reinterpretation of traditional design. While historic styles continued to lead a sort of underground existence, since the 1940s only Modernist design was considered serious or important by the architectural establishment. This began to change in the 1960s, largely under the influence of Robert Venturi, a Philadelphia architect who frequently taught courses at Yale's school of architecture. Under the banner of Postmodernism, Venturi advocated using traditional and vernacular building styles, reinterpreted to suit the modern age. However, what that reinterpretation meant for actual structures often remained unclear. Carter Wiseman, in his history of twentieth-century American architecture, writes that Venturi and his followers seemed more interested in the *idea* of rethinking traditional forms than with the actual results.

Salisbury's architects, the husband-and-wife firm of Robert Kliment and Frances Halsband, belonged to the Venturi school. They resisted the idea of a columned portico, maintaining that columns had lost their symbolic meaning as a result of being tacked mindlessly onto cheap commercial buildings. But the old portico had been much loved and a popular meeting place, and the plan was rejected in a townwide referendum. So, Kliment and Halsband provided a portico, albeit their own version of one. While the columns are fairly orthodox, part of the entablature has been trimmed away, leaving individual square blocks atop the columns, with the rest simply a flat board. In the center of the pediment, the architects cut a big semicircular opening, like an oversized fanlight, with paired radial dividers like window muntins. This motif is repeated in two dormers, one at either end of the hipped roof, to light the second-story meeting rooms.

Like someone making wisecracks to avoid expressing a serious thought that might seem corny, the town hall appears to use traditional forms while denying the meanings they had acquired over the centuries as part of a widely accepted architectural language. Perhaps this is the point: whether intended or not, the design reveals modern discomfort with traditional civic virtues. This may be why some observers prefer the building's rear elevation, which with its shed-roofed lean-to and slight asymmetries has more of the artlessness of vernacular buildings.

THE PLACE
SALISBURY TOWN HALL

1986–1988, R. M. Kliment and Frances Halsband
    Architects
27 Main Street, Salisbury. Open to the public.

FURTHER READING

Ransom, David F. "Salisbury Historic District." National Register of Historic Places, reference number 97001115, listed September 11, 1997.

Wiseman, Carter. *Shaping a Nation: Twentieth-Century American Architecture and Its Makers.* New York: W. W. Norton, 1998.

FIGURE 186. Salisbury Town Hall. Patrick L. Pinnell

Part Eleven

MEANING AND MESSAGE

What style is it? That is often the first, and the last, question people ask about a building or other work of architecture. But style is more than a label to slap on a building and then move on. Considered as a menu of design choices that fit together—including form, plan, materials, construction technology, ornament, colors, and, most important, ideas—style can define a whole way of building.

Another way to think of style is as a means of expression, a language with its own vocabulary and grammar. Asking *what* a work of architecture says and *how* it says it are vastly more important than merely identifying which language it is using. Connecticut architecture features an ongoing parade of styles, some conservative and some innovative, some flamboyant and some reticent, some used strictly and some spiced up with off-menu items. All have something to say, and finding out what that is is all the fun.

87

CONNECTICUT VALLEY BAROQUE
EBENEZER GRANT HOUSE, SOUTH WINDSOR

In the eighteenth century, an interrelated network of families dominated the Connecticut River Valley in Connecticut and Massachusetts. This small group, who supplied the majority of the region's public officials, ministers, and merchants, has come to be known as the "River Gods." By the middle of the century, they had not only made their mark on the valley's economy, society, and politics, but had also developed an architectural style distinct from that of coastal cities like Boston or Newport or New Haven.

One of these River Gods was Ebenezer Grant of East Windsor Hill, in what is now the town of South Windsor. Grant made a fortune shipping livestock, tobacco, and produce to the West Indies in exchange for sugar and rum, or to New York and Boston in exchange for luxury goods. His house, built in 1757, epitomizes the River Gods' style in its imposing size, its spacious center-hall plan, and its exterior ornamentation such as quoins and pedimented window hoods.

The chief attraction of the Grant House, and the architectural trademark of the River Gods, is the doorway. Like their coastal counterparts, the River Gods framed their doors with classical pilasters and pediments whose bold proportions and sensuous curves were based on Baroque precedents from England. In the Connecticut Valley these doors were given their own distinctive twist.

A well-trained coastal craftsman would unhesitatingly dismiss Grant's door as the work of an inept provincial. The opening is too broad for its height. The entablature simply repeats the same few moldings in place of the modulated sequence of varied elements decreed by classical precedent. The pilasters are too squat, and their capitals a clownish caricature of a proper Corinthian order—merely plain blocks each with a single leaf-shaped cutout nailed onto it.

But by insisting on classical correctness, the coastal craftsman would miss the door's power. There is a wealth of curves: on the capitals, on the moldings, on the door panels, on the great scrolls of the pediment. These were difficult to execute and would have sent the budget skyrocketing. Rusticated blocks form a background for the pilasters (compare the New London courthouse, place 9), giving the doorway a sense of three-dimensionality. The multiplication of molding upon molding is highlighted by the way the entablature steps out over the pilasters and in the center. The outlines of the pilasters and step-outs are doubled, as if a narrow column is superimposed on a slightly wider one (or as if the builder suffered from double vision). Finally, the bases of the pilasters are decorated with miniature versions of the doorway, complete with rustication and scrolled pediments: three doorways for the price of one.

There is nothing subtle about this doorway; it is vigorous and bold, qualities valued in the still-raw civilization of inland New England. In fact, it seems likely that its unorthodoxies weren't the result of ignorance of classical precedents, but were rather a conscious manipulation of those precedents for the specific purpose of proclaiming Grant's wealth and influence in ways that his neighbors would best understand. Two hundred and fifty years later, the doorway is still doing just that.

THE PLACE
EBENEZER GRANT HOUSE

1757, Aaron Grant, Abiel Gray, Josiah Vining, Abiel Grant, Isaac Clark, et al., joiners. 1913, moved.
1653 Main Street, South Windsor. Private residence.

FURTHER READING
Cunningham, Jan. "East Windsor Hill Historic District." National Register of Historic Places, reference number 86001208, listed May 30, 1986.
Miller, Amelia F. *Connecticut Valley Doorways: An Eighteenth-Century Flowering*. Boston: Boston University for the Dublin Seminar for New England Folklife, 1983.
Ward, Gerald W. R., and William N. Hosley Jr., eds. *The Great River: Art & Society of the Connecticut Valley, 1635–1820*. Meriden, Conn.: Stinehour Press for the Wadsworth Atheneum, Hartford, 1985.

FIGURE 187. Ebenezer Grant House, South Windsor, door. William Hosley

88

REPUBLICAN SIMPLICITY
OLD STATE HOUSE, HARTFORD

After the Revolution, when the United States was establishing its identity as an independent nation, many states built new capitol buildings. In Connecticut, Hartford joined the trend in 1792 by commissioning a state house from Boston architect Charles Bulfinch (1763–1844). It was a building intended to showcase the city's prosperity and sophistication—and, no doubt, as a salvo in Hartford's long-running rivalry with its co-capital, New Haven.

With Bulfinch far away in Boston, many design decisions would have fallen to the master builder, John Leffingwell. Without original drawings, it is impossible to know how closely the completed building reflected Bulfinch's intentions. The historian Abbott Lowell Cummings has posited that it was much simplified to keep costs down.

Nonetheless, the State House was the first important Neoclassical public building in the Connecticut River Valley. Its first story and trim are of Portland brownstone (the artist John Trumbull lobbied unsuccessfully for marble). A continuous row of arches, framing windows and entries, leavens the visual weight of the masonry. Above the stone is brick, painted until the early twentieth century to hide the mortar joints and emphasize the overall geometric form. The verticality of the first-floor arches and the shorter third-story windows call attention to the building's height, and the monumental Doric portico dominated the view up State Street from the Connecticut River.

All in all, the State House was larger and finer than anything else in Hartford; yet it was far from elaborate. At this point it had neither roof balustrade nor cupola, and in relation to comparable structures in fashionable coastal cities interior detail was sparse, including, for some reason, unfinished capitals on the Corinthian columns lining the Senate chamber. Nonetheless, the public approved. Anne Royall, a writer known for her sharp-tongued criticisms, reported in 1826 that "the State House ... is a very handsome plain building. The representatives' apartments are entirely void of ornament, representing one of the most striking pictures of republican simplicity."

Although the United States was asserting its independence politically, culturally it remained a part of Europe. One aim of the State House and other public buildings was to demonstrate that the young nation could conform to international standards of Neoclassical taste, with appropriate adaptations for local conditions. The desired message was that America was no longer merely a collection of remote colonies, but rather a full and equal member of European civilization. Within this framework, some designers employed overt symbols like eagles or tobacco leaves to express national character in architecture and furnishings. But for the most part Americans sought to express their identity in more general terms, notably the "republican simplicity" that Anne Royall praised. Thomas Jefferson reflected this notion when he praised the "chaste and good style" of ancient Roman and Greek buildings. The Commissioners of the City of Washington also echoed it in describing their wish that the federal city "exhibit a grandeur of conception, a Republican simplicity, and that true elegance of proportion which correspond to a tempered freedom excluding Frivolity."

Later alterations to the Old State House have included the addition of the roof balustrade (1815) and cupola (1827); enclosure of the first-floor passage; and extensive redecoration for use as Hartford's city hall (from 1878 to 1915). In the 1910s, restorers sought to return the building to Bulfinch's design, but also gave it a number of Colonial Revival upgrades. The 1990s brought a different kind of restoration, with rooms finished to represent various phases in the building's history. Through all these changes, the building has continued to stand as an expression of the beginnings of American nationhood.

THE PLACE
OLD STATE HOUSE

www.ctoldstatehouse.org

1792–1796, Charles Bulfinch; John Leffingwell, master builder. 1913–1917, Smith and Bassette; Robert Day Andrews, consultant. 1994, Smith Edwards Architects. 800 Main Street, Hartford. Open to the public.

FURTHER READING

Dillon, James. "The Old Hartford Statehouse." National Historic Landmark. National Register of Historic Places reference number 66000878, designated December 19, 1960.

Maynard, W. Barksdale. *Architecture of the United States, 1800–1850.* New Haven, Conn.: Yale University Press, 2002.

(*top*) **FIGURE 188.** *Jeremiah Halsey,* by Joseph Steward, ca. 1796, showing, in background, Old State House as originally built. The Connecticut Historical Society

(*bottom*) **FIGURE 189.** Old State House, Senate Chamber. Patrick L. Pinnell

89

FEDERAL PRESENCE

UNITED STATES CUSTOM HOUSE, NEW LONDON

Custom houses were among the first federal government buildings built outside the national capital, so the task that Robert Mills (1781–1855) faced was not only to provide adequate accommodation for the customs office, but to devise an appropriate expression for the federal presence. The New London Custom House is one of four, all very similar, that he designed at the same time. The others were in Middletown, demolished in 1916, and two in Massachusetts.

Mills claimed to be the first native-born, professionally trained architect in America, having served an apprenticeship under the English-born Benjamin Henry Latrobe. Mills was particularly interested in fireproofing, and persuaded the secretary of the treasury to specify fireproof construction for the four New England custom houses. As a result, the New London Custom House is built almost entirely of granite and brick, with vaulted masonry ceilings and a stair of stone blocks cantilevered from the wall. Only the second-floor ceilings and roof framing are of timber. The thick walls and vaulted ceilings inside create cellular spaces with a strong sense of enclosure, more so than the usual timber construction.

The Custom House stands out among contemporary buildings on Bank Street. The National Whaling Bank, just a few doors away at 40 Bank Street, is more typical of its time. It was built in 1833 by speculator John French, who hoped to sell it to the federal government. Like many commercial structures of the time, the bank is nearly indistinguishable from a dwelling. This resemblance was beginning to erode in the 1830s, as businesses and institutions grew larger and more complex, requiring bigger and more specialized buildings. Perhaps a desire for a more recognizable presence also contributed to the government's decision to reject French's building and commission a purpose-built one instead.

What does the New London Custom House say about the federal presence? Although it has Greek columns and moldings, the building is not a copy of a Greek temple like the Samuel Russell House (place 16). Instead, Mills creates an abstract version of ancient motifs. There is no overt symbolism or identification—indeed, scarcely any ornamentation at all, apart from the cornice and a small

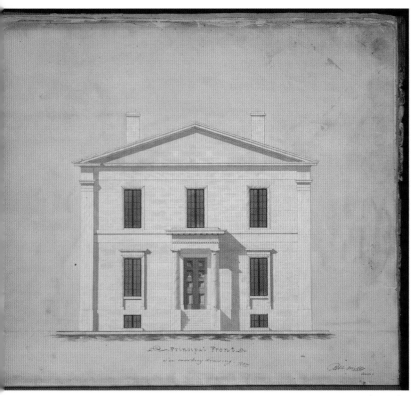

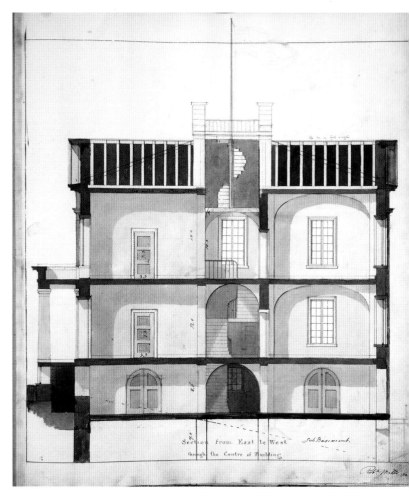

FIGURES 190 AND 191. U.S. Custom House, New London, elevation (*above*) and section drawings (*right*) by Robert Mills. New London Maritime Society

porch with Doric columns. This austere simplicity is partly a function of the hardness of the granite, but it also gives the building a sense of solidity and dignity—qualities appropriate to a civic structure.

More than anything else, it was this all-masonry construction that would have distinguished the Custom House from its neighbors. At the time, the vast majority of American buildings were made of wood, like the nearby New London County Courthouse (place 9). Even when brick or stone were used, interior framing, floors, partitions, and trim still were of wood. Mills's use of durable, fireproof materials promised that the Custom House would endure, even surviving fires or floods. For the federal government, still less than fifty years old, this idea

of permanence was perhaps the most important message that the building could convey.

THE PLACE
UNITED STATES CUSTOM HOUSE

www.nlmaritimesociety.org

1833–1835, Robert Mills. 1987–1991, restored, Lindsay, Liebig, Roche Architects and Noyes/Vogt Architects.

150 Bank Street, New London. Open to the public.

FURTHER READING

Luyster, Constance. "New London Custom House." National Register of Historic Places, reference number 70000706, listed October 15, 1970.

90

ONE STYLE, TWO MESSAGES
TWO HOUSES IN PLAINFIELD

Beginning in the 1850s, a revival of Renaissance-style architecture took place in France, just as Napoleon III was reviving his namesake uncle's empire. With its lavish ornamentation, the new architectural style reached a peak of popularity in the United States in the boom years of the Gilded Age. It is usually known as "Second Empire," after the younger Napoleon and his imperial ambitions.

It is all about the roof. High, double-pitched roofs called "mansard" after the seventeenth-century French architect François Mansart are the hallmark of the Second Empire style. The roofs' height gives a vertical emphasis to buildings, and they are almost invariably richly decorated, with patterned slates or shingles, elaborate cornices and dormers, and iron cresting to create a festive skyline.

Two Second Empire houses in Plainfield warrant a closer look. One was built in 1877 for Edward P. Hall, a successful farmer. A nineteenth-century historian called it "a tasty little residence," its tastiness coming from a high mansard roof rich with patterned slates, an outsized monitor, elaborately framed dormers, and brackets on everything. All of this accentuates the house's small size, making it look almost like a child's toy left out on the street.

Down the street, Lemuel Cleveland, the heir to a real-estate fortune, built a house in 1871 that also has a mansard roof. Instead of busy ornament, though, Cleveland's house relies for effect on bold three-dimensional massing originally emphasized by smooth flush-board siding. A central pavilion projects from the façade, but then has a deep, cavelike recess carved into it. Countering this recess are two thrusting bay windows, whose heads are part of a continuous cornice that wraps around the house like a rubber band holding everything together. Repeated curves—on big brackets, arched windows, barrel-vaulted dormers, the central recess, and the convex mansard roof—create a sense of opulence.

An architectural style is a language, a means of expression with its own vocabulary and rules for assembling the various terms. So, asking "What style is it?" is akin to asking in what language a book is written. It is important to know, but by itself of limited use. A more meaningful question would be, "What is the author (or the builder) *saying* in this language?" For the Hall House, the combination of small size and frilly ornament produces a message of sprightliness, or, as the nineteenth-century historian put it, tastiness. The Cleveland House, on the other hand, with its big scale, smooth surfaces, and more restrained ornament, speaks of monumentality, richness, dignity. One style, two messages.

As with any work of art, the message depends on the viewer or user as well as the creator. Different people may see different things in the same building. There is almost never a single correct answer. So just look. What do *you* see?

THE PLACES
EDWARD P. HALL HOUSE
1877

513 Norwich Road, Plainfield. Private residence.

LEMUEL CLEVELAND HOUSE
1871

550 Norwich Road, Plainfield. Private residence.

FURTHER READING
Clouette, Bruce, and Matthew Roth. "Plainfield Street Historic District." National Register of Historic Places, reference number 91000350, listed April 11, 1991.

FIGURES 192 AND 193. Edward P. Hall (*top*) and Lemuel Cleveland (*bottom*) Houses, Plainfield. Connecticut Trust for Historic Preservation

91

THE ARCHITECTURE OF CITIZENSHIP

CONNECTICUT STATE CAPITOL, HARTFORD

Since the eighteenth century, Americans have tended to prefer classical design for official buildings. The orderliness and clarity of classical architecture resonates with the vision of the people's government and its philosophical roots in the Enlightenment and classical antiquity. Connecticut's State Capitol is an exception, built at a moment when an alternative, a modern reinterpretation of medieval Gothic architecture, was considered acceptable.

The architect's pedigree may have played a role in his choice of style. He was Richard M. Upjohn (1828–1903), the son of the Gothic Revival pioneer Richard Upjohn. The younger Upjohn's design, which he classified as "modern secular Gothic," emerged after a convoluted process that involved two competitions plus months of political infighting and negotiation. Adding to the complication, the builder chosen was James G. Batterson, himself an unsuccessful competitor for the design contract (with his in-house architect, George Keller). The marble for the Capitol came from Batterson's quarry in East Canaan.

There is nothing shy or reticent about the Capitol. Mighty in scale, decked out with images and symbols from the state's history, and crowned with a pinnacled and gilded tower/dome, the building was a proclamation of Connecticut's wealth and taste, a monument to its proud past, and an ornament for the city of Hartford. (It was also a trophy for Hartford, which in 1875 became the state's sole capital after sharing the title with New Haven since 1701.)

Underneath all the Gothic finery, the Capitol has a sense of orderliness that owes much to classicism, and vast portions of the building are devoted to circulation space, reflecting the massively greater scale of government in the years after the Civil War. But it is also here that the picturesque qualities of Upjohn's modern Gothic play a crucial role. Though the plan is generally symmetrical and rectilinear, Upjohn manipulates the spaces to create a varied and romantic setting—an architectural version of the naturalistic landscape of Bushnell Park outside. Ceilings range from low and cavelike, at the lobby to the House of Representatives chamber, to soaring under the dome. Sweeping plains of open floor give way to grotto-like nooks and alcoves. There are groves of columns, and open clearings in the light wells. Stairs ascend like mountain paths, with branching trails and switchbacks offering

**FIGURES 194, 195, AND 196. Connecticut State Capitol.
Connecticut Trust for Historic Preservation**

ever-changing views of the surrounding scenery between columns and arches and statuary.

Like nature, this architecture abhors a vacuum. Carving, painting, stained glass, and patterned pavements create an all-over sense of pattern and texture. Many of the motifs are abstracted from nature, from stylized leaves and flowers to a constellation of stars high in the dome. A single designer, William James McPherson of Boston, oversaw the interior decoration, which gives the Capitol greater coherence and unity than many public buildings of the period.

The combination of Upjohn's architecture and McPherson's decoration (all sensitively restored in the 1980s) enhances the Capitol's magnificence. More important, the generous public spaces provide the setting for the informal meetings and conversations—the *lobbying*—that are an inescapable part of the legislative process. It is a place for seeing and being seen, for

FIGURE 197. Connecticut State Capitol. Robert Gregson

schmoozing and chatting, for taking part in the rituals of citizenship.

THE PLACE
CONNECTICUT STATE CAPITOL

1872–1879, Richard M. Upjohn; interior decoration, William James McPherson. 1977–1987, restored, Dominick C. Cimino Architect, Canning Studios.

210 Capitol Avenue, Hartford. Open to the public.

FURTHER READING

Curry, David Park, and Patricia Dawes Pierce, eds. *Monument: The Connecticut State Capitol*. Hartford, Conn.: Old State House Association, 1979.

Snell, Charles W. "Connecticut State Capitol." National Historic Landmark. National Register of Historic Places, reference number 70000834, designated December 30, 1970.

MEANING AND MESSAGE

92

AMERICAN RENAISSANCE

JAMES BLACKSTONE MEMORIAL LIBRARY, BRANFORD

"In a very plain village in Connecticut ... in a lonesome little old town called Branford ... there is a public library that has cost nearly $600,000," reported the Boston *Sunday Herald* in December 1898. The building actually cost only about half that; but it also came with a $300,000 endowment. Despite that lower price, the Blackstone Memorial Library, completed in 1896, was a building worthy of notice, even by Bostonians.

Like many small-town libraries of the time, it was a gift from a native son who had moved away and made a fortune in a distant city. In this case it was Timothy Beach Blackstone, who left Branford for Chicago, where he became president of a railroad company. To design his gift (a memorial to his father), Blackstone hired Solon S. Beman, a Chicago architect best known for creating the company town of Pullman, Illinois.

Many leading architects of the late nineteenth and early twentieth centuries were trained at the École des Beaux-Arts in Paris. Beman was not, but he nonetheless absorbed the rich interpretation of classical architecture and the theories of planning and decoration that together are known by the school's name: the Beaux-Arts style.

From the Erechtheum, an ancient temple in Athens, Beman copied the Ionic columns that frame the library's entrance, the stylized leaf finials atop the pediment, and the egg-and-dart moldings that line many of the building's parts. The dome crowning the building is a feature from Roman, not Greek, architecture and an example of the eclectic mixing of styles that was characteristic of the age. The materials are as luxurious as the design: marble walls, bronze doors, mosaic tile floors, oak and chestnut woodwork create an atmosphere of wealth and dignity.

Underlying the classical orders and rich materials, Beaux-Arts designs always start with the plan, and the plan always starts with circulation: how will people get around in this building? The Blackstone Memorial Library revolves around a spacious and light-filled rotunda under the dome. All the important rooms open off this space, allowing a visitor standing in the middle of it to see easily where everything is located.

Decoration expresses and reinforces the building's purpose. Lining the dome are paintings that depict the development of book making, beginning with *Gathering*

the Papyrus and ending with *A Book Bindery–1895*. Just beneath the paintings are portraits of great American authors: William Cullen Bryant, Henry Wadsworth Longfellow, Oliver Wendell Holmes, Harriet Beecher Stowe, and others. The message is clear: in both technology and culture, the United States was claiming its rightful place among the older civilizations of the world.

The point of this magnificence was to uplift and inspire. If Bryant, Longfellow, and their like could achieve great things on the world's stage, so too—with hard work and dedication—could the sons and daughters of Branford's farmers, fishermen, and factory workers. The key to their future success was in the books gathered together in this marble temple that was open to all. In spite of its Greek and Roman and French roots, the Blackstone Library is a monument to the American promise of opportunity for all.

THE PLACE

JAMES BLACKSTONE MEMORIAL LIBRARY

www.blackstone.lioninc.org

1893, Solon S. Beman; murals, Oliver Dennett Grover. 1996, restored, Buchanan Associates.

758 Main Street, Branford. Open to the public.

FURTHER READING

Loether, J. Paul. "Branford Center Historic District." National Register of Historic Places, reference number 87000636, listed May 6, 1987.

FIGURE 198. James Blackstone Memorial Library, Branford, rotunda. Robert Perron; courtesy of Buchanan Associates Architects

93

IMMIGRANT SUCCESS
VILLA FRIULI, TORRINGTON

In the late nineteenth and early twentieth centuries, foreign immigrants flocked to Connecticut, most attracted by the promise of jobs in the state's flourishing factories. The largest group was Italians, whose numbers in the state increased from approximately 20,000 in 1900 to more than 227,000 by 1930. In 2000, 18.6 percent of Connecticut's population claimed Italian ancestry, compared to fewer than 6 percent nationwide.

Many Italian Americans went into the building industry, particularly as masons and decorators. Among them were John and Matthew DeMichiel, two brothers from Friuli in northeastern Italy. Trained as stonemasons, they immigrated to the United States in the 1890s, eventually moving to Torrington, where they advertised themselves as "stone cutters, carvers, and dealers in building stone." They branched out into road building as well, as towns and states sought to keep up with the demands of proliferating automobiles. As the brothers prospered, they became leaders in Torrington's Italian American community, founding or supporting several community institutions. John DeMichiel was politically active as well, as a founder of the Torrington Italian-American Republican Club and a state representative.

By 1915 the brothers were able to build this big double house for themselves, on a residential hillside overlooking downtown Torrington. Proclaiming their position as successful businessmen and influential members of the community, the house reflects both the brothers' Italian roots and the current architecture of their chosen homeland.

With its simple rectangular massing, broad eaves, hipped roof, stuccoed walls, and balustraded terrace, Villa Friuli resembles Italian farmhouses and villas. Variously called "Italian Renaissance" or, simply, "Mediterranean," this style was popular in the eclectic atmosphere of the early twentieth century, among Yankees as well as immigrants. Reflective of the builders' Italian American background and their profession was the high quality of the masonry, seen in the ornamental posts flanking the front walk, and in the granite curbing, carved to resemble tree trunks, lining the front lawn. The DeMichiels are said to have carved some of this themselves, along with mantel ornaments inside.

Also distinctively Italian American was the house's color scheme. The stucco is tan, with recessed panels painted red and quoins and other trim highlighted in white. Such multicolored surfaces are found in many parts of the state on buildings associated with Italian Americans, and can perhaps be considered a primary marker of Italian American architectural taste in early twentieth-century Connecticut. Builders achieved the effect by using brick in different colors, or by mixing materials such as brick with stucco, stone, or decorative concrete. Quoins or bands almost invariably outline building corners, and often doors and windows as well. The effect is typically colorful and lively. Villa Friuli is comparatively restrained, perhaps a function of its big scale and its owners' aspirations.

While the house's Italian origins are obvious in its design and, of course, its name, it also is clearly an American building. The rough-textured stucco, along with stained woodwork and chunky mantelpieces inside, belong to the Arts and Crafts taste of the time.

Villa Friuli stands as a symbol of the DeMichiels' commercial and civic success in their new country, rooted in their pride in their origins. With its imposing size, fine craftsmanship, and elaborate design, and its mixture of architectural influences, the house represents their dual heritage. Like its owners, it is both Italian and American.

THE PLACE
VILLA FRIULI
1915, Ferruccio (Fred) Guarda, architect; DeMichiel
    Brothers, contractor
58 High Street, Torrington

FURTHER READING

Clouette, Bruce, and Matthew Roth. "Villa Friuli." National
    Register of Historic Places, reference number 91000349,
    listed April 11, 1991.

FIGURE 199.
Villa Friuli,
Torrington.
Connecticut
Trust for Historic
Preservation

94

NATIVE AMERICAN RENAISSANCE

MASHANTUCKET PEQUOT MUSEUM AND RESEARCH CENTER, MASHANTUCKET

In 1667, remnants of the Pequot tribe who survived a 1637 massacre at their fort in Mystic by English colonists and the colonists' Native American allies were granted a reservation at a place called Mashantucket, in what became the town of Ledyard. (This branch of the tribe is called Mashantucket Pequot, to distinguish them from the inhabitants of another Pequot reservation in Connecticut.) Over the years, pieces of the reservation were sold off, and the tribe scattered. By 1970 the original two thousand acres had been reduced to fewer than two hundred, and only a handful of people remained at Mashantucket.

Change came in the 1970s when the tribe began a concerted effort to repopulate the reservation. In 1983, the federal government officially recognized the Mashantucket Pequots as a sovereign nation, today formally known as the Mashantucket (Western) Pequot Tribal Nation. Recognition freed the Pequots from state and local regulation, allowing them to open Foxwoods Resort Casino in 1992. Since the neighboring Mohegan tribe built its own Mohegan Sun casino in 1997, in Montville, southeastern Connecticut has seen explosive economic growth and a revival of Native American culture.

Although native peoples in eastern North America constructed few permanent buildings before the European invasion, the revival has produced highly visible architecture that attempts to express Native American cultural identity. At the casinos, cultural expression serves the goal of attracting and entertaining visitors while separating them from their money, so a theatrical approach is integral to the program. Foxwoods, the first built, is a generic Postmodernist design embellished with isolated Native American motifs. At Mohegan Sun, the effect is more unified, with an overall scheme that includes lampposts containing corn kernels and beans, and terrazzo patterns symbolizing the seasons of the year. The approach, though, is still primarily decorative.

The Modernist design of the Mashantucket Pequot Museum and Research Center offers a less literal vision of a Native American architecture, incorporating abstracted cultural motifs. The research wing is clad in slabs of different-colored stone set in an aluminum grid to suggest wampum belts. The overlapping half-circles of the atrium

recall the bird's-eye view of the Pequots' palisaded Mystic fort as depicted in a 1638 engraving of the massacre.

Expressing the tribe's harmony with the land, a defining cultural characteristic, was a primary consideration in the museum's design. Galleries are buried, to reduce the building's apparent size, while large windows provide views to the surrounding forest. Local materials further link the building to its site: shells embedded in the lobby's terrazzo floor, and elm and ash wood in display cases. The museum's grandest architectural gesture, a 185-foot observation tower, represents a more expansive link to the landscape. From it—since property lines and municipal borders don't show from the air—the viewer can imagine the Pequots' realm in its original extent, stretching across the rolling hills, and is reminded of the tribe's claim of continuous identity based on the land.

THE PLACES

MASHANTUCKET PEQUOT MUSEUM AND RESEARCH CENTER

1998, Polshek Partnership Architects

110 Pequot Trail, Mashantucket. Open to the public.

FOXWOODS RESORT CASINO

1991 and later, JCJ Architecture

350 Trolley Line Boulevard, Mashantucket. Open to the public.

MOHEGAN SUN

1996, Brenner Beer Gorman Architects; interior, Rockwell Group. 2001, Kohn Pederson Fox; interior, Rockwell Group. 2002, Kohn Pederson Fox; interiors, Hirsch Bedner Associates.

1 Mohegan Sun Boulevard, Montville. Open to the public.

FURTHER READING

Mashantucket Pequot Museum and Research Center. *History and Culture eBook*. www.pequotmuseum.org/eBook.aspx.

Bodinger de Uriarte, John J. *Casino and Museum: Representing Mashantucket Pequot Identity*. Tucson: University of Arizona Press, 2007.

Part Twelve

TRANSFORMATIONS

A work of architecture is never truly finished. In big and small ways, its users continue to reshape it. Changing times and tastes and fortunes leave their mark on individual buildings, as can cycles of neglect, deterioration, and repair. Ad hoc landscapes or collections of buildings can grow into well-integrated, attractive compositions, or functioning neighborhoods can be torn apart. Adaptation to new uses allows obsolete structures to continue to be part of their communities, either as a matter of frugality or because they are valued for their meaning or design. Often, the richest, most interesting places are those that have many layers of meaning.

95

HOW BUILDINGS LEARN

TAINTOR HOUSE, HAMPTON

"Form follows function," modern architects often say. But what happens when function changes? As the writer Stewart Brand explains in *How Buildings Learn*, the history of most buildings is a story of ongoing alterations to meet changing needs and desires, or to correct the ways in which every structure falls short of perfectly performing its intended functions.

Brand distinguishes two kinds of buildings in which change happens in different ways. Utilitarian "Low Road" buildings, "where no one cares what you do," get ad hoc, temporary, or make-do alterations. "High Road" buildings, on the other hand, are designed for durability and aesthetic appeal. Change comes to them more carefully, with thoughtful planning and attention to visual coherence. One might also apply this distinction to different parts of a single structure—High Road for the façade and the parlor; Low Road at the rear or in the attic. Sometimes, High Road buildings fall on hard times and get Low Road treatment.

Like many eighteenth-century Connecticut buildings, the Taintor House has gone through numerous changes. But unlike many of its contemporaries, it has never been "restored" to what someone thought was its original appearance. Better yet, the house's history has been thoroughly told in a book by James and Janet Robertson, who owned it for more than thirty years.

Although best known for its long occupancy by the Taintor-Davis family, the house was constructed sometime between 1790 and 1793 for Thomas Stedman Jr., probably by his uncle, a local builder also named Thomas Stedman. Roger and Solomon Taintor, brothers and farmer-merchants from Windham, bought it in 1804. The Taintors, who married sisters, shared the house for the rest of their lives, and it remained in the hands of their descendants until 1967.

Over the years, the Taintors remodeled the house several times. The most obvious work could be classified as High Road, reflecting the family's continuing prosperity and prominence in Hampton. In the 1820s, the brothers removed the center chimney and replaced it with twin chimneys serving twin front parlors—one for each family—on either side of a new center hall. Federal-style interior woodwork completed the transformation from a simple farmhouse to (in the Robertsons' words) "the residence of gentlefolk." In the 1850s, Solomon Taintor's son Henry added front and side verandas with slender Italianate posts, cut the front windows down to the floor, and installed new woodwork in the front rooms. But he left the upper story unaltered, giving the house a split personality, 1850s below and 1820s above.

Low Road alterations included reusing old paneling and trim in out-of-the-way places like closets and the attic stair. In the early twentieth century, the space between the front and side porches was filled in, apparently to end the inconvenience of having to jump the gap or go through the house to get from one porch to another. To save on maintenance, the louvered shutters added in the 1850s were stored away in the barn.

With layers of stylish improvements, needed repairs, and make-do changes, buildings like the Taintor House make the passage of time visible. In them we can track changes in tastes, in technology, in the economy, or in the fortunes of their inhabitants.

THE PLACE
TAINTOR HOUSE

ca. 1792, Thomas Stedman (attributed). ca. 1824, 1854, 1857, etc., remodeled.

273 Main Street, Hampton. Private residence.

FURTHER READING

Brand, Stewart. *How Buildings Learn: What Happens after They're Built*. New York: Penguin Books, 1994.

Ransom, David F. "Hampton Hill Historic District." National Register of Historic Places, reference number 82004408, listed September 23, 1982.

Robertson, James Oliver, and Janet C. Robertson. *All Our Yesterdays: A Century of Family Life in an American Small Town*. New York: HarperCollins, 1993.

FIGURE 201. Taintor House, Hampton. Connecticut Trust for Historic Preservation

96

CITY BEAUTIFUL
DOWNTOWN NAUGATUCK

John Howard Whittemore (1837–1910), president of the Naugatuck Malleable Iron Company, far outdid most philanthropic industrialists of the 1890s and 1900s. Rather than donate a building or two, Whittemore, working with McKim, Mead & White, the foremost architectural firm of the day, completely transformed downtown Naugatuck.

It was a moment of change in American architecture. The exuberance of the 1870s and 1880s (see places 17 and 91) was giving way to a restrained classicism. Building silhouettes were simpler, surfaces cleaner, colors paler and subtler. Landscape and town design also moved away from picturesque irregularity to symmetry and formality, with strong organizing axes that visibly knit together buildings, landscapes, or entire towns. This change is called the City Beautiful movement, based on its proponents' insistence that beauty itself was a valuable civic asset. As embodied in the World's Columbian Exposition of 1893, the movement inspired ambitious civic-improvement efforts nationwide.

McKim, Mead & White were leaders in the new style. In Naugatuck, they designed two Whittemore houses (both demolished), the Howard Whittemore Memorial Library (1891), a bank (1892; demolished), two schools (1892, 1902), the Congregational Church of Naugatuck (1901), plus the town green (1894). Whittemore initiated or contributed to all these projects.

What Whittemore and his architects produced was more than individual buildings. They gave the town a new core. The buildings enclose three sides of the town green, strengthening its sense of place. On the east, the library (and the demolished bank) established a human scale and introduced a classical vocabulary and color scheme that later construction would emulate. On the west, the Salem School forms a solid wall centered on the axis of Maple Street, the entry to the town center from the east. On the north, the Congregational Church and its earlier parish house form another enclosing wall. The church's massive tower and stubby spire form a giant "Here it is!" sign, identifying the green from afar.

The church and the Salem School replaced two older buildings located on the green. Once those earlier structures were removed, the firm laid out new paths and installed a fountain that reinforced the existing Civil War monument as a focal point of the newly open landscape.

Most interesting is the Naugatuck High School (now the junior high school) perched on the hillside overlooking the green. A walkway and stair, aligned with Division Street, link the school to the street grid. But the building sits at an angle to the streets below, with Hillside Avenue curling around it—an unexpected departure from the axial principles of City Beautiful planning. In addition to fitting the topography, this position accentuates the school's dramatic site overlooking the downtown.

John Howard Whittemore gave Naugatuck a new identity, which the town has carefully guarded ever since. After fire gutted the high school, in 1961, the town restored the surviving exterior and rebuilt the interior. Since then, unfortunately, Naugatuck's rubber plants and iron foundries have closed and been demolished, and the economic base is largely controlled by out-of-town interests. Who now will take up Whittemore's legacy of commitment to the public realm?

THE PLACE
DOWNTOWN NAUGATUCK
1891–1905, McKim, Mead & White
Church, Division, and Meadow Streets; Hillside Avenue

FURTHER READING
Cunningham, Jan. "Naugatuck Center Historic District." National Register of Historic Places, reference number 99000859, listed July 30, 1999.
Roth, Leland. "Three Industrial Towns by McKim, Mead & White." *Journal of the Society of Architectural Historians* 38, no. 4 (December 1979): 317–347.
Smith, Ann Y. *Hidden in Plain Sight: The Whittemore Collection and the French Impressionists.* Roxbury, Conn.: Garnett Hill Publishing and the Mattatuck Historical Society, 2009.

FIGURES 202 AND 203. Naugatuck High School (*top*) and the Howard Whittemore Memorial Library (*bottom*). Daniel Sterner (school); Robert Gregson (library)

97

CHANGE AND SIMILARITY
CANAAN INSTITUTIONAL
BAPTIST CHURCH, NORWALK

A few blocks from Norwalk's SoNo shopping and restaurant district stands a vinyl-sided Baptist church crowned with two exotic-looking onion domes. The building originally was a synagogue called Beth Israel, built in 1906 for a congregation of Orthodox Jews. In the nineteenth century, European and American Jews turned to Middle Eastern design (called "Oriental" at the time) to express the Middle Eastern roots of their faith, and to avoid the Gothic or Romanesque styles that were considered specifically Christian. The transformation from synagogue to church was a common story in working-class urban neighborhoods, where various immigrant groups moved in and established themselves before moving on to more desirable areas. In the process, synagogues were converted to churches, and churches were converted to synagogues or churches of different denominations. The buildings' shifting identities tracked the changing demographics.

These changes were made easier by the similarity of the buildings. Traditionally, most houses of worship in the West took the form of a gabled box with its narrow end to the street and one or more towers as eye-catching symbols of heavenward aspiration. Inside, rows of seating faced forward to a platform from which leaders conducted worship. Galleries usually provided additional seating, and sometimes a place for musicians. Stained-glass windows obscured views to the outside, setting the building apart from worldly cares.

The interior of Beth Israel was designed for Orthodox worship that primarily consists of words—prayers and teaching and reading from scripture. The most important physical action of the service occurs when the Torah scroll is taken from the ark in which it is stored and carried through the congregation. Traditionally, this procession ended at a platform, called a *bimah*, in the center of the room, from which the service was led. By the turn of the twentieth century, Jewish congregations increasingly combined the bimah platform with the ark at the front of the room, creating a single focal point for worship. (In Connecticut, only one synagogue, Beth Israel in New Haven, still has a central bimah.) Beth Israel in Norwalk followed the new pattern. Its ark was set in paneling embellished with a Star of David and Hebrew inscriptions.

FIGURE 204. Canaan Institutional Baptist Church, Norwalk. Tod Bryant

In front of it was the platform, with a pulpit and branched candelabra that have been a symbol for Judaism since Roman times. Men and boys sat on the main floor; women and girls (and infants) in the galleries, so as not to distract the men from their prayers.

In 1972, Beth Israel moved and sold its old building to Canaan Institutional Baptist Church, an African American congregation founded in 1959 by a pastor originally from Virginia. The Baptists made remarkably few changes to their adopted building. Baptist worship also focuses on

FIGURE 205. Canaan Institutional Baptist Church, Norwalk. Tod Bryant

FIGURE 206. Canaan Institutional Baptist Church, interior as Beth Israel Synagogue. National Register of Historic Places

words, including scripture reading and a sermon, as well as prayers and singing. Ritual actions, baptism and Holy Communion, take place less frequently. The Baptists removed some obviously Jewish symbols, such as the Star of David and inscriptions over the ark, and replaced the pulpit and the pews on the main level. The only entirely new elements are the altar and a baptistery for full immersion. Clad in wood to match the existing trim and tucked under the gallery, the baptistery is almost invisible when its lid is closed.

Beth Israel's transition from synagogue to church was, physically, not much of a change. This reflects the similarity of Jewish and Christian religious traditions and practices—similarities grounded in the origins of Christianity as a Jewish sect, and no doubt also by the influence of Christianity, as the European-American majority religion, on Judaism. But understanding even

the modest changes made to the building reveals the changing makeup of the neighborhood in which it is located.

THE PLACE
CANAAN INSTITUTIONAL BAPTIST CHURCH

(Originally Beth Israel Synagogue)
www.canaanibc.org
1906
31 Concord Street, Norwalk

FURTHER READING

Ransom, David F. "Beth Israel Synagogue." National Register of Historic Places, reference number 91001684, listed November 29, 1991.

———. "One Hundred Years of Jewish Congregations in Connecticut: An Architectural History." *Connecticut Jewish History* 2, no. 1 (Fall 1991): 7–147.

98

HAZARDOUS DUTY

WILCOX, CRITTENDEN & COMPANY FACTORY, MIDDLETOWN

Factory work could be dirty and dangerous, something that is not always obvious when industrial buildings have been converted to new uses. A series of changes made to the former Wilcox, Crittenden & Company factory in Middletown offers a glimpse into the hazards of industrial work.

The largest manufacturer of marine hardware in the United States, Wilcox, Crittenden produced equipment for ships that ranged from grommets and swivels to thirty-ton steel anchors. The company's factory was located on Middletown's South Main Street, next to a deep ravine that had provided waterpower for mills since the seventeenth century. Mill C, built in 1907, was the company's galvanizing and forge shop. The mill is a utilitarian structure, 350 feet long, with concrete-block walls and an interior frame of steel, up-to-date materials that promised advancements in strength and durability.

Despite these promises, Wilcox, Crittenden had to make a series of alterations to Mill C in ongoing efforts to cope with corrosion caused by the galvanizing process. Galvanizing, in which iron or steel pieces were dipped into molten zinc, was crucial for protecting items in constant contact with seawater from rust. Since zinc emits powerful fumes that can eat away at iron or steel, Mill C was built with a monitor to vent the fumes, but it proved inadequate. In 1913 the company added a ventilation tower to the west side of the building and by 1924 had enlarged the tower to increase its capacity. Further changes came in the 1940s, when big air scoops of Monel metal (a corrosion-resistant alloy of nickel and copper) were added to the roof. By that time, the zinc fumes had eaten away the steel framing in the southern portion of the building. The company replaced the steel with timber, an old-fashioned choice but a less vulnerable one in this situation.

According to the National Register nomination, the main reason for these changes was to ensure the stability of the building. But the effect on the workers may have been another factor behind them. Zinc vapor has been connected with a condition called "metal fume fever," which produces symptoms including fatigue, chills, muscle pain, fever, coughing, and shortness of breath in both workers and neighbors of industrial plants. Today, Mill C has been converted to apartments, but its monitor,

FIGURE 207. Wilcox, Crittenden & Company Factory (the Wilcox apartments), Middletown. Patrick L. Pinnell

its ventilation tower, and the row of metal scoops that line its roof are potent reminders of the human cost of Connecticut's industrial achievements.

THE PLACE
WILCOX, CRITTENDEN & COMPANY MILL C
(The Wilcox apartments)
1907 and later
305 South Main Street, Middletown

FURTHER READING

Cunningham, Jan. "Wilcox, Crittenden Mill Historic District." National Register of Historic Places, reference number 86003349, listed December 3, 1986.

99

MODEL CITY

DIXWELL PLAZA, NEW HAVEN

Since the nineteenth century, the area along Dixwell Avenue has been New Haven's principal African American neighborhood. Residents from the 1940s remember the community's vibrant social and commercial life. Yet by 1960, years of neglect had taken their toll. According to the New Haven Redevelopment Agency, Dixwell suffered from substandard housing, poor planning, traffic congestion, inadequate parking, and a lack of open space.

Beginning in 1960, the Redevelopment Agency set about remaking Dixwell as part of the new model city that Mayor Richard C. Lee (1916–2003) hoped to create through the nation's most ambitious urban renewal program. City planners reorganized land uses, improved traffic patterns, built parking lots, flagged deteriorated buildings for demolition or renovation, and planned new construction. At the neighborhood's heart they created a public square with stores and community institutions around an open plaza.

Impressive architecture was central to the renewal program. Three key commissions in Dixwell went to John M. Johansen of New Canaan, who at the time was experimenting with dramatic, irregular forms in place of the simplicity of earlier Modernist designs. For the Dixwell Avenue Congregational United Church of Christ (1968), Johansen produced a crystalline shape that seems solid from the street yet has a light-filled sanctuary. In his Florence Virtue Homes (1964; altered) and Helene Grant School (1964; demolished), striated concrete blocks created textural interest. A bell tower made the school a neighborhood landmark.

Local architects participated as well. Carleton Granbery's East Rock Lodge (1967) has concrete colonnades that recall classical porticoes. Edward Cherry and Herbert S. Newman gave the Dixwell Community Center, or Q House (1967; demolished), a monumental stair that provided seating for events in the plaza or informal gatherings.

More dramatic than the individual buildings was the new shape of the neighborhood as a whole. Before renewal, blocks were lined with buildings erected individually but conforming to a uniform type: narrow and deep, two to four stories high, and closely spaced to form a continuous street wall. Post-renewal Dixwell is made up of big

FIGURE 208. Dixwell Avenue Congregational United Church of Christ, New Haven. Connecticut Trust for Historic Preservation

superblocks with inward-turning clusters of buildings in a wider range of sizes and forms, each conceived as a distinct entity rather than as a part of the larger urban fabric and surrounded by open space.

Although overall conditions were improved, particularly for housing, Lee's vision of a city without slums was never realized. Dixwell remains poor, and its renewal-era architecture has not fared well. The shopping center has lost its covered walkway, and Johansen's school and the Q House have been demolished. Some housing also has been razed, and what remains has been encased in vinyl or stucco. Only the Congregational church has escaped mutilation or destruction.

Some of these losses resulted from inherent structural

problems or years of neglect. But in many cases planners want to heal the disruptions of urban renewal by erasing evidence of it from the cityscape and replacing it with something new and better. Ironically, this only repeats the strategies of the 1960s. It places too much responsibility for social ills, and too many hopes for curing them, on architecture. Even in troubled neighborhoods, smaller steps—renovation, infill construction, targeted redevelopment—seem more likely to result in improvements. Meanwhile, urban renewal remains a difficult legacy, a noble but tragically flawed effort to invest heavily, if misguidedly, in improving life for the nation's citizens.

THE PLACES
DIXWELL AVENUE CONGREGATIONAL UNITED CHURCH OF CHRIST
1968, John M. Johansen
217 Dixwell Avenue, New Haven
DIXWELL PLAZA
1968, Douglas Orr, DeCossy, Winder & Associates
230 Dixwell Avenue, New Haven

FURTHER READING

Brown, Elizabeth Mills. *New Haven: A Guide to Architecture and Urban Design*. New Haven, Conn.: Yale University Press, 1976.

Carley, Rachel. *Tomorrow Is Here: New Haven and the Modern Movement*. New Haven, Conn.: New Haven Preservation Trust, 2008.

New Haven Modern Architecture. http://newhavenmodern.org.

Wigren, Christopher. "Preserving Dixwell as a Model." *Connecticut Explored* 11, no. 2 (Spring 2013): 44–45.

FIGURE 209. Dixwell Avenue, New Haven, before urban renewal. Courtesy of the New Haven Museum

100

NEW LIFE FOR OLD BUILDINGS

CHENEY YARN DYE HOUSE, MANCHESTER

For almost as long as people have erected buildings, they have adapted them to new uses. From the medieval Romans who lived and worked in the Colosseum to the nineteenth-century manufacturer who took over the Middletown Alms House (place 58), reuse usually was simply a matter of frugality. But sometimes the motivation was the desire to retain the building for its historical or architectural significance—in short, historic preservation. In the twentieth century, preservationists gave this age-old practice a formal name: "adaptive reuse," or, less commonly and, to my mind, less redundantly, "adaptive use."

One of Connecticut's biggest adaptive-use efforts has been the gradual conversion of the former Cheney Brothers silk mills in Manchester to new purposes. At its peak in the 1920s, Cheney Brothers was the nation's biggest silk producer, occupying approximately 1.3 million square feet of space in eight principal buildings. After World War II, however, business faltered; in 1954 the family sold the company, and the mills soon closed. Beginning in the 1970s, the Town of Manchester initiated redevelopment of the vacant mills. The most recent to be completed is the former Yarn Dye House, converted to apartments in 2009.

Public funding has helped make adaptive use feasible. Since 1976, the federal government has offered tax credits to developers who renovate historic buildings. States, including Connecticut, have also instituted similar programs. To qualify, projects must adhere to a set of preservation guidelines called the Secretary of the Interior's Standards for Rehabilitation. Commonly known as the Secretary's Standards, their goal is to retain a building's original materials and appearance as much as possible.

Renovating a building under the Secretary's Standards typically requires balancing preservation requirements against the alterations needed to accommodate a new use. For example, converting the Yarn Dye House to apartments required subdividing the open manufacturing spaces. Yet industrial character still comes through in the exposed brick walls, concrete ceilings, and steel-and-concrete structural columns. The original windows were too deteriorated to retain, but the replacements imitate their glazing pattern, while modifying their construction to allow the addition of screens. Particularly noteworthy are the seventeen-foot-tall first-story windows, which provided ventilation to dry the dyed yarn and vent off fumes. To avoid dividing the windows, the first-floor apartments are double-height spaces with twenty-three-foot ceilings and lofts inside.

Other financing possibilities also influenced the reuse of the Yarn Dye House: in addition to the historic rehabilitation tax credits, federal and state affordable-housing funding was available, so the building was developed as subsidized housing for tenants who meet low-income qualifications. Satisfying the requirements of that funding source further complicated the design process. Finally, contamination had to be cleaned up, and structural deterioration corrected.

Despite the complexity of the issues that had to be addressed, reusing the Yarn Dye House was seen as worth the effort by the Town of Manchester, the federal and state governments, and the developer. The building's historic significance, as part of the larger Cheney complex, accounts for part of this, as does the availability

of financing for reuse that couldn't be tapped for new construction. But the appeal of the building's industrial character also played an important role. The Yarn Dye House conversion is one of many that show us that buildings can live multiple lives, continue to be occupied, maintained, and even loved long after their original purpose has disappeared.

THE PLACE
CHENEY BROTHERS YARN DYE HOUSE
(Dye House Apartments)
1914. 2009, Crosskey Architects; Simon Konover Company, developer.
31 Cooper Hill Street, Manchester. Private residences.

FURTHER READING
Adams, George R. "Cheney Brothers Historic District." National Historic Landmark. National Register of Historic Places, reference number 78002885, designated June 2, 1978.

FIGURE 210. Cheney Brothers Yarn Dye House (now Dye House Apartments), Manchester. Crosskey Architects LLC

AFTERWORD

Although best known for Colonial houses, Federal churches, and Georgian and Gothic Revival schools and universities, Connecticut boasts a rich array of architecture of every type. It has residences ranging from urban tenements to great estates. It features industrial complexes from early textile mills to mammoth red-brick factories to suburban industrial parks, some with traditional and progressive worker housing. It is the site of landmarks of Modernist architecture and planning.

Moreover, Connecticut's architecture is not limited to individual buildings, but also encompasses town greens and urban parks, entire neighborhoods and communities, and infrastructure projects from reservoirs to parkways. Among those who have contributed to the state's physical environment are colonial master builders, architects, landscape architects, and engineers from New York and Boston, a steadily growing network of well-known and little-known local professionals, and idiosyncratic folk builders.

This architectural variety is a living record of the people of Connecticut and the active and varied lives they have pursued. They have tried many ways of making their living. They have absorbed influences from other places and periods. They have been intellectually curious and prosperous enough to keep up with—and sometimes contribute to—changing fashions. They have been technologically innovative. As the nineteenth and twentieth centuries progressed, the state's population grew ever more diverse socially and ethnically, introducing new tastes and lifestyles and aspirations to influence the ways residents shaped their environment.

This book is a starting point. I hope it will inspire you, its readers, to learn more about Connecticut and its architecture, but more than that, to see and experience it for yourselves. As always, the historian Elizabeth Mills Brown put it perfectly ("The Nifty Fifty," typescript, 1984, 4): "Architecture is for everyone, and there's enough to go around if we'll only learn to take care of it. We can't write it all down on convenient lists that we can carry in our pockets, but it's all around you wherever you go. Go out and keep your eyes open. Enjoy every bit of it whether it's on somebody's list or not. And, above all, guard it."

584

ARCHITECTURAL GLOSSARY

Adamesque: A neoclassical style characterized by slender proportions and elliptical forms; named for the eighteenth-century Scottish architect Robert Adam.

Art Nouveau: An early twentieth-century style characterized by sinuous curves and plant-based ornamental forms; rare in the United States.

balloon frame: A method of constructing buildings developed in the nineteenth century in which standard-size boards are nailed together to form a structural frame. To people used to heavier timber frames, such buildings seemed as insubstantial as balloons.

bargeboard: A decorative board lining the slope of a gable, found in Gothic and Gothic Revival buildings.

Baroque: A classical style of the Renaissance characterized by elaborate curved forms used to create emotional effects; in Connecticut, it appears in a much-simplified version.

battered: Said of a wall that slopes inward.

bay: A structural unit of a building, particularly one with a timber frame, defined as the space between two bents.

bent: In timber framing, a two-dimensional frame of posts, beams, and diagonal braces; bents define structural bays.

bond: A pattern of arranging bricks in a wall, with stretchers (bricks laid lengthwise) and headers (bricks laid with their narrow end exposed to tie, or *bond*, parallel courses of brick together). Flemish bond has alternating stretchers and headers in each course and is most common in Georgian, Federal, and Colonial Revival buildings. Dutch-cross bond is uncommon in Connecticut.

campanile: Italian term for a bell tower.

chamfer: A bevel along the corner of a beam, cut off at a simple angle or molded.

clerestory: Windows set high in a wall to admit light and/or air but not views.

Composite: The most elaborate of the classical orders, with column capitals combining acanthus leaves from the Corinthian with large scrolls from the Ionic.

Corinthian: A classical order, with column capitals bearing leaf forms derived from the acanthus plant, a member of the thistle family.

cornice: Projecting moldings forming the topmost part

of an entablature, or ornamenting the top of a wall or another architectural element.

cusped arch: An arch whose inner curve is scalloped.

dado: The lower portion of an interior wall, sheathed with wooden boards or panels.

dendrochronology: A method of determining the age of a piece of wood by comparing tree rings to those from known examples to tell when the tree it came from was felled.

diapering: All-over repetitive surface patterning, especially on a diagonal or rectangular grid.

Doric: A classical order characterized by columns with simple molded capitals and an entablature with plain squares, called metopes, alternating with vertically grooved rectangles, called triglyphs.

eared: Moldings around a rectangular opening that step out at corners; also "crosseted."

egg-and-dart: A decorated molding carved into alternating egg-shaped and arrow-shaped forms.

entablature: Part of a classical order, forming the crosspiece or lintel atop the columns. The entablature is made up of a series of moldings that vary by order but fall into three main subdivisions: architrave, frieze, and cornice.

flèche: In Gothic architecture, a narrow, ornamental spire.

gambrel: A roof with gable ends and sloping sides broken into two pitches.

Garden City movement: A planning movement of the late nineteenth and early twentieth centuries that sought to create communities with a high proportion of open, landscaped space.

Georgian: English late-Renaissance design employing classical orders and solid proportions; named for the four kings named George who ruled England from 1714 to 1830.

Gothic: A medieval style characterized by pointed arches and vaults and efforts to make masonry walls as light and insubstantial as possible; revived in the nineteenth and twentieth centuries under the name Gothic Revival and especially common in religious and educational buildings.

half-timbering: Construction of timber frame filled in with a different material, typically stucco or brick, used in Gothic and Tudor buildings or buildings modeled on them.

Ionic: A classical order characterized by columns with large scrolls for capitals; the entablature has a plain frieze and, usually, dentils (small blocks resembling teeth).

keystone: The large central wedge-shaped stone at the top of an arch, or an imitation of one.

loggia: A recessed porch with columns, typical of Italian buildings.

mansard: A hipped roof with each side broken into two different slopes, characteristic of French Renaissance and American Second Empire design.

Miesian: Referring to architecture of or influenced by the Modernist architect Ludwig Mies van der Rohe (1886–1969), known for simple rectilinear forms constructed of meticulously detailed steel frames typically filled with glass or brick.

monitor: A raised section of a roof with clerestory windows; usually wider and lower than a cupola.

muntin: A dividing bar separating the panes of a window; distinguished from a mullion, which is a heavier bar separating sections of a window.

obelisk: A monumental stone pier of a type first used in ancient Egypt, having a tapered shaft and a pyramidal cap.

order: In classical architecture, the combination of column and entablature that are used together. The Greek orders are Doric, Ionic, and Corinthian; the Romans added Tuscan and Composite. Each order has a standard set of components and proportions, which become systems for ordering an architectural design—hence the name "orders."

palazzo: Italian for "palace"; in American architecture a large rectangular building with a low-hipped roof and Renaissance or classical design.

Palladian window: A three-part window with narrow side sections and wide central section with an arched top. Named for the Italian Renaissance architect and writer Andrea Palladio (1508–1580).

parapet: A low wall surrounding a terrace, stair, or roof.

parterre: An ornamental garden on a level plane or terrace, planted in geometric patterns to create a carpet-like effect.

pavilion: A shallow projecting section on the façade of a building, often crowned with a pediment.

pediment: In classical design, a formal gable ornamented with moldings.

pilaster: In classical design, a rectangular pier attached to a wall, often ornamented to resemble a classical column.

porch: In early colonial buildings, an enclosed projecting portion of a building containing an entry.

quoin: Prominent stone blocks at the corner of a building, or brick or wooden forms imitating such blocks.

Romanesque: A medieval style, earlier than Gothic, which employs semicircular arches and heavy masonry walls; it was revived in several phases in the nineteenth century, most notably by the architect H. H. Richardson, whose interpretation of the style became widely influential. English Romanesque is sometimes called Norman.

rusticated: Stonework with stones beveled to accentuate their individual character, or brick or wooden elements imitating such work.

timber framing (post-and-beam): A method of constructing buildings of large wooden posts and beams fitted together with a variety of joints to form a framework.

Tudor: The final phase of English Gothic design, characterized by very flat pointed arches and rectangular paneling; in the early twentieth century, the term could be applied to any Gothic-inspired residential structure.

vault: An arched ceiling; strictly speaking, it should be constructed of masonry, but the term can refer to any arched form.

Victorian Gothic: A subset of Gothic Revival, a nineteenth-century movement to reinterpret Gothic design for current circumstances, characterized by flat surfaces with crisp corners and multicolored surface patterning; the wooden version, featuring applied sticklike elements, is sometimes called "Stick Style."

Page references in *italics* indicate illustrations and photos.

Garnet Books

ABOUT THE AUTHOR

Christopher Wigren is an architectural
historian and deputy director of
the Connecticut Trust for Historic
Preservation, where he edits and writes
for *Connecticut Preservation News*,
the Trust's bimonthly magazine. His
articles and essays also have appeared in
the *Hartford Courant*, the *New Haven
Register*, and *Connecticut Explored*.
Chris serves on the Merritt Parkway
Advisory Committee and the Connecticut
State Historic Preservation Board, which
reviews nominations to the National
Register of Historic Places.
The Connecticut Trust for Historic
Preservation was established by the
General Assembly in 1975. The Trust
works throughout the state to protect
and promote buildings, sites, structures,
and landscapes that contribute to the
heritage and vitality of Connecticut
communities.